Irish People of Colour

A social history of mixed race Irish
in Britain and Ireland between 1700-2000

Conrad Koza Bryan and Chamion Caballero

With contributions by:
William Hart, Mark Doyle and Maurice Casey

Non-Commercial, Limited Edition
Published by
The Association of Mixed Race Irish
London, United Kingdom.

Irish People of Colour

Published in 2024
by The Association of Mixed Race Irish
41 Raymond Avenue, Ealing
London W13 9UY
United Kingdom
www.mixedraceirish.ie

ISBN 978-1-3999-7603-9

Copyright @ Conrad Bryan and Chamion Caballero 2024

The rights of Conrad Bryan and Chamion Caballero have been
asserted to be identified as the authors of this work in
accordance with the Copyright, Design and Patents Act 1988

All rights reserved. No part of this publication may be reproduced,
stored in a retrieval system, or transmitted, in any form, or by
any means (electronic, mechanical, photocopying, recording,
or otherwise) without prior consent of the authors.

A CIP catalogue record for this book is available
from the British Library

This non-commercial limited edition book is distributed
by the publisher subject to the condition that it shall not
by way of trade or otherwise, be lent, hired out, or otherwise
circulated without the authors' prior consent in any form of
binding or cover other than that which it is
published in this edition.

Cover illustrations @ Anisha Bryan
Cover design by Novus Innov8

Printed and bound by CPI Group (UK) Ltd
Croydon CR0 4YY

Typeset in 8pt to16pt Garamond

Irish People
of
Colour

Acknowledgements

This publication emerged from the online Mixed Race Irish People in Britain, 1700-2000 ('AMRI exhibition') launched in July 2020, which was a joint collaboration between The Association of Mixed Race Irish (AMRI) and The Mixed Museum. The AMRI exhibition content and curation were organised by Chamion Caballero of The Mixed Museum, with Conrad Bryan and Peter Aspinall. We are very grateful for the written contributions in this book provided by William Hart, Mark Doyle and Maurice Casey, all of whom worked tirelessly, over many years, to uncover the hidden stories of black people in Ireland over past centuries. This publication has been expanded significantly to include more content about Ireland, which was not previously included in the AMRI exhibition.

In addition, we are deeply grateful to all those who have provided their support and encouragement during this project and contributed to the production of this book. In particular, thanks to our project team, Anisha Bryan, Tilly Lyons, Oona Colin and Jack Crangle who worked on the design, editing and proofreading of this edition, and for the support of AMRI board members Jude Hughes, Alan Powderly and Phil Mullen. Also, we would like to thank the following for all their support and assistance: Elizabeth Anionwu OM DBE, Peter Aspinall, John Kennedy CBE, Enya Egan, Leeds Irish Centre, SuAndi, the Buckley family, William Laffan, Brendan Rooney, Daniel Livesay, Kerri McLean and Mammoth Screen, Pauline Nevins, Tam Joseph and also Stuart Kinsella, Research Advisor and Ruth Kenny Head of Learning, Christ Church Cathedral. The publisher would also like to thank all individuals and organisations for permissions to reproduce images and archival content included in the list of illustrations in this book. In addition, we would also like to thank all those who supported us in producing the AMRI exhibition in 2020.

We are especially grateful to our sponsors and donors for their continued support and encouragement, without which this book would not have been possible. We wish to thank the many individuals who have given donations, directly and through our online crowd funding platform.

Acknowledgements

In particular, we wish to thank our sponsors, for their generous support and grants, such as the Department of Foreign Affairs through its *Government of Ireland Emigrant Support Programme*, the Department of Children, Equality, Disability, Integration and Youth through its *International Decade for People of African Descent Fund*, University of Maynooth through the *Irish Research Council New Foundations Scheme 2023* and the Mixed Museum.

 An Roinn Leanaí, Comhionannais, Míchumais, Lánpháirtíochta agus Óige
Department of Children, Equality, Disability, Integration and Youth

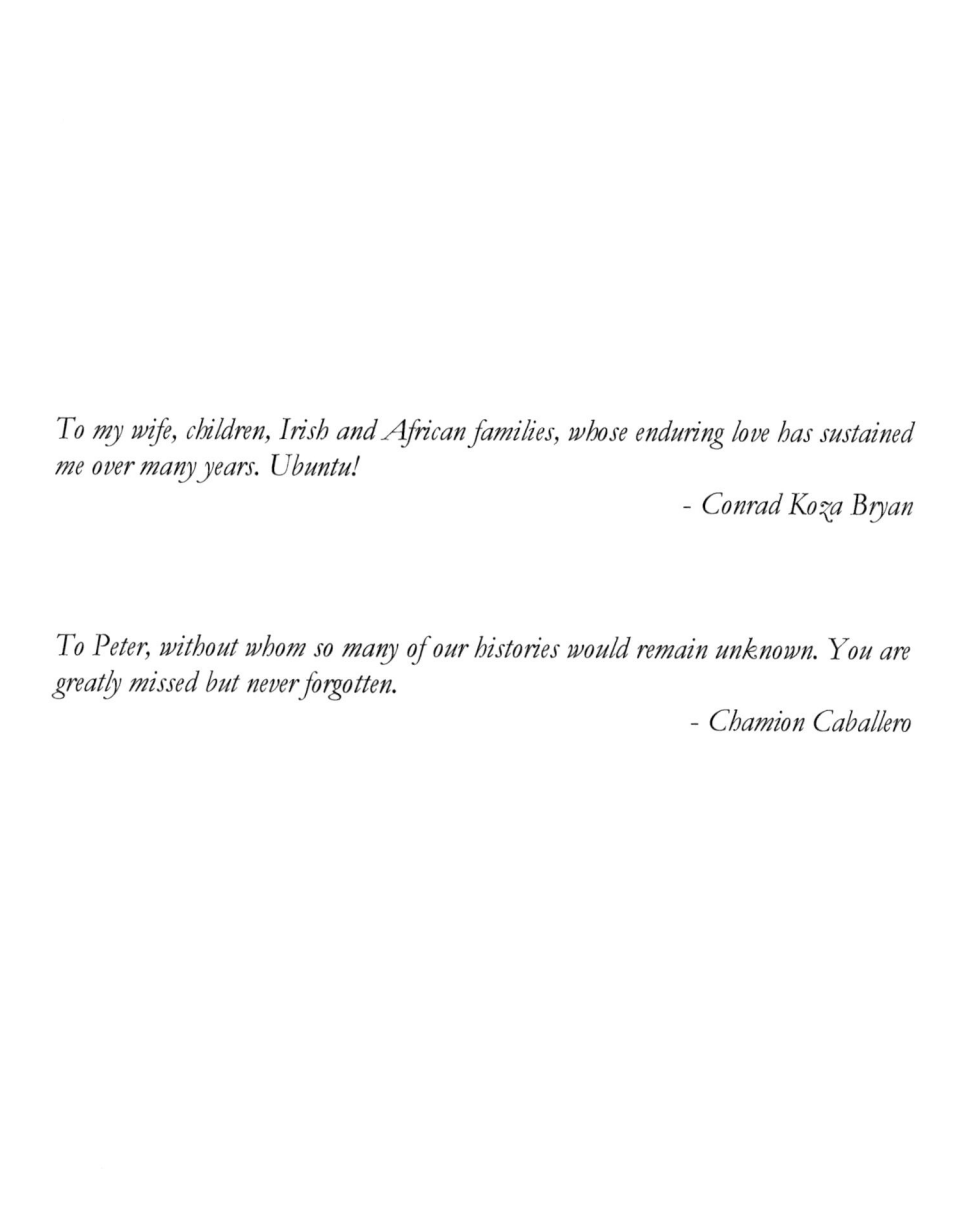

To my wife, children, Irish and African families, whose enduring love has sustained me over many years. Ubuntu!

- Conrad Koza Bryan

To Peter, without whom so many of our histories would remain unknown. You are greatly missed but never forgotten.

- Chamion Caballero

A Note on Language and Terminology

This book uses several terms to refer to people from different ethnic and cultural backgrounds. The histories presented to our readers here include people who arrived in Britain and Ireland over the centuries, such as Africans, Asians and Chinese as well as black people of African descent from America and the Caribbean. Many of these people integrated into Irish communities in Britain and Ireland and formed what were seen as 'mixed race' families. Today, their children and subsequent generations also identify as being of mixed race or heritage, as well as black, brown or ethnic and national descriptions - all terms which are frequently used by others to identify them too. We use these generally accepted terms throughout this book.

However, other terms feature in this book too, some of which are not acceptable today. Terminology and language about race changes over time, as groups and communities themselves challenge and redefine the words that describe them. What was standard usage, even in the recent past, is now outmoded or offensive. In this book, where words are considered offensive today, we put these in quotation marks to indicate their original historical usage, which is important for understanding how those of different races and ethnicities were viewed by others at the time.

It is important to note that, given the incredible diversity among and between people, the term 'race' is a biologically meaningless category. However, racial categories were used extensively during the centuries of African enslavement and retain their salience today. With this in mind, our use of the term 'Irish people of colour' aims to capture the wider group of people, from ethnic minority communities, who were connected to Ireland and its people, across the British Isles. In addition, this descriptor is not about nationality, though technically people in Britain today are 'Irish citizens' if they have a grandfather born in Ireland. Hence, this is less relevant within an historical context when Ireland was part of the British Empire.

A Note on Language and Terminology

Although our project sprung from a focus on mixed race families and people, this book is not solely about this group, even though much of our work relates to mixed race families and people in later generations, many of whom self-identify in multiple ways.

Note that there are several extracts and images in the book taken from archival material, such as newspaper articles and literature, which contain terms that are considered pejorative today and should be understood within the context and times within which it was written. However, given the 'n' word is generally considered offensive and inflammatory today and even in historical contexts, we have decided to star out this term so that it reads as 'n*****'.

Contents

Acknowledgements v
A Note on Language and Terminology ix
List of Illustrations xiii
Foreward xxi
Preface xxiii
Introduction xxv

Chapters:
1. Early Irish History 1
2. Irish Roots 41
3. Racial and Ethnic Diversity in Britain 99
4. Early Twentieth Century Migration 133
5. Racial Mixing During and Post – WW2 187
6. Racial Mixing in the Era of Mass Migration 199
7. Racism and Daily Life 207
8. Celebrated Personalities 229
  Afterword 253
  Selected Bibliography 257
  References 265
  Index 281

List of Illustrations

No.		Page
1.	Portrait of the Earl of Mulgrave and the 'African Boy'	2
2.	St. Werburgh's Church	3
3.	The Ely Family, by Angelica Kauffman (1741–1807)	4
4.	A Show for the Benefit of the Celebrated Mrs. Ellis.	9
5.	Bristol Hot Wells in 1773	10
6.	The Celebrated Mrs. Ellis, formerly Miss Baptist	11
7.	Mrs. Ellis at the New Theatre in Birmingham	12
8.	Rachel Baptist acting in *Romeo and Juliette*	14
9.	A Genlteman's Poem to Mrs. Crow	15
10.	The sinking of the *Mary Ann* on 13th March 1783	16
11.	Auction of the cargo of the sunken Mary Ann ship	17
12.	Auction at Dunany in May 1883	18
13.	Public Cant at Drogheda Custom House	18
14.	Marriage of John Suttoe and Margaret Brien	19
15.	George Forbes, 6th Earl of Granard	21
16.	Painting of Dido Elizabeth Belle, 1779	25
17.	Baptismal record of Sabina Eleanor Tierney, 1785	27
18.	Destination of mixed race Jamaicans 1773-1815	28
19.	City of Cork, by T. Roberts, 1799.	29
20.	Mir Aulad Ali, 1875	30
21.	'Irish Negro Falls Heir to Property', 1896	33
22.	All Black Drummers in 1757	34

List of Illustrations

No.	Page
23. Cudjo the State Trumpet	34
24. A runaway 'Negro Man'.	36
25. Frontispiece of John Jea's autobiography	42
26. Blossom Alley, near Hawke Street, Portsea, 1906	43
27. Jack Tar admiring the Fair Sex, 1815	44
28. Sea Stores, 1812	44
29. Burial record of 'Anthony Small a Black aged 40'	47
30. Bold Sir William (a Barb) and an Indian Servant	49
31. Sake Dean Mahomed	51
32. *The Travels of Dean Mahomet*, 1794	52
33. Irish baptism entry for the Mahomed's son Dean	52
34. Sake Dean Mahomed	53
35. Plaque for Mahomed's Indian restaurant	54
36. Jane wife of S.D. Mahomed	54
37. Sake Dean Mahomed's Baths, Brighton	55
38. Mahomed's Medicated Baths	55
39. Ladies Baths superintended by Mrs. Mahomed	56
40. James Dean Keriman Mahomed	57
41. New gymnasium opened by Mr. Frederick Mahomed	57
42. Marriage of Sake Dean's grandson	58
43. Pablo Paddington in Wellington in 1840	59
44. Spectacle at Batty's Circus in Cork 1842	60

List of Illustrations

No.	Page
45. Paddington takes his benefit as a 'Corkman himself.'	60
46. Pablo Paddington the 'Flying African'	61
47. Two female impostors	62
48. Pablo, the first slack rope vaulter.	63
49. The 'celebrated man-monkey, Pablo Paddington'	64
50. Appreciation extended to Fanque and Paddington	65
51. George Van Hare, 1888	65
52. Pablo over the fire in 1853	67
53. Greatest Novelties ever produced in Cork	68
54. Mr. Van Hare 'In the Lions' Cage'	69
55. George Paddington gains a doctorate in Theology	70
56. M. McCarty rents from Rev. G. J. Paddington	71
57. The Riots in Belfast in 1872	76
58. Paul Robeson and wife visiting Dublin in 1935	97
59. Changing the Guard at St James's Palace, 1792	99
60. Sketch of Charles McGee in *Vagabondiana*, 1817	100
61. Sketch of Joseph Johnson in *Vagabondiana*, 1817	100
62. John Orde, His Wife, Anne, his Eldest Son	101
63. A musical club, Truro, 1808	102
64. 'Dudley Street, Seven Dials', a wood engraving	103
65. 'Black Brown & Fair' with song sheet	104
66. Four men and a 'black woman' break into house	105

No.	Page
67. Lowest "life in London" by Cruickshank (1821)	106
68. 'Midnight' by Cruickshank (1821)	107
69. "Lemonade. Bal-loon say, and Swing" in Dicken's	109
70. High Life Below Stairs; or MUNGO	111
71. 'a lusty black Woman'	112
72. 'Discordant Harmony' in 1860	114
73. Irish woman in a mixed race marriage in 1798	115
74. 'The Irish Sphinx'	116
75. "Another Ugly One!"	117
76. Irish girls marrying Chinese men	118
77. Edward Marcus Despard	120
78. Day and Son, Cutting and Trucking Mahogany	121
79. 'London Corresponding Society, alarm'd.'	123
80. Colonel Despard in bed with a black woman	124
81. The hanging of Edward Marcus Despard	127
82. Kerri McLean as Kitty Despard	128
83. Lady Hamilton abandons Catherine Despard	131
84. Widow of the 'unfortunate Colonel Despard'	132
85. Catherine Despard's burial record, 1815	132
86. 'White Girls Marry Black Men'	133
87. Secrets of the Freak Show	134
88. Racial problem of black and white	135

List of Illustrations

No.	Page
89. Indian Princesses marry two English brothers.	136
90. Madame Wellington Koo	138
91. Lionel Montgomery Caulfield-Stoker	139
92. The Norseman ship passing Barton, 1894	140
93. 'The Landing of Savage South Africa', 1899	144
94. 'Savage South Africa'	144
95. Peter Lobengula and Kitty Jewel	146
96. Death of Prince Lobengula	147
97. Painting of Len Johnson by Tam Joseph	148
98. John Archer in his mayoral robes	151
99. Mrs. Archer, a 'Coloured Mayoress'	152
100. John Archer's speech	154
101. The Black Mayor	155
102. James Clarke, a celebrated swimmer	156
103. Wild Scenes in Wales in 1919	158
104. Racial Riots in Cardiff. Sensational Scenes	159
105. 'You Ought to be Burned'	160
106. "Canton Kitty" and "Lascar Sally"	164
107. 'Among East End Asiatics and Africans'	165
108. Wedding Procession of Canton Kitty	166
109. Cover of *Limehouse Nights* (1920)	168
110. Image of Crown Street children, 1930	172

List of Illustrations

No.	Page
111. Soldiers Wives in India	174
112. Count of pejorative terminology	175
113. A Warning to English Girls	178
114. Illustration from *The Englishwoman*, 1912	180
115. Aubrey Menen, the Irish-Indian author	181
116. Book cover of *Indian or British?*	184
117. The Satar family, Butetown in Cardiff, 1943	187
118. Map of Canning Town, 1940	188
119. Elizabeth Nneka Anionwu	192
120. Lilian Bader	194
121. Stow-Away Girl	198
122. Dolores Mantez - actress	202
123. Singer and Comedian Kenny Lynch	203
124. Enoch Powell and the Race Bill	208
125. K. Lynch, S. Milligan and E. Sykes in 'Curry and Chips'	212
126. The Gbadamosi family, Vauxhall, c.1965	214
127. Phil Lynott of Thin Lizzy, at a recording session	217
128. Statue of Phil Lynott	218
129. John Conteh holds his trophy aloft	220
130. 'Band on the Run' album by Wings'	221
131. John Conteh escorting Veronica Smith	221
132. A still image of *A Touch of Eastern Promise*	223

List of Illustrations

No.	Page
133. Extract from 'My Joy at Chris, by Mrs. Hughton'	225
134. Chistine Buckley, 20 May 2009	229
135. Christine Buckley with her father in the 1980's	233
136. Christine Buckley in 2010	234
137. SuAndi's father	236
138. SuAndi, aged 8	236
139. SuAndi receiving her honorary degree	237
140. Book cover of *Sister Josephine*	238
141. *Lara*, a debut novel by Bernardine Evaristo	240
142. Paul McGrath, footballer	243
143. Phil Babb and Paul McGrath with Rep. of Ireland team	244
144. Kanya King MOBO Founder	245
145. Terry Phelan footballer	246
146. Wilf O'Reilly, speed skating champion	248
147. UK 2001 Census ethnic categories	249
148. White married people by ethnic group	250
149. UK Census: Irish born and resident	251
150. Framed picture of John Mulgrave, the 'African Boy'	253

Foreword

Professor Dame Elizabeth Nneka Anionwu

It is a pleasure to contribute this foreward to the first social history book about Irish people of colour and mixed race Irish families in Britain and Ireland. I have had the privilege to get to know Conrad Koza Bryan personally over several years, as The Association of Mixed Race Irish was developing in London. Although the association had its provenance in the legacies of the abuse of mixed race children in Irish childcare institutions, Conrad has always had his eyes on the future and how people can learn more about the hidden history of mixed race Irish figures, who had followed similar migration patterns from Ireland to Britain in the past. Conrad has worked on this excellent project in collaboration with Chamion Caballero, Director of The Mixed Museum. Both Conrad's and Chamion's passion for interesting mixed race and ethnic minority histories shines through in this book. We are so lucky to now have the fruits of their successful research for this book.

There are several aspects of the stories in this publication which resonate with my own (see page 192). I am sure this will also be the case for many of the second and third generation Irish in Britain, who want to know more about the history of integration and relationships with other non-Irish and black communities. This book is also about an evolving Irish identity within the Irish diaspora in Britain and how moving from shades of white to black impacts our view of what it is to be Irish. I know Conrad, the son of a black South African and a white Irish mother, emigrated from Ireland to Britain in 1989. He always wondered and asked where are all the Irish people in Britain who look like him! Well, the answer is here in the stories of all the mixed race and black families who were in Ireland in past centuries, working in various roles, such as domestic servants, soldiers, labourers, circus acrobats, even a black priest in Cork etc. Many of these black people inter-married in Ireland and often emigrated to Britain. In the 20th Century we read about the migration of ethnic minorities into Britain as sailors, labourers and students etc, from Africa, India and the West Indies. They integrated into the white British communities and often had families with mainly white Irish women and women of Irish descent in Britain.

Importantly, the book also provides the unsavoury accounts of racial prejudice and racism faced by these mixed race families in Britain in the past. It seems the prejudice faced by white Irish people in general, especially during the Troubles, might have been avoided by Irish people of colour who faced the racial prejudice. Some research[1] has been carried out, which compared racial discrimination between white Irish and black people in Birmingham. However, the short narratives in this book raise provocative questions about our multi-ethnic society and there are plenty of book references for further reading. In this respect, it also acts as a great reference point for further in depth reading. This has been a great read and I thoroughly enjoyed the family stories. In particular the one about Ireland's black priest Fr George Paddington and his acrobat brother "Pablo" with his circus escapades in Britain and Ireland.

– Professor Dame Elizabeth Nneka Anionwu
Patron of Irish in Britain

Preface

Conrad Koza Bryan

There are often unexpected encounters, we all experience, which remain deeply embedded within our memories long afterwards. One of these chance encounters was when I met a British man over a cup of tea at a friend's house in Cork in 2022. I was fascinated with his story about being born in England and his discovery of a photo of his great grandfather hanging on the wall at his grandfather's house in England. He was intrigued at his skin tone and hair and was convinced he was mixed race and possibly of African descent. He inquired within the family to see if there were any family stories about his Irish ancestors and in particular his great grandfather's. Dead silence! Nobody seemed to know and no stories were passed down the generations either. He showed me the photo of his great grandfather and I became curious as I could see his face looked very Irish but his hair appeared to be afro, tight cut and he wore what appeared to be a well-tailored suit, shirt and tie. This was a photo of a man whose appearance was clearly of a well-groomed Irish gentleman, with unusual hair!

It turned out that this British man I met in Cork and his family are the quintessential immigrant third generation white Catholic Irish family, living in the United Kingdom. Nobody would ever suspect they could possibly be mixed, let alone of African and Irish descent. But when his father took a DNA test they found traces of African ancestry, possibly a few generations back. This provided further evidence to support his suspicions. His great grandfather was born in Ireland in the early 1800s and his son had emigrated to England. Questions abounded as to how the African ancestor ended up in Ireland? Was it as part of a foreign army at war in Ireland in the 17th or 18th Centuries or as some servant brough in by an Anglo-Irish aristocratic family from a far-away plantation? The heritage, especially the African line, of this family is still

Preface

unknown and we are excitedly digging to find out! However, this is a story of emigration which is mirrored in some of the interesting histories of families you will find in this book. Many involve migration between the islands, which make up the British Isles, along with the mixing between different ethnic groups, which make up Britain today.

Chamion Caballero

The idea for this book came out of the online AMRI [1] exhibition in July 2020 curated by The Mixed Museum. Dr Chamion Caballero and I felt that as we had done so much research from our respective archives for the exhibition why not turn it into a book for the benefit of students in schools and Irish communities in Britain and Ireland? This would help raise awareness about this hidden group with mixed ancestry and heritage. This book has been a real pleasure to compile and has been a passion of labour and discovery, searching for Irish families who cross racial and ethnic lines, forming new Irish Britain identities. The book spans three centuries from 1700 to 2000 and provides accounts of the lives and challenges of mixed race families and people of colour living during this time.

– *Conrad Koza Bryan*

Introduction

The popular conception of interraciality in Britain is one that frequently casts mixed racial relationships, people and families as being a modern phenomenon. Yet, as scholars are increasingly discussing, interraciality in Britain has much deeper and diverse roots, with scholars uncovering a substantively documented presence at least as far back as the Tudor era. From the outset, this study of racial mixing and mixedness has predominantly taken the form of white women partnering and raising children with men of colour; however, despite a growing body of scholarship highlighting the racial and ethnic diversity of the men, little attention has been paid to that of the women.

Yet, as research at The Mixed Museum is revealing, it is clear that the blanket term 'white women' encompasses a range of ethnicities, not least that of women from white Irish backgrounds – a fact clearly reflected by the existence and work of The Association of Mixed Race Irish (AMRI). The fascinating history of mixed race Irish families in Britain highlighted here is the result of a collaboration between AMRI and The Mixed Museum. Drawing on materials held in both our collections as well as research especially commissioned for the project, this publication provides an insight into the presence and experiences of these families in Britain and Ireland, the range of reactions towards them, as well as the social contexts in which they lived. By creating an Irish perspective, we aim to contribute to knowledge about the diversity of Britain's changing ethnic and racial mix over the last few centuries. The accounts of the lives described in this book also challenge the notion that the diversity we see in Ireland today is somehow a recent phenomenon.

This book, based on the online AMRI exhibition at The Mixed Museum, shows many mixed-race Irish families formed as the result of migration to Britain and Ireland. Here we present a number of accounts that highlight how Ireland's own multicultural history played a part in the growth of Britain's racially diverse society. This is in addition to the increasing scholarship in this area, which is discovering new stories and increasing our knowledge of the diverse racial presence in Ireland that dates back to the early modern period, including the formation of mixed race people and families.

We are delighted to have included the contributions of William Hart, Mark Daly and Maurice Casey in this book, which can be read in chapter 2, Irish Roots. Their narratives and research have greatly added to the rich tapestry of histories and themes reflected in this publication. We have also added a short commentary at the end of their contributions, where we have made any further discoveries or have other observations on the characters or themes they have written about.

Chapter 1

Early Irish History

Ireland's Early Multiracial History

Passing references to people of colour in Ireland can be found in accounts as early as 1578 when Sir William Drury of Kilkenny ordered that a 'blackamoor' and two witches be burned at the stake. This is in addition to the mentions of black servants and 'slaves' that creep into records during the course of the seventeenth century.[1] William Hart is the first person to estimate the population of the black people in Ireland. He identified reports of black people in Irish newspapers and estimated that there were between 1,000-3,000 black people in Ireland during the latter part of the eighteenth century.

This estimate makes the Irish black presence in the eighteenth century as large as that of France which had a population four times the size of Ireland.[2] It appears that though the country's black population was small, it was not necessarily strange or unknown to the white population. In recounting the reporting on a 'female black and child' who were terrified by a jostling, staring crowd in Dublin in 1777, Hart notes that the newspaper commented that:

> *'Had she in any manner differed from others of her colour and country so common to meet with, it might have been some apology, to gratify curiosity; that not being the case, it reflects both scandal and ignorance on the company, and the more so, as the time and the place considered, much better behaviour might be expected.'* [3]

Evidence of the historical black presence in Ireland can also be seen in other records, such as in art and on stone. If you had entered St. Werburgh's Church, on Werburgh Street in Dublin, a few years ago you would have been surprised to see a black and white portrait (see page 253) of John Mulgrave, an African Boy, with Lord Mulgrave. The title written on the portrait states: 'In Christ Jesus there is – Neither Bond nor Free' and below the picture it states: 'John Mulgrave, The African

Boy. Buried at St. Werburgh's. Feb. 28th 1838 – Aged 17 Years –'. Today, there is a tablet on the wall, inside the church, dated 1838, which reveals how John Mulgrave, an enslaved African boy, was rescued and brought to Ireland by the Lord Mulgrave, an Anglo-Irish statesman and novelist.

1. Portrait (1835-38) of Constantine Henry Phipps, 1st Marquess of Normanby (1797-1863), also known as the Earl of Mulgrave (1831-1838), with the 'African Boy', John Mulgrave (detail). Oil on Canvas by Nicholas Joseph Crowley (1813-1857). The framed picture of both, in St. Werburgh's Church, was identified by Stuart Kinsella, Research Advisor at Christ Church Cathedral, Dublin, as most likely reproduced from Charles O'Mahony, *The Viceroys of Ireland* (London, 1912), opp. p. 240, which was based on the above painting. Image reproduced by permission of the National Gallery of Ireland (NGI.202).

The following words are inscribed on the tablet at St. Werburgh's Church:

Sacred to the Memory
of
JOHN MULGRAVE
an African Boy. Shipwrecked in
a Spanish Slave Ship on the
Coast of Jamaica in the year 1833,
When he was taken under the protection
of the EARL of MULGRAVE.
The Governor of that Island,
in whose family he resided
till the 27th of February 1838, when
it pleased God to remove him from
this life by severe attack of Small Pox.

His Integrity, Fidelity, and kind
And amiable qualities, had endeared
Him to all his Fellow Servants, at
Whose desire this Tablet is erected
By his Godmother.

The 'Earl of Mulgrave', engraved on the tablet of John Mulgrave, was Constantine Henry Phipps (1797 – 1863), who was known as the Earl of Mulgrave between 1831 and 1838 and served as Ireland's Lord Lieutenant from 1835 to 1839, after returning from Jamaica.[4] His grandfather, also called Constantine Phipps (1722-1775) was an Irish peer and, in 1767, became the 1st Baron of Mulgrave of New Ross, in County Wexford.[5] Phipps returned from Jamaica to take up his role as Lord Lieutenant of Ireland, bringing the African boy, John Mulgrave, with him. John Mulgrave would most likely have lived his short life in the Viceregal apartments in Dublin Castle, along with his 'Fellow Servants' who had 'endeared' him.

St. Werburgh's Church was originally built by the people of Bristol, in the reign of Henry II (1133 – 1189), but was destroyed by fire in 1300. It was burnt down again in 1754 and rebuilt in 1759 in the style existing today in Werburgh Street, Dublin.[6] It is the burial ground of several leading Protestant figures, such as Lord Edward Fitzgerald. He famously brought home from America a black escapee called Tony Small who rescued him during the American Revolutionary War (see page 46).

2. St. Werburgh's Church,
Werburgh Street, Dublin. Photo taken by
C. Bryan on 22 November 2023

St. Werburgh's burial register also records John Mulgrave, referenced in the wall tablet, as having been buried at St. Werburgh's Church in 1838. This child was brought back from Jamaica to Ireland to live with the Mulgrave family in Dublin and died of small pox.

In art, we see depictions of black children, seemly living as child pageants or servants, with Irish aristocratic families. Kauffmann's 1771 portrait of an Irish aristocratic family below highlights the fashion amongst eighteenth century European elites to have black and Indian enslaved people or servants in their household.

3. The Ely Family, 1771, by Angelica Kauffman (1741–1807).
Presented, 4th Marquess of Ely, 1878.
Image courtesy of National Gallery of Ireland (NG1.200).

Around the time of this painting, in the 18th Century, Ireland had a strong anti-slavery movement, particularly in cities such as Belfast, Cork and Dublin. The formerly enslaved Olaudah Equiano (1745-97)[7] visited Ireland in 1791-2 as part of the abolition movement in Ireland, to speak against slavery and to promote his autobiography called *The Interesting narrative of the Life of Olaudah Equiano or Gustavus Vassa, the African*. The Dublin edition printed in 1791 sold an impressive 1,900 copies and had significant supporters and subscribers such as the archbishop of Dublin, the lord mayor, Henry Howson, the earls of Ormond and Milltown, the duke of Leinster, David La Touche and Lady Moira. However, there were no subscribers from the Ely family.[8]

Regarding the above painting, Phillip McEvansoneya notes the following in this extract:

> *'The black servant figure could only have been included by Kauffman with the consent of her patron, Lord Ely, who may even have suggested it. The presence of a black servant figure in portraits had been an established artistic convention since the seventeenth century. Therefore, if not a demand of the patron, the black servant in the Ely group may have been a gesture by Kauffman to show that she had, after five or so years in Britain, learnt what were the prevailing elements in group portraiture, which she then applied to Irish sitters.'*[9]

The following is also noted by William Laffan and Brendan Rooney in their book, *Thomas Roberts 1748-1777. Landscape and Patronage in Eighteenth-century Ireland* (2009) in this extract:

> *'As Philip McEvansoneya has observed, such figures, however well treated, "were human commodities in an age which indulged its appetites for the colours, tastes and textures of the world beyond Europe, the expanding world of imperial possession"'*[10]

Irish aristocrats were no different to their European colonial counterparts when it came to new and exotic European trends, fads and fashion associated with black bodies. However, below we see other accounts of the lived experiences of some of these people of colour in Ireland.

'Mulatto Jack'

As with people of colour in Britain during the early modern era, many in Ireland are likely to have entered into relationships with members of the local white population, such as the parents of 'Mulatto Jack'. In 1736, investigators looking into an uprising plot by enslaved black people in Antigua, sought advice from the island's Governor on how to deal with 'a person called Mulatto Jack' who was brought before them as 'a criminal slave concerned in the plot' but who 'alleged he was free born in Ireland and stolen thence and sold here as a slave'. After several months' imprisonment, it was agreed that Jack not be brutally executed as the majority of the accused enslaved people were but be released provided that he was sent immediately back to Ireland. We do not know Jack's full name and few details are known about his life, but scholars have estimated that he was likely kidnapped around 1720, raising fascinating questions about his family and upbringing in early 18th century Ireland.[11]

Rachel Baptist – Celebrated 18th Century Black Singer

Rachel Baptist (fl. 1750–1773), was a celebrated black singer in Ireland and England, who had a musical career, lasting almost a quarter of a century. William Hart has researched and written extensively on the hidden and somewhat fragmented story of Baptist. Like many black entertainers and stage performers in the past, such as the circus acrobat Pablo Paddington, her family life and background was sparsely recorded. However, thanks to Hart, we know a lot more today about her musical performances and movements in Ireland and Britain. His important, painstaking research provides us with what we know today as outlined below. Here we also add some insights and a little further information from our research to build on his excellent work.

Baptist first appeared in Dublin in the 1750s, entertaining and singing to audiences in the city's pleasure gardens.[12] Her singing repertoire was contemporary for this time and included popular Irish and Scottish airs and concert arias by G. F. Handel (qv), Boyce, and Thomas Arne. She made her debut in Dublin in February 1750 when she performed at a benefit concert for her music teacher Bernardo Palma. She was described then as a "native of this country."[13] She would have been about 13 years old at this time, judging by a later marriage bond in England, we have seen, dated 1758, which stated she was 21 years old, indicating she was born around 1737 (see below). A month after her first performance, she appeared in a double bill at the Music Hall in Crow Street, in Dublin, alongside an 'Indian Gentleman' in a show advertised as one in which 'The two Performers hope to convince, that the Power of Music is not confined to Colour.'[14] This is a remarkable public statement made by the organisers of the event on behalf of the two performers and gives an indication of attempts to overcome racial prejudice at that time.

No church records of Baptist's birth or baptism have yet been found. Hart suggests that, with the name 'Baptist', her forebears may have arrived earlier from the French West Indies. It is also possible that, given her entry into the world of music and stage, her background was within a musical and aristocratic Irish family, as a child servant brought into the country from abroad. As David Livesay noted, wealthy planters in the Caribbean also sent their mixed race children to relatives in Britain and Ireland to receive a good education.[15] However, given the little we do know, we currently assume she was born in Ireland.

Between 1750 and 1753 Baptist sang regularly at Marlborough Green in Dublin. The Irish actor and playwright, John O'Keefe (1747–1833), attended the concerts in Marlborough-Green Dublin as a young boy (Marlborough Green was west of Marlborough Street, between Cope Street, now called Talbott Street, and Lower Abbey Street). O'Keefe had a great fondness for songs and he went there in 1758 and saw Rachel Baptist singing "among the many fine singers" and described her as:

> *"a real black woman, a native of Africa: she always appeared in the orchestra, in a yellow silk gown, and was heard by the applauding company with great delight, without remarks on upon her sables"*[16]

Clearly, no one was concerned about Baptist's "sables", which in literary terms means dark colour, referring to her skin and hair. O'Keefe noted that she sang one of the popular songs, at that time called "Fair Kitty, beautiful and young" by Lord Chesterfield. He described Dublin's Marlborough Green as:

> *"a sort of tea drinking place, with singers, bands of music…and was greatly frequented. It was a large square, kept in capital order as a bowling green: at the far side was a slope, leading up to a terrace: in the centre of this rose the orchestra, at the back of this there was a gravel walk which…led to a tea room."*[17]

This is the venue where Baptist sang and it is possible that she saw or heard about some of the abhorrent duels that occurred at this period, such as that described by O'Keefe, which took place at this venue in Marlborough Green. The duel he witnessed one evening on the Green, was between two noblemen which resulted in the death of a Lord, unnamed by O'Keefe.[18] In fact, it was the 19 year old drunk Lord Devlin (Richard Nugent), the eldest son and heir of the 6th Earl of Westmeath, who was fatally wounded by Captain George Reilly, on 5 July 1761, at this pleasure garden where the nobility "whiled away their time in the pursuit of pleasure."[19] Baptist had left for England by this time and the incident caused "a *grande monde* of Dublin society to desert Marlborough Green" and it was closed shortly afterwards.[20] The patrons of these music venues and pleasure gardens were of the higher social classes and aristocracy, amongst which Baptist would mingle during her lifetime and musical career. O'Keefe described her a 'native of Africa' which was likely based on his observation of her as black singer, which fascinated him as a boy of about 10 years old, rather than on his real knowledge of Baptist and her actual family background.

She left Ireland to perform in England between 1757 and 1767, but records of her time there are somewhat patchy and minimal. During this period, she toured several cities such as Liverpool, Newcastle, Ipswich, Denham, Bath, London, and Birmingham, though, as Hart points out, her appearances in Bath and London do not appear in any of the standard reference works on the eighteenth-century London stage.[21] However, her performances in Liverpool are well reported in local newspapers which reported that 'Miss Baptist, the celebrated singer from the gardens of Dublin', sang in the *Ranelagh Gardens* in Liverpool in the spring and summer of 1758. The pleasure garden at Ranelagh in Liverpool was the city centre's first public recreation space, opened in the 1720s, modelled on gardens of the same name in London. Its "fish pond surrounded by flowers, shrubs and alcoves made it a popular green spot for wealthy residents on what was then the edge of an emerging industrial and slave port."[22] Baptist would possibly have seen some of the 'slave' auctions held in public houses and on the steps of Liverpool's Customs House around this time.[23] Liverpool's *Ranelagh Gardens* closed in the 1790s and is now the site of the Adelphi Hotel.

On 26 June 1758, 'Rachel Baptist' married a mariner called Thomas Ellis. They married at Our Lady and St Nicholas, Church of England, Liverpool.[24] The marriage bond was signed the previous day on 25th June,[25] which stated that Thomas Ellis was a mariner, resident in Liverpool. Her age was stated as 21 years old, therefore her year of birth is estimated at around 1737. The record notes her as a 'Spinster' and her abode was stated as Liverpool. The witness was Daniel Conway, a surgeon, also from Liverpool. Rachel Baptist now started to perform under the name of "Mrs Ellis".

In June 1762 a concert was arranged in the Assembly Hall in Ipswich "by Desire of Lady Barker" for the benefit of the "Celebrated Mrs ELLIS, Formerly Miss Baptist". The vocal part of the instrumental music session was performed by Mrs Ellis. See extract of the newspaper notice for this event below:

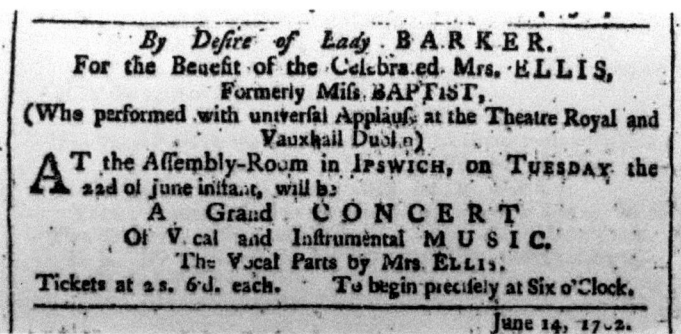

4. By Desire of Lady Barker, For the Benefit of the Celebrated Mrs. Ellis. *Ipswich Journal* 19 June 1762. Image @ The British Library Board. Shelfmark: 013923465.

Interestingly, this notice is specifically at the request of Lady Barker, which hints at some form of connection between her and Miss Ellis. It would be useful to know which Barker family[26] this was, as it may give some more clues about Baptist background with further research. At this time, Sir William Barker 3rd Baronet of Bocking Hall, Essex, and Kilcooley Abbey, Ireland was married to Lady Mary Barker (née Quin), daughter of Valentine Quin from Adare in Co Limerick, an Irish political family. This Barker family had homes in both Ireland and Sussex which is near Ipswich. Kilcooley Abbey is not far from Kilkenny, where the Barkers owned land, and where Baptist was later to return for further musical performances. After Ipswich, 'Mrs Ellis' performed on 14th July 1762 at the Assembly Hall at Dedham for the 'benefit of Joseph Gibbs'.

In 1764 and 1765 Baptist appeared in Bath and Birmingham newspapers as "Mrs Ellis", formerly the celebrated Miss Baptist. The *Pope's Bath Chronical* reported that "Mrs Ellis (the celebrated singer)" arrived at Bristol Hotwells on 18 August 1764 along with several other dignitaries. The Bristol Hot Wells lies in Avon Gorge at the River Avon, and was popular during the Georgian period for treatment of illnesses and diseases.[27] The sketch of Bristol Hot Wells in 1773 on the following page, as depicted in the 1867 book by the author Emma Marshall, gives a sense of what recreation was like around the time of Mrs Ellis's visit.

5. Bristol Hot Wells in 1773
Sketch by unknown artist in the book
Bristol Diamonds or The Hot Wells in the year 1773
by Emma Marshall (1867). Image courtesy of
the British Library Board. Shelfmark: 012633.m.5.

Perhaps Mrs Ellis was suffering from some illness at the time and sought some form of treatment and recovery. This was a resort for socialites and the aristocracy, who could afford time at the local hotels. In the picture above it is clear that life included balls and music (see musicians under the trees). Mrs Ellis, 'the celebrated singer', arrived at the Hot Wells without her husband.

The new discovery here of 'Mrs Ellis' in a Birmingham newspaper, once again, points to the painful and slow process of building the full story of a black entertainer in the 18th century. As Hart mentions, Baptist "made the claim that she had performed in London, Bath and other principal parts of England" and only now we see that 'other principal parts' included Birmingham. Thanks to the Library of Birmingham, we now know that in early 1765 "Mrs Ellis appeared in the *Aris's Birmingham Gazette*. Below is an advertisement for a musical event, in the Sawyer's Room in Birmingham, for the benefit of 'The Celebrated Mrs. Ellis, formerly Miss BAPTIST".

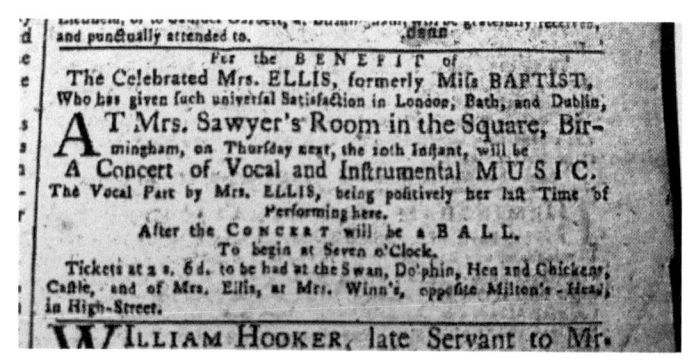

6. The Celebrated Mrs Ellis formerly Miss Baptist.
Aris's Birmingham Gazette, 7 January 1765.
Reproduced with permission of the Library of Birmingham.

In the same newspaper it was advertised, on 21st and 28th January 1765, that she will perform at the New Theatre in King Street Birmingham. This stated that this would be her last time performing here, suggesting she had performed here earlier, but also that she had plans to move on to another or bigger stage (see page 12). The advertisement is telling in that it mentions Mrs. Ellis performed to universal applause at Bath, London and Dublin and shows her hand in providing 'Boxes' tickets to members of the public, pointing to her role in the business management of the show. There were 35 Boxes available for sale. The advertisement also stated that the show would include the *Prologue* of "the Celebrated Mr Foote's", called the *Author*. The celebrated Mr Foote referred to in this advertisement, refers to Samuel Foote (1720 – 1777), who was a well-known actor, dramatist and theatre manager.

> (For One Night Only)
> AT the New-Theatre in King-Street, Birmingham, this present Evening wil be perform'd the Tragedy of
> VENICE PRESERV'D, or a PLOT DISCOVER'D.
> The Characters by a Set of young Gentlmn, and a Lady,
> Being their first Appearance on any Stage.
> To which will be added the farce of
> LETHE; Or, ÆSOP in the SHADES.
> The Characters by the same Performers.
> Between the Play and Farce will be spoke the favourite Prologue to the Farce, (of the celebrated Mr. FOOTE's) call'd the AUTHOR.
> Between the Acts of the Play will be introduced several capital SONGS by Mrs. ELLIS, formerly Miss BAPTIST, who perform'd with universal Applause at London, Bath, and Dublin.
> Being positively her last Time of Performing here.
> The Orchestra to be composed of a most select Band.
> Boxes 3s. Pit 2s. Gallery 1s.
> The Doors to be open'd at Five, and to begin precisely at Seven o'Clock.
> Places for the Boxes to be taken at Mrs. Ellis's, at Mrs. Winn's, at the Hen and Chickens.
> Tickets to be had at the Swan, Dolphin, Hen and Chickens, Castle, George, Red-Lion, of R. Pearson and S. Aris, Printers, and Mr. Sketchley, Bookseller.
> N. B. Proper Care is taken to have the House well air'd, and No-body to be admitted behind the Scenes.
> BIRMINGHAM, January 21, 1765.

7. Mrs Ellis at the New Theatre in Birmingham.
Aris's Birmingham Gazette, 28 January 1765.
Reproduced with permission of the
Library of Birmingham.

The cast in this performance were all on stage for the first time, so one wonders if Mr Foote attended this show as a scout, as it is surprising to see his *Prologue* being read out. Foote reopened the Haymarket Theatre in London in May 1767 and called it the Theatre Royal Haymarket following the granting of a licence in 1766 to operate the theatre legally.

The gap in Baptist's history and whereabouts after her appearance at the New Theatre in Birmingham in 1765 has probably been resolved by Hart, after he discovered an unnamed black singer at the Theatre Royal in Haymarket London he believes is likely to be Rachel Baptist.[28] If this revelation is true, it is a remarkable story of a professional singer faced with racial prejudice in London, despite her brilliant singing talent. On 7th September 1767, an advertisement, for the Theatre Royal Haymarket, announced the plays: *The Busy Body* and *The Mayor of Garratt* to be followed by the *Entertainments*. Part of the entertainment for this show was to be Foot's Occasional Prologue 'in which will be introduced - the real BLACK-A-MOOR LADY'.[29] In none of the earlier advertisements, in England and Ireland, was Baptist ever racialised as singer or performer. Her colour was never mentioned, even when visiting the Hotwells in Bristol, with the exception of her debut in Dublin in 1750, when colour was mentioned in the context of promoting her as a promising new talent and as a challenge to the prejudices of any doubters. Furthermore, Hart also points to this use of racialised terminology when he notes that the diarist Sylas Neville, who attended this show in 1767, wrote of his feelings on her performance as follows:

> *"Her confusion was so great, that seeing her gave me pain. On this occasion Foote gave us a stroke of humour; When the Blackamoor Lady had retired, he asked Snarl what character he thought she should play first. Snarl said in Imoinda.*
> *Foote replied "Don't you think Callista would do better? for it would have a good effect in the Bills--The Fair Penitent by a Black Lady."* [30]

It is worth noting that, unlike the other actors, nowhere in the programme is the, so-called, 'Blackamoor Lady' identified by name, which was in itself dehumanising and would have made it virtually impossible to promote herself elsewhere to progress her career. This is unlike the earlier advertisements where Baptist was recognised and identified as "the Celebrated Mrs Ellis, formerly Miss Baptist". As an accomplished singer, with several years of experience, it is surprising that she should have come across as "confused" at Haymarket theatre. Hart notes that there was quite some resistance from Foote's associates, to having a black person on stage in London. Perhaps she felt this on the night, but we do not know how the general audience reacted to her performance when singing the Scottish air *Thro' the Wood laddie*, which Baptist was known to have sung before. The actor and theatre manager, John Jackson, knew of Baptist from earlier performances in Lancashire, when he said he saw her acting as the character Polly Peachum in *The Beggars Opera* and said he was informed that she had performed as Juliet in *Romeo and Juliet*. This was a remarkable breakthrough for Baptist, as a person of colour, to perform these two leading roles. Nevertheless, it seems this counted for little in Haymarket and the performance at the Theatre Royal Haymarket in London is currently her last known (or likely known) stage performance in England.

8. Rachel Baptist acting in *Romeo and Juliette*.
Artist's impression. Courtesy of @Anisha Bryan

Earlier in the same year (1767), Baptist had announced her new name as Crow, in an advertisement for two concerts at Wrigley's Great Room in Liverpool. She now renamed herself 'Mrs Crow'. We don't have a record of her ever remarrying. The church marriage records of Rachel Baptist's marriage to Mr Crow have not yet been identified, so we do not know where, or if it actually took place. We know nothing about her husband's ethnicity or what country he came from. However, she now decided to move back to Dublin with her new husband.

On returning to Ireland, 'Mrs Crow' and her husband toured the major towns and cities, such as Limerick, Cork, Clonmel, Durrow, Bandon and Kilkenny where she made a positive name for herself. The audiences in Kilkenny were so impressed by her performances that even one "gentleman of Kilkenny", so moved by what he saw and heard, turned to poetry to convey his high opinion of the singer. His poem was published in the *Finn's Leinster Journal*, see the extract on page 15.

The last newspaper report of the couple is in Belfast. They began performances in Belfast in October 1772, attending concerts and balls once a month throughout the winter at the Assembly Room, and held other performances in Lisburn, Downpatrick, and Carrickfergus. Their final concert was held in Belfast on 30 April 1773 'for the benefit of Mr Richard Lee' who had fallen on hard times. The story of their lives then goes cold after 1773 and we do not know if they emigrated or had a family or when they died.

This is a remarkable story of the times and one which will not end, as other researchers find new information. There are so many unanswered questions about Baptist's life and how she survived as a person of colour in Ireland and Britain. She comes across as the lone "Syren", as noted in the Kilkenny poem, who appeared in Irish history out of nowhere.

In ancient Greek mythology, a siren is a hybrid human creature, usually a female, who lures mariners to their doom by their singing. We know for sure that Baptist married a mariner, but we know nothing about his fate.

Written by a Gentleman on the excellent perform-ance of the celebrated Mrs. CROW (formerly Miss BAPTIST) at her Concert in Kilkenny the first instant.

FAME's done thee right, thou hast the lulling art,
That can soft Music's melody impart;
Envy herself must thy perfections own,
And say thou'rt worthy of the laurel crown.
   Let the white Fair-ones swell with proud disdain,
Despise thy colour, and thy dusky mein;
Yet what of that—even these nor want their charms,
Nor grace to lure the lover to thine arms:
Such was *Amaryllus*, of a dusky hue,
If what the poet *Virgil* says be true;
And tell us now, ye Fair, the reason why
Ye think, ye boast a more bewitching eye:
Here's eyes as bright, nor yet inferior shine,
Tho' she wont b'lieve the foplings they're divine;
But hark t'her voice, sweet music in her tongue,
As if the fibres by *Apollo* strung;
Her voice will chant ye with melodious sound,
And *Echo* from the vaulted roof rebound.
The rapture-giving note will charm each ear,
Chear the sad heart from melancholy care;
Wil't think of colour then? wil't think of face?
When charms more moving seem to merit grace?
Disgust will vanish, b'lieve me, and disdain,
Nor wil't thou say, the Syren sung in vain,
But wil' be forc'd to clap her o'er again.

9. A Gentleman's Poem to Mrs. Crow.
Finn's Leinster Journal, 5 – 9 December 1767
Image courtesy of the National Library of Ireland.

John Suttoe and Margaret Brien – Mixed Marriage

Another glimpse at interraciality later in the 18th century can be found in the account of John Suttoe and Margaret Brien. Thanks to the research carried out by Turtle Bunbury[31] on the McClintock family of Drumcar and their black servant, we have been able outline the story of John Suttoe. This has enabled us to locate and provide some images of archived material from that time, referring to parts of his life. It is still a challenge to find a complete story of how he lived till the end despite extensive searching for more detail of when he died and if he had left a family behind.

Suttoe was a black man who survived a ship-wreck at Dunany, Co. Louth in 1783. He stayed on in Ireland and became a servant at Drumcar. The sinking of the *Mary Ann* ship, on which John Suttoe sailed, was described in detail in a letter from Dublin to the *Caledonian Mercury*, which can be read from the extract shown below.

> *Extract of a letter from Dublin, March 14.*
> "Yesterday se'nnight, in a violent storm, a ship named the Mary Ann, of New York, laden with rum, tobacco, and slaves, bound for Liverpool, was stranded opposite the house of Robert Sibthorpe, Esq; at Dunneany, in the county of Louth. When the vessel struck, great part of the crew mutinied and quit the ship, being intimidated by the country people, who they discovered assembling on the shore in great numbers, with intent to plunder the vessel, and soon after boarded her, and threatened to throw the captain and the remaining hands overboard if they made any resistance. In this dilemma the captain continued for sometime, until he was relieved by the appearance of Stephen James Sibthorpe, Esq; whose spirited and prudent conduct on this occasion, cannot be sufficiently applauded. This young gentleman, upon hearing the account, immediately armed himself and his servants, and repaired to the vessel, where he found great numbers of the country people aboard in a state of inebriety, having before his arrival broke open the locks, and tore all before them in plundering the vessel, and were preparing to carry away part of the cargo, but Mr Sibthorpe, at the hazard of his life, obliged them immediately to desist, and took one of the ringleaders with his own hands, who had the audacity to make a blow at him with a drawn hanger, and sent for the proper officers, put the ship and cargo under their care, with a sufficient guard to assist the officers, and attended in person both day and night, by which means the ship and cargo has been preserved for the benefit of the owners. The fatigued passengers were also taken care of, having been conducted to Dunneany, where they met with proper refreshment and attention."

10. The sinking of the *Mary Ann* on 13th March 1783 off the Dunneany coast. *Caledonian Mercury*, 19 March 1783. Image courtesy of The British Library Board. Shelfmark: MFM.M71181. Public Domain.

It is possible that John Suttoe was one of the mutineers who abandoned the ship, along with other passengers that were picked up at Dunneany coast by Mr Stephen Sidthorpe and given "proper refreshments and attention". From here he ended up with John McClintock as a labourer at Drumcar House. As the ship was a New York vessel, it is not clear if Suttoe would have been enslaved, though slavery was at its height in the Americas at this time. The word "Stave", written in newspapers at the time, can be misinterpreted as old writing for 'slave' but this is very unlikely to be the case. As the letter said, the Ship was laden with "rum, tobacco and staves" which does imply cargo. In subsequent advertisements for the auction of this cargo the word is associated with Barrels of produce, see the extracts below of the auction arranged by Stephen Sidthorpe for the ship's master, Thomas Quill, at his home in Dunany, on 25th March 1783, see extracts below.

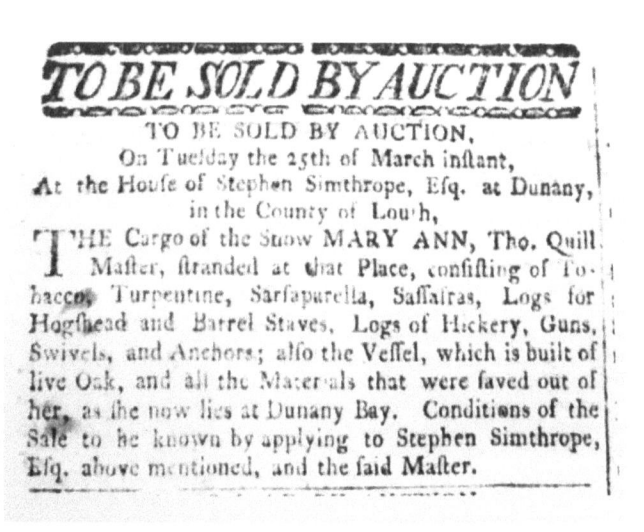

> **TO BE SOLD BY AUCTION**
>
> TO BE SOLD BY AUCTION,
> On Tuesday the 25th of March instant,
> At the House of Stephen Simthrope, Esq. at Dunany, in the County of Louth,
>
> THE Cargo of the Snow MARY ANN, Tho. Quill Master, stranded at that Place, consisting of Tobacco, Turpentine, Sarsaparilla, Saffafras, Logs for Hogshead and Barrel Staves, Logs of Hickery, Guns, Swivels, and Anchors; also the Vessel, which is built of live Oak, and all the Materials that were saved out of her, as she now lies at Dunany Bay. Conditions of the Sale to be known by applying to Stephen Simthrope, Esq. above mentioned, and the said Master.

11. Auction of the cargo of the sunken *Mary Ann* ship on 25 March 1783. *Saunders Newsletter* 21 March 1783. Image @The British Library Board. Shelfmark: 013943613.

This places "Barrel Staves" among several other cargo products. Further auctions took place at Dunany in May 1783 and at the Drogheda Customs House in December 1784, see the extracts on page 18.

> TO BE SOLD BY AUCTION,
> For Account of the Underwriters,
> At Dunany, in the County of Louth,
> On Friday the 9th instant,
> 60 Barrels best American Turpentine,
> 3 Bales Sarsaparilla,
> A Parcel of Saffafras,
> A Quantity of White Oak Logs for Hogshead Staves,
> A Quantity of Hickery ditto, for Hand Spikes,
> Guns, Swivels, and old Anchors, lately saved out of the Snow Mary Anne, Thomas Quill, Master, from New York.
> Terms.—Cash, or approved Bills on Dublin, not exceeding 21 Days. Dunany, 2d May, 1783.

12. Auction at Dunany in May 1883.
Saunders Newsletter, 3 May 1783.
Image @ The British Library Board.
Shelfmark: 013943613

> CUSTOM-HOUSE, DROGHEDA,
> DECEMBER 29, 1784.
> TO be SOLD by Public Cant, at the said Custom-house, on Tuesday the 11th of January, 1785, the undernamed goods, saved out of the Mary Ann, of Liverpool, Thomas Quill, Master, from New-York, stranded at Dunany, in this district, the 5th of March, 1783.
> 61 Barrels of TURPENTINE.
> 760 OAK LOGS.
> 139 HICKERY HANDSPIKES.
> 194 OAK STAVES.
> 4 Bags SASSAPARILLA.
> 70 Pieces of SASSAFRAS.
> 1 Cask of SNUFF.
> THOMAS SHEPHERD, Col.

13. Public Cant at Drogheda Custom House.
Dublin Evening Post, 8 January 1785.
Image @ The British Library Board.
Shelfmark: MFM.M19510.

In these auctions we see the terms Oak Staves and Hoghead Staves. Staves are wooden sticks used by coopers to make barrels and must have been cargo shipped for trade along with other products at this time. Shortly after this last auction in Drogheda in 1785, Suttoe had by now settled into Irish life and met with a local Irish girl with whom he fell in love and married.

The *Dublin Evening Post* reported a story from the *Faulkner's Journal*, on 23 April 1785, about a marriage between Margaret Brien and a 'Black' in Clintontown, see the extract on page 19.

> The following extraordinary match took place last week at Drumcar, near Dunleer:—About two years ago a ship was wrecked near that place, on board of which there was a Black, who very soon afterwards became a servant at Drumcar; he often expressed a desire of marrying a white woman, this coming to the ears of Miss Margaret Brien, of Clintonstown, in that neighbourhood, she took several opportunities of dancing with him at the little parties in the neighbourhood; this encouraged him to propose for her, and he got some friends to interfere; they had several meetings, and at last settled every thing and they were married before a vast crowd of people. No young girl could behave with more propriety or modesty; there was a very elegant supper prepared, and the bride and bridegroom seemed as happy as possible, and are now enjoying all the comforts of a married life.—— *Faulkner's Journal.*

14. Marriage of John Suttoe and Margaret Brien.
Dublin Evening Post, 23 April 1785.
Image @ The British Library Board,
ref. no. MFM.M8262.

On hearing that he was keen to marry a white woman, Brien inveigled a series of meetings and Suttoe proposed. The pair 'married before a vast crowd of people' and the press reported that 'there was a very elegant supper prepared, and the bride and bridegroom seemed as happy as possible, and are now enjoying all the comforts of a married life'.[32]

Unlike Margaret Brien, for some unknown reason the groom's name is not mentioned in the above article. However, we know from the *Journal of Henry McClintock*,[33] the son of John McClintock (1744-1799) of Drumcar, that a black man worked for John McClintock for many years and, on McClintock's death in 1799, John Suttoe probably transferred to the son Henry McClintock. Henry work at the Customs House in Dundalk and owned a black horse called "Mungo",[34] a name which was often used for black people. On the 16th December 1812 Henry McClintock mentions John Suttoe in his journal as follows:

> "Wednesday 16th December, 1812, Dundalk. Very Cold stormy day – I went as usual to the Customs House – I have a painter, a carpenter and two labourers at work at my own house – poor old John Suttoe (the black man who lived so many years with my father) is one of my labourers - I walked out for an hour or two before dinner with my gun and killed one green plover and three staires – dined at home with my mother and Bessy – Louise much better."[35]

It is difficult to find any further information about Suttoe and his wife Margaret. The description by Henry McClintock as "poor old John Suttoe" does not suggest he lived an entirely happy life. However, it does appear from newspaper reports that the McClintocks treated their labourers well. In October 1814 the *Saunders Newsletter* reported that:

> "Harvest House at Drumcar, County Louth ...are happy in having the pleasing task of making public the laudable practice followed by John McClintock, Esq. of crowning the labourers of the year at this season, with a convivial meeting, for the amusement of the peasantry. On Wednesday the 5th Inst. Nearly one hundred persons were assembled at two o'clock, on the lawns opposite Drumcar House, and exhibited in grotesque figure, decked in the usual way on such occasions.
>
> After sporting some time in this manner, they were summoned to an excellent and plentiful dinner with ale and punch etc. after which the joyful sound of fiddles and pipes, inspired the happy groups to quit the pleasures of the table and join in a round of dancing" [36]

This event happened just two years after Henry McClintock mentioned Suttoe in his journals, but there is no mention in his 1814 entries that he attended this event for the "peasantry" at Drumcar. Therefore, it is probably unlikely Suttoe attended as he now lived at Henry's house rather than at Drumcar where he previously worked.

Lord Granard's Black Drummer and Black Servant

We have found an interesting story about a black drummer, connected with Lord Granard (George Forbes 6th Earl of Granard). Lord Granard, was an Irish peer and general in the British army, whose ancestors, the Forbes, arrived in Ireland from Scotland in the 17th century. The family was granted lands in Ireland by the King under the Act of Settlement in 1667. Today, Castle Forbes in county Longford, near Newtownforbes, remains the seat of the Forbes family in Ireland. The black drummer was in Ireland during the uprising of the United Irishmen in the latter part of the 18th century. In 1798, Ireland erupted into rebellion, following the wave of republican revolutions across Europe during the period. In the run up to this rebellion, the United Irishmen wanted more autonomy from the British crown and collaborated with the French to carry out a military insurrection.

15. George Forbes, 6th Earl of Granard.
Stipple engraving by James Heath (1757-1834)
Image courtesy of The National Library of Ireland.

The French landed on the west coast of Ireland but were beaten by the militia and yeomen under the command of the wealthy Anglo-Irish class and English soldiers who had arrived to defend the British Empire. The battles, such as the battles of Ballinamuck and Castlebar, in the west of Ireland were brutal and many of the rebels were slaughtered even when attempting to surrender. In September 1798, Captain Cottingham defeated insurgents gathered at Granard, in county Longford, killing 100 rebels, "the Yeomanry experienced no losses…. On the same evening Lord Longford, at the head of a body of yeomanry, assisted by a detachment of the King's troops, attacked a body of rebels at Wilson's Hospital and put them to flight with much slaughter."[37] On 9 July 1798, it was reported that numerous people were charged with "dissenterism, one of whom, after receiving 75 lashes from the drummers of the garrison, promised to make important discoveries, on which he was let down, and re-committed by order of Lord Granard; who humanely remitted the punishment of another, on account of his youth and contrition."[38]

Thirty years later, in 1828, the horrors of these lashings by the 'drum major', a black drummer called "Fury", were recounted at the County

Clare bi-election[39] hustings at the Kilrush courthouse, in which Daniel O'Connell debated in the political hustings for the County Clare constituency seat. Mr Steele spoke about the experience he and his friend Francis Wheatstone witnessed at a lashing, reported in a newspaper in 1828, see the extract below:

> *"That Gentleman ... and I were in a window at the opposite side of the street, from this Court House; we were school fellows then, and we have always been friends. We observed a procession; O how different from the procession of last night! A regiment marched to the market-place with a large group of prisoners. There then stood two pumps close to each other; one of the prisoners, his name was Walsh, was brought forward and stripped; his hair was cut, and he was tied up to the pumps. The regiment formed around the prisoners and the hands were placed within its circle, the drum major took his station,* **the Drummer, a black,** *commenced the work of the torture, on the back of the Prisoner – the man's name was Walsh; from the nature, colour was empurpled and ensanguined, and he fainted; after he revived, a jug of water was put to his mouth, he drank, and when he was a little renovated the work of the torture was recommenced by* **a drummer whose name was "Fury."** *I saw a little more – when I became sick, and went home to my mother, and never again did I go to witness such a scene. We lived in that very street, said Mr. Steel, (pointing out of the Court,) between this Court and the Old Jail, and we could frequently see parties of prisoners, whose shrieks we heard while they were under the torture, marched past the windows, with their backs all bloody from the lashes of the drummers. I say this, furthermore, that the scene that I have described, the memory of which is as vivid – it is before me this moment, as if it was now acting – it was that scene that made the agitator that I am, for I have said to myself, O God! Are such scenes ever again to be renewed? I say that on that day could be heard in this very Court, called a Court of Justice!!! The echoes of the shrieks of agony of Walsh – of his wild prayer for mercy –Lord Granard, Lord Granard, take me down and shoot me – the voice of the drum-major, the sound of the cat, the wild raving cry to Heaven in extremity of the torture – Oh! Christ Jesus – O! Saviour of the world can I bear this? And then at intervals as informal symphonies, to the shrieks of the tortured man's agony – the music of the military band!!! ... will you return any supporter of such*

an Administration? ... to Heaven for the return of Daniel O'Connell!! The mighty Agitator! – the Liberator – the Catholic Liberator of his Country!!!"[40]

Earlier in 1783, during the Longford elections, it was reported that Lord Granard (George Forbes 6th Earl of Granard) had a black servant who was also freeholder of land. As the black servant was a freeholder, he was entitled to vote in the County Longford election, which caused much debate and delay in the hustings and proceedings in the Courthouse in Longford. In a public letter, by one of the contestants, Henry Gore wrote;

> To the Gentlemen, Clergy and freeholders of the County of Langford.
> Gentlemen
> As the High Sheriff has appointed Tuesday the 12th of August for holding the Election at Longford, for Knights of the Shire for that County, I must humbly request that those Gentlemen who are pleased to honour me with their support on that occasion, will be so good as to meet me at the Court-house of Longford that day at 10 o'clock…most faithful and obedient servant. HENRY GORE."[41]

Note this letter was addressed only to "Gentlemen, Clergy and freeholders", i.e. those with voting rights. Lord Granard's black servant, called *Mungo*, was produced at voting proceedings in the Court-house. A newspaper reported the incident as follows:

> 'Extract of a letter from the country Longford, "Saturday last ended our election, it continued but five days and would have been over the fourth", but for a black servant of Lord Granard's that was produced as a freeholder. The business was new, and gave rise to great debate, the point Mr. Duquery, and other gentlemen of the long robe, to the no small entertainment of the court and after four hours, Mungo was allowed to vote. Early on Saturday, Mr. Harman and Mr Gore were declared duly elected, by a very great majority, after which Col. Gore addressed the court, which was remarkably full…'[42]

Both Gore and Harman were elected to Ireland's House of Commons, representing County Longford. Lord Granard did not contest this Election as he was already a member of the house of Lords in England, which he later lost following the Act of Union, which came into force on 1st January 1801. According to the *Memoirs of the Earls of Granard* (George Forbes), Forbes "displayed the strongest aversion" to the Union with Great Britian and took little involvement in politics after he lost his seat and devoted his time to managing his estates. He had been a "consistent liberal" and supporter of Catholic Emancipation.

However, during the 1798 rebellion he commanded the Longford Militia and was present at the battle of Castlebar where his regiment deserted him "secretly wishing the triumph of their enemy."[43] He subsequently, fought at the battle of Ballinamuck, where the French troops surrendered to Lord Cornwallis in 1798. Lord Granard was a military man and part of the British establishment as part of an Anglo-Irish family, originally from Scotland, that had been granted lands in 1619 as part of Plantation of County Longford. The origins of the black servant and drummer and how they ended up in Ireland with Lord Granard is unclear, but it is possible they emerged through the wider family's activities in the British Admiralty and through its expeditions to the West Indies. However, more research is required to establish the facts and whether there were more black people working for the Forbes family in Ireland. This story provides an interesting insight into a certain hidden past of the Anglo-Irish Ascendancy and how they employed or used people of colour.

Wealthy Planters

'Mulatto Jack's journey from Ireland to the Caribbean - and back again - is the converse of the mixed race children of wealthy Irish planters and black or mixed race women, both enslaved and free. Elite white English and Scottish families in the colonies frequently sent their sons or daughters to be educated in the father's homeland - Dido Belle being probably the most well-known example - but Daniel Livesay's analysis of probate wills shows that some Irish plantation owners in late eighteenth and early nineteenth century Jamaica followed this pattern too.[44]

Dido Elizabeth Belle was born in the West Indies in 1761 to Sir John Lindsay, a British naval officer, and Maria Belle, an enslaved African woman. Like numerous other colonists who had fathered mixed race children, when Lindsay returned to England in 1765 he brought Belle with him where she was raised and educated by her father's maternal uncle, Lord Mansfield, William Murray, 1st Earl of Mansfield, as a free person in England. One wonders about the power dynamics that would have played out within mixed race families such as Dido's. However, Livesay notes that, in the early 18th century, few upper-class white families in Britain commented significantly on the heritage of their relatives of colour, who arrived in Britain from Jamaica and "incorporated them into the fold with little protest".[45] Lord Mansfield is famous for his legal judgement in the *Somerset Case* of 1772, prohibiting slavery in England, which had an impacted on Irish case law, as highlighted in the legal case of *James Jordan* (see page 39).

16. Dido Elizabeth Belle and Lady Elizabeth Murray, 1779.
Painted by David Martin (1737 – 1797). Image provided courtesy of the Earl of Mansfield, Scone Palace.

A further example of mixed race children brought home is found in a will written in 1795 by Eugene Calnan, which stipulated that he wished to 'bequeath unto William Calnan and John Calnan my reputed Mustee Sons, the sum of One thousand pounds sterling each to be paid them when they respectively arrive at the age of nineteen years' and for them to be placed under the care of his brother William Calnan, in Ireland, for their maintenance and education.

The Jamaican Church of England 'Register of Birth Christenings' show the following details for the two Calnan sons:

"Calnan, John and William Calnan, mustees, late Eugene Calnan. Children were baptised on 28th day of June 1796" [46]

In the same year, another planter with links to Ireland, John Durney left money to two free women of colour as well as individual sums between £300 and £500 to his 'reputed' daughter and two sons, all of whom he wished to be sent to Ireland for education, with the bequest to be null and void if any of the three ever returned to Jamaica.[47]

The Tierney family is another fascinating example of a personal history in which the worlds of Ireland, England and the Caribbean were intricately connected and traversed. James Tierney was the barrister son of a wealthy Irish merchant from Limerick and brother of the prominent nineteenth century MP George Tierney (MP for Southwark and Knaresborough).

He was a Jamaican plantation owner who named two mixed race 'mustee'* daughters in his will: his 'reputed' daughter, Eleanor Frances Tierney, born in 1782 to a 'native girl' named Fanny Brice; and Sabina Eleanor Tierney, born in 1784 to Margaret Dunbar a free 'quadroon' woman.

On his death in 1784, Tierney specified that £1000 should be invested in the benefit of Eleanor Frances, whether this be to ensure her status as a free woman, or to support, educate and maintain her and her descendants. He also named Dunbar as his housekeeper and specified £1000 to be left to her as well as 'all my household furniture and utensils, pictures, plate, china, linen and carriages and any one of my horses which she may choose for herself.' In 1790, a private Act of Assembly was passed to entitle Margaret, as well as Margaret's mother Mary Blake ('a free mulatto woman') and Margaret's children, including Sabina, 'to the same rights and privileges with English subjects, born of white parents, under certain restrictions.'

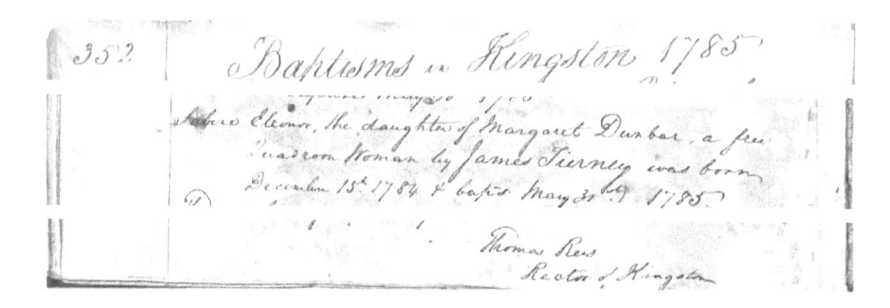

17. Baptismal record of Sabina Eleanor Tierney
on 31 May 1785 at Kingston, Jamaica. Mother recorded as "a free Quadroon Woman".
Image of extracts courtesy of the Registrar General's Department, Spanish town, Jamaica.

Later in her life, Sabina moved to England, possibly accompanying her stepfather and half siblings who settled in Beverley, Yorkshire. At Sabina's death at the age of 60 in 1844, she was registered as living in the affluent area of Marylebone in London. Unmarried, she left everything to her half-brother Ebeneezer.[48] The finances within Ebeneezer's inheritance are likely to have contained the wealth Sabina gained in the wake of the 1833 Abolition Act which recompensed slave owners for their diminished income: in 1836, she received compensation for 6 enslaved people, who, like other enslaved people, received no compensation. This slice of the Tierney family history demonstrates how the descendants of an Irish family became English elites and slave owners, despite being of mixed race. It also shows how easily racial, ethnic and national lines were not only crossed but also blurred and obscured in the passing of time during the eighteenth and nineteenth centuries.[49]

The destinations of mixed race Jamaicans, by percentage between 1773-1815 are shown in the chart on page 28.

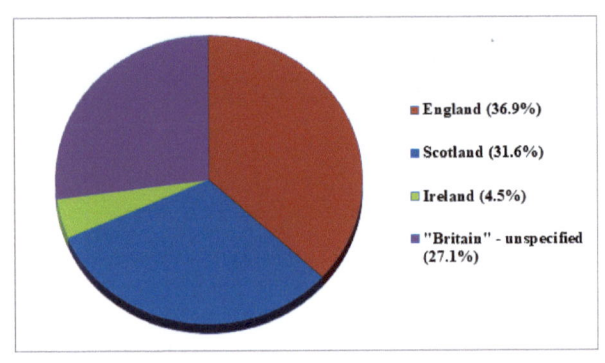

18. Destination of mixed race Jamaicans 1773-1815.
Provided courtesy of Daniel Livesay (2010).

- England (36.9%)
- Scotland (31.6%)
- Ireland (4.5%)
- "Britain" - unspecified (27.1%)

Mixed Race Possibilities

As the size of the black population in Ireland, in the eighteenth century, has been estimated by Hart to be between 1000-3000, there are likely to be numerous accounts of mixed race Irish families still to be uncovered from this period. Tantalising glimpses of such possible histories are suggested by a number of narratives. The acclaimed opera singer Rachel Baptist (see page 6) who first appeared on the stage in Ireland in 1750 was described as a 'native' black woman. However, no references have yet been found as to her or her second husband's racial backgrounds and family origins. As the race of people of colour was often commented upon in the press during this period, could this suggest that her husband was a white Englishman?

Similarly, Stella Tillyard notes that in 1775, Emily, 1st Duchess of Leinster, received a letter from her third son - the naval officer Charles Fitzgerald who later became Baron Lecale - in which he declared 'the jet black ladies of Africa's burning sands have made me forget the unripened beauties of the north'. A few months later he followed this up with the news that among the number of her grandchildren, she'd soon have one of copper colour'.[50] Although it was noted in his obituary that Fitzgerald died 'without issue', he appears to have had two illegitimate children: the Hon. Henry Fitzgerald, a midshipman who died in 1803 at sea boarding a French ship of war, and Anna Maria Fitzgerald who entered into a morganatic marriage with a British diplomat, the Hon. Algernon Percy, the second son of Lord Lovaine. Anna-Marie Fitzgerald's marriage contained the caveat that neither she nor any children would inherit her husband's titles or privileges. This may suggest that she was 'the grandchild of 'copper colour' referred to in Fitzgerald's correspondence.

Early Indian presence

Similar to West Indian plantation owners, Michael Fisher notes that Irish men who had served in the East India Company sometimes brought their Indian wives, mistresses or mixed race children to Ireland with them. This, he speculates, may have been the case for William Massey Baker who was the brother of Godfrey Evans Baker and patron of the Indian entrepreneur Sake Dean Mahomed, the most well-known Indian resident of Ireland during the late seventeenth century. Like his brother, William also served as an officer in the East India Company's army in India, where he had an Indian mistress and a teenage Anglo-Indian daughter, Eleanor. In 1796, Massey Baker, returned to Cork on leave from the Company's army where Fisher notes he may have been accompanied by Eleanor.[51]

19. City of Cork, by T. Roberts, 1799.
Image @The British Library Board. Shelfmark: Maps KTop.52.18.b.

Certainly, the British army and navy played an important role from the eighteenth century onwards in creating multicultural populations in both Britain and Ireland. Domestic servants were imported as cheap labour by returning Irish East India Company men, while traders, soldiers and sailors also found their way to Irish shores. Narain remarks that "Indian domestics and lascars often received one-way passages and if they parted ways with their employers or ship, they usually were left to fend for themselves without any resources." Many were reduced to vagrancy in port towns, such as Cork.[52] Like many other Irish ports, numerous people of colour passed through Cork during the eighteenth century, some even making the city their home.

Glimpses of racial mixing in 19th century Ireland
Further glimpses of the presence of mixed race families in Ireland continue throughout the nineteenth century. Mir Aulad Ali, appointed in 1861 as Professor of Arabic at Trinity College, a position he held for thirty years, married an Englishwoman named Rebecca and the pair's son, Arthur, was baptised at the Church of Ireland in Rathmines.[53]

20. Mir Aulad Ali, 1875.
Courtesy of The Board of Trinity College,
ref. No. TCD MS 4896 p 10.

In 1898, Arthur - who had trained as a doctor in Ireland and went on to practise medicine in London - had a legal action brought against him by a Miss Kathleen Wilson of Pembroke Road, Dublin, for 'breach of promise of marriage'. The pair had met during one of Arthur's visits to his father.

On 14 June 1898, *The Belfast News-Letter* included the extract below under the heading 'Dublin Day By Day: myriads of love letters'.

> *"Miss Kathleen Wilson, of Pembroke Road, has brought an action against Dr Arthur Aulad Ali, son of Professor Weir Aulad Ali, of T.C.D., for breach of promise of marriage. He is practicing at Defoe Road, Tooting London. While on a visit to his father last year became enamoured of the plaintiff, and myriads of love letters passed between them, ending in a proposal of marriage. Leave was given to-day to issue and serve a writ out of jurisdiction upon him."*

In 1884, the St James's Gazette featured the story of Andrew Tobias, an 'Irish negro' living in New York who spoke with 'a brogue which left no doubt' that he was 'a coloured Irishman'. In response to the incredulous magistrate in front of whom he appeared on a charge of theft, Tobias remarked:

> *'I was born in county Cavan, as was me father and grandfather before me. Me grandfather, I was tould, was the body servant of an Irish lord and settled in Cavan.[sic]'*

An extract from *St James Gazette* on 3 May 1884, headed 'Tobias', reads as follows:

> *'An Irish negro is an ethnological rarity; but that at least one representative of the species exists the report of a recent New York police case attests. Andrew Tobias, "a full-blooded negro," was brought before Justice O'Gorman one day last month to answer to a charge of theft. "Where were you born?" asked the magistrate, aghast, after a glance at the case paper. "Do you see a coloured Irishman?" "Indeed an' you do," answered Tobias, with a brogue which left no doubt about the on the point. "I was born in county Cavan, as was me father and grandfather before me. Me grandfather I was told, was the body-servant of an Irish lord, and settled in Cavan." An additional evidence of his nationality was presently forthcoming. "The officer tells me you were drunk," said the justice, eying the prisoner severely. "An' maybe he's right," answered the prisoner. "I did take a sup too much; but I never drink anything but Irish whiskey." One does not quite see relevancy of this addition to his confession, though*

possibly Mr. Tobias may have thought it would be accepted as a plea in extenuation by his compatriot on the bench. No prosecutor, however, appeared, and the magistrate allowed the "phenomenon" to go with a reprimand.'[sic]

The *Gazette* gasped that Tobias was an 'ethnological rarity'; however, in 1896, the *New York Journal* ran a feature on Paddy Murphy, a fellow 'Irish negro' living in New York. Born in 1833 to a black father and Irish mother in county Cork, Murphy's father died at sea shortly after he was born and he spent his early years as a servant to a Colonel in the Fourth (Royal Irish) Dragoon Guards. Travelling all over the world with the army as well as in the service of an English gentleman, in his sixties Murphy settled in New York where he found work as a waiter, being popular with customers due to his 'native wit, together with his remarkable intelligence'. He spoke over six foreign languages fluently and was also 'one of the few Irishmen in New York who [were] able to speak perfect Gaelic.' See the extract on page 33 which shows a report from the *New York Journal* printed in the *Supplement to The Cork Constitution* paper of 19 September 1896.

The *New York Journal* above noted that 'with the exception of his colour he has all the facial and racial characteristics of an Irishman, and he speaks with a brogue that couldn't be cut with a knife.' At the time of the article, Murphy was planning to return to Ireland after being informed that his aunt had died and had left her house to him:

'Sure, it's only a bit of land that me mother's sister has left. But, begorra, there's a nate little house on it, and it's there I'm going to be after spending me last day. Paddy Murphy's knocked about this worruld long enough, and sure, it's high time he had a rest at last.[sic]'

While there is still more work to be done to trace these types of mixed race families in Ireland hinted at in nineteenth century reports, there are a fascinating number of accounts of those who first met in Ireland before moving to other countries, including Britain.

IRISH NEGRO FALLS HEIR TO PROPERTY.

"PADDY" MURPHY, A STRANGE MIXTURE OF RACES, EXPERIENCES AND FORTUNES.

Paddy Murphy is his name, and he is an Irish negro. He was born in the County Cork, Ireland, June 16, 1833, and now at the age of sixty-six he is as hale and hearty as a man of twenty. He is short, blacker than any ace of spades, has kinky gray hair and a cast of features that would have driven the late Pat Rooney out of the theatrical profession.

With the exception of his color he has all the facial and racial characteristics of an Irishman, and he speaks with a brogue that couldn't be cut with a knife.

Murphy is at present employed as a waiter in Charles A Tubby's cafe at No 10 Union square, but he recently received a letter from lawyers in Dublin stating that an aunt had died there and left him a modest little home, and it is likely that he will shortly return to the land of his birth to spend his declining years.

Murphy has had a varied and interesting career. He was borne in a barracks in a little country place just outside of Cork. His father was a negro and his mother an Irishwoman. His father was a sailor, and shortly after the birth of the child, who inherited his father's color, but his mother looks and nature, the father went to sea and was never heard of afterward.

At an early age young Murphy entered army life as an under servant in the Fourth Dragoons, of Her Majesty's service, commanded by Colonel T F Townsend. He remained with the Dragoons thirty years and finally became the Colonel's private servant. During this time he travelled all over Europe and also witnessed the principal battles of the English Army in the Soudan.

He visited France, Italy, Germany, Russia, China, Japan, South America, and three years ago drifted to the United States with an English gentleman, who intended to take up his residence here. Three months ago, however, his employer determined to return to London, and when he went he left Paddy Murphy behind.

Murphy was not long in securing employment, and his native wit, together with his remarkable intelligence, soon made him a general favourite about Tubby's cafe. The place is frequented by foreigners of various nationalities, and it was soon found that the Irish negro was capable of acting as interpreter for all of them.

In the course of his travels he has mastered French, Spanish, German, Portuguese, Chinese, Italian, and other languages. He speaks all of these tongues fluently, and he is also one of the few Irishmen in New York who are able to speak perfect Gaelic.

Murphy is proud of his lineage. In the old days he used to be quite a factor in athletic sports, around the camps of the English army, stationed in Ireland, and he tells with great gusto of a flight he once had in which he whipped Peter Maher's brother, and says that if Peter himself could only get down to weight now he thinks he could get away with him.

The other day an Irishman happened into Tubby's restaurant, and, seating himself at a table, gave his order to Murphy. Murphy, in repeating the same to the cook, showed his brogue. The Irishman, looking at the negro, thought that Murphy was making fun of him, and for a few moments it appeared as though there was going to be trouble. The matter was straightened out, however, by the proprietor, after which the fellow countrymen got along famously together.

Murphy, in speaking of his sudden windfall said:

Sure, and it's only a bit of land that me mother's sister has left. But, begorra, there's a nate little house on it, and it's there I'm going to be alter spending me last day. Paddy Murphy's knocked about this worrald long enough, and sure, it's high time he had a rest at last."—*New York Journal*.

21. 'Irish Negro Falls Heir to Property', 1896.
Supplement to The Cork Constitution, 19 September 1898.
Image @ The British Library Board,
Shelfmark: MFM.M7761.

Other early reports of black people in Ireland and Britain

Archival newspaper records also provide us with some useful glimpses into the lives of black people, albeit in short notices. To give an example of the military careers of black people as drummers in Ireland, we see in 1757, the Royal Scotch guards parading in Dublin with all black drummers described as "distinguished", in this extract under the heading 'Dublin' on page 34.

> patch of bonnets.
> This Week the First Battallion of the Royal Scotch marched out of our Barracks to Country Quarters, and are replaced by Col. Boscawen's Regiment. This is one of the finest and most uniform Regiments on this Establishment, and is distinguished by having all Black Drummers.

22. All Black Drummers in 1757.
Pue's Occurrences, 7 June 1757.
Image @ The British Library Board,
Shelfmark: MFM.M34866.

As noted above, Lord Granard employed black drummers in his Militia who also acted in meting out punishment, such as lashings, to prisoners and the enemy. However, it is not clear from the above if the expression "All Black" refers to costume or ethnicity. Nevertheless, it is worth noting that "during the Seven Years War (1756-63), 2nd Battalion served in North America and the Caribbean, fighting at Louisburg (1758), Guadeloupe (1759) and Havana (1762),"[54] so it is possible the Royal Scots brought back some black people, from these expeditions in the Caribbean and the Americas, to the garrison in Ireland.

In addition, the character of *Cudjo*, the State Trumpeter, was reported in 1772, which gives us further clues as to how some Africa children, like John Mulgrave (see page 2), were brought into Ireland by leading Statesmen, such as the Lord Lieutenant of Ireland, Lord Halifax. The notion of African children being transferred to British aristocrats, as gifts, feeds into the idea that children were regarded as fashion items, or even commodities, as depicted in art works across Europe at this time. See the newspaper extract below:

> One Cudjo, a Black, by the death of an aunt became last week possessed of a fortune of 2000l. This Black was sent over as a present to Lord Halifax, as a grateful acknowledgement for his having interested himself so warmly in the cause of the two young African Princes, who were here in the last reign. When Lord Halifax was Lord Lieutenant of Ireland, he made this Cudjo State Trumpet, which place he still enjoys.

23. Cudjo the State Trumpet.
Jackson's Oxford Journal, 23 May 1772.
Image @ The British Library Board.
Shelfmark: MFM.M9776.

Although this report is dated 1772, Lord Halifax, (George Montagu-Dunk 2nd Earl of Halifax, 1716-1771) was in Ireland as the Lord Lieutenant between 1761 and 1762. Therefore, Cudjo must have arrived in Ireland about 10 years earlier and was still in Ireland in 1772 at the time of the report (about a year after Lord Halifax's death). Halifax was known as the "The Father of the colonies",[55] which explains his relationship with African Princes who gifted this child to Lord Halifax. He also helped to found the province of Nova Scotia, with its capital called Halifax after him. The name *Cudjo* is an African name which originates from the *Coromanti* tribe, along the Gold Coast region in west Africa (Ghana).[56] The name is based on the days of the week. Cudjo is a male name meaning Monday, the female equivalent is Jaba. The African names found in archived newspapers at the time give us some indication of a person's origin. Where black people arrive in Ireland with European names this indicates they may have travelled from the Americas or Caribbean and have been part of the transatlantic salve trade. Ports, such as Belfast, Cork and Bristol, were often entry points for 'elopements'.[57]

We can also see the occupations of black people, through newspaper notices about runaway household servants such as the 'Young Negro' runaway, *Jeremiah or Jack*, who was seemingly owned by his master Patrick Burk, which is a typical Irish name. In 1769 Jeremiah was reported as a man who could read and write, though badly, and he could play pretty well on the Violin, as well as shave and dress a wig. Runaway notices were common in papers in Ireland and Britain at this time. They reveal fragments of the lives of servants and the relationships with their so-called Masters, which can, at times appear to be forms of enslavement, rather than a servant-employer relationship in which the servant is paid a wage. It seems from the above notice that Jeremiah is not a paid servant but could possibly gain this position if he wishes to have his "Freedom" or if "Freedom be what he wishes for". Whether Patrick Burk's affection is genuine or just a ruse for the advert, it is clear that he very much wants Jack back in the household, see the extract on page 36.

> MARCH 14, 1769.
>
> RAN away on WEDNESDAY Night last, From his Master PATRICK BURK, Esq;
>
> A Young Negro Man, called *Jeremiah* or *Jerry*, about 5 Feet 8 or 9 Inches high, large boned, well set, but not fat, has large strong Negro Features, and a large Scar on the upper Part of one of his Wrists, just upon the Joint, and supposed to be on the right Hand, slightly marked with the Small-Pox; had on when he went away a light-coloured Great Coat, dirty Leather Breeches, and White Stockings, and wore a Curl behind, that match'd the other Part of his own woolly Hair; he reads and writes badly, plays pretty well on the Violin, and can shave and dress a Wig.
>
> Whoever delivers him to Capt. Oliver, of the Ship Coltreen, at Mill-Stairs, Rotherhithe, London; or to Messrs. Recve, Son, and Hill, Merchants in Bristol, shall receive *Twenty Guineas* Reward, or *Five Guineas* for such Intelligence of him as may enable his Master to apprehend him.
>
> ☞ As the said Negro knows his Master's Affection for him, if he will immediately return, he will be forgiven; if Freedom be what he wishes for, he shall have it, with reasonable Wages; if he neglects this present forgiving Disposition in his Master, he may be assured that more effectual Measures will be taken. He has been pretty much at Bath, and the Hot-Wells, Bristol, with his Master.

24. A runaway 'Negro Man'.
Bath and Bristol Chronicle, 16 March 1769.
Image @The British Library Board.
Shelfmark: MFM.M17957.

Similar runaway notices appeared in Irish newspapers, such as at coastal ports where black sailors abscond from their ships. In the example below, in 1766 a 'Negro Sailor' abandoned the ship which was moored at Belfast. See this extract from the *Belfast Newsletter* below:

> '*RUN-AWAY from on board the Sloop Mary Ann of Whitehaven, John Angus, Master, now lying at the Kay of Belfast, on Friday the 3d Instant, a Black Negro Sailor called Jack, aged 22 years, about five Feet four Inches high, set made, and scratched down both Cheeks, the Property of Mr Robert Waters of Whitehaven, Merchant. Whoever will apprehend said Negro Sailor and bring him to Messrs. Gregs and Cunningham, Merchants in Belfast, Mr Darby Kane in Newry, or Mr. William Ledger on Aston's Kay, Dublin, shall receive two Guineas Reward and all expenses attending: And it is requested that if he applies to any Masters of Vessels to take him on board, that they will secure him and give Information thereof to the Persons aforesaid, or to the said Robert Waters, and they should be entitled to the said Reward. Said Negro had on when he went off a blue Jacket, strip'd Waistcoat, and Trowsors. Dated 6 October 1966*'.[58]

This notice refers to 'Messrs Gregs and Cunningham' who are included in the *Legacies of British Slavery* database under Mr Waddle Cunningham (1729 – 1797),[59] and Thomas Greg, also a Belfast merchant.[60] The biography of Cunningham states that he was a "Belfast Atlantic merchant and industrialist, partner with Thomas Greg (d.1796) ...., with whom he shared ownership of an estate and enslaved people on Dominica." It further goes on to say that the estate in Dominica was a sugar plantation and that he was the founder of the Linen Hall in Belfast and member of the Belfast Harbour Corporation. In the Greg family papers the estate in Dominica is identified as *Belfast*, adjoining John Greg's *Hertford* estate. Thomas Greg, Cunningham's partner, died in 1796 and, in his will, he left his share of enslaved people and cattle to his two sons Thomas and Samuel. The Hillsborough sugar plantation in Dominica had 128 enslaved people when awards were made to 'slave owners' after the abolition of slavery. On 7th December 1835, Thomas Greg was awarded £2,830 15s 9d (equivalent to £460,034 in today's money)[61] as compensation for the loss of 128 enslaved people on the Hillsborough estate.[62] The enslaved people received no compensation under the British compensation scheme. This story gives some insight into the activities of certain Irish merchants and their treatment of and attitude towards black people at this time.

Earlier in 1784, Cunningham "proposed fitting out a ship to engage in the Atlantic slave trade"[63] but his proposal was rejected and no ships ever officially engaged directly in this trade from Ireland. His Dominican estate was sold in 1797, for £17,000 (worth £2.7 million today),[64] which was probably sold in anticipation of the abolition of the slave trade by the British State. He died in December 1797 and the Slave Trade Act was signed into law in 1807 which prohibited the slave trade in the British Empire.

It is worth noting the reference by Jones and Youseph, to the movement of black people between Bristol and overseas plantations, which was most likely the case at Cork and Belfast ports: "There were also the negro sailors who visited the port, as well as family servants who left the city with their employers, some of whom went on to the plantations in the West Indies, especially when emancipation in England was imminent."[65] These were not ships engaged in the transatlantic slave trade but ships used by families to travel, which included black sailors and black family members and servants.

Slavery and Irish People of Colour

It is clear from the above that chattel slavery, *per se*, was not practiced on a large scale in Britain and Ireland prior to the 1772 Mansfield Judgement outlined below. However, the Atlantic Slave Trade was at its height during this period and the appearance of black people in Ireland and Britain is linked to this wider story and merchant or military shipping. It does appear that many people described above had freedoms enjoyed by other white citizens, such as Mungo, who was a freeholder and was able to vote in County Longford, during the elections to the Irish Parliament. However, there were some interesting advertisements in the newspapers which perhaps suggested otherwise. In the British Isles, it seems there was sometimes a very thin line between household servants, who received wages, and enslaved black domestics, whose "masters" restricted their freedoms.

The first British legal case to deal, head on, with the enslavement of back people in Britain, of which Ireland was a part, was the renowned 1772 anti-slavery *Somerset Case*.[66] This case concerned James Somerset, an enslaved man owned by Charles Stewart in Virginia and originally purchased from Africa in the slave trade. He was brought from Virginia to England on Captain Knowles vessel, the *Ann and Mary*.[67] An application of *habeas corpus* was made on his behalf requesting Knowles to present Somerset to the court and to explain his seizure and detention without his consent. The lawyer for Somerset, Mr Hargrave, argued against Mr Stewart's supposed right to slavery in England saying that "[t]he question on that is not whether slavery is lawful in the colonies...but whether in England? Not whether it ever has existed in England; but whether it be not now abolished?"[68] In his defence against perpetual servitude or chattel slavery, he invoked principles of Natural Law and the ideas from legal scholars, such as Grotius, Lock, Pufendorf and others, justifying temporary slavery in circumstances such as in captives in war or through contracts, stating that moderate slavery may be tolerated "though slavery in its full extent be incompatible with natural rights of mankind". Lord Mansfield decided to discharge and free "the black" on the grounds that slavery was so odious that only positive law could support it. In his final judgement, Lord Mansfield stated that the "power of a master over his slave has been extremely different, in different countries. The state of slavery is of such a nature, that it is incapable of being introduced on any reasons, moral or political; but only positive law, which preserves its force long after the reasons, occasion, and time itself from whence it was created, is erased from memory: it's so odious, that nothing can be suffered to support it, but positive law…therefore the black must be discharged."

The impact of the *Somerset Case* was later to be seen in Cork, Ireland, in 1848 in a case concerning *James Jordan*, a who arrived at Cork on a ship. In the case of *Captain Attridge v James Jordan*,[69] Jordan was described as a "coloured man" who worked for Captain Attridge, as a steward, on the American brig called the *Growler*, which was docked in Cork harbour in Ireland. After being attacked by the Captain, Jordan managed to escape and take him to a district court in Cork. In the court, when the magistrate asked Captain Attridge what charge he was making against Jordan, he stated that Jordan had disobeyed his orders and was tied up and put in custody, in the local gaol, for singing, being drunk and making noise on board. He went on to say that "it was a customary thing; it is a thing I have done to those fellows several times". He said: "I went to our Consul for advice, and he told me to tell Captain White to take him up and put him in gaol as that was the punishment for disobedience of orders". The Magistrate, Mr Spearing, told the captain that in his opinion "we ought to dismiss this case, and we regret to see you were so ignorant of the laws of this country, for you have not the slightest right to interfere with that man's person or liberty after he has entered this or any other port of the United Kingdom". The case was dismissed by the judges who left Jordan to adopt any course of action he wished to take and "he intimated his intention of proceedings against the captain for the outrage that had been committed on him". These two cases above show how James Somerset and James Jordan had their legal personality recognised on landing in Britain and Ireland under domestic laws, which would not have been available to them in their countries of enslavement.

Chapter 2

Irish Roots

This chapter highlights the migratory experience of several people of colour identified in our research during the 19th century. We had initially assumed that this community would have remained settled in either Ireland or Britain. However, like other Irish people, they moved back and forth between Ireland and Britain, mainly in search of work.

John and Mary Jea

Sold into slavery at the age of two along with his entire family, John Jea, a Nigerian from Calabar who was born in 1773, grew up experiencing horrendous brutality and cruelty under the hands of his Dutch slave owners in New York. Forced to attend church, Jea was gradually drawn to the Christian religion of his owners that he initially despised and, at the age of 15, began sharing the gospel with other enslaved people. Declaring that he had received a vision from God, the illiterate Jea then caused astonishment by being able to read the chapter of the Gospel of John from the bible.

Granted his freedom as a result of his ability, Jea began his life as a roving preacher, conducting evangelical rallies throughout rural New York and New Jersey to a growing audience of enslaved people, eventually working with white missionaries to found a church tending to a congregation of 1500. Jea then set off preaching across the United States before becoming a ship's cook, a position which allowed him to travel and preach across the world, including in South America, East Asia and Europe. Arriving in Liverpool in 1801, his sermons proved very popular amongst the working-class seafaring community and word of his preaching spread to other parts of the country. In 1803, Jea arrived in Ireland where he travelled across the country to preach his radical Methodism to crowds, attracting hostility from Calvinists as well as Catholic priests, though finding an ally in the Mayor of Limerick who protected Jea from death threats.

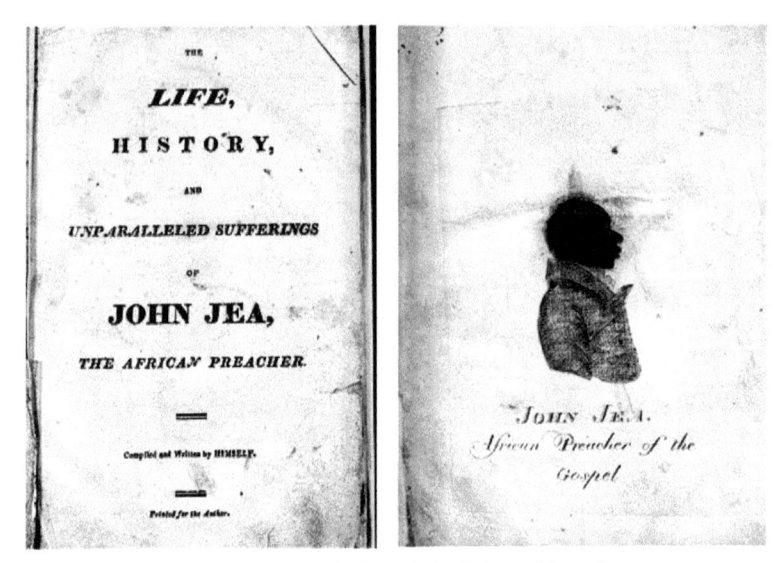

25. Frontispiece of John Jea's autobiography.
Image courtesy of The British Library Board.
Shelfmark: DRT 4985.bbb.28.

It was during his two years in Ireland that Jea met Mary, the woman who would become his third wife. His first wife, Elizabeth, was of native American descent, who suffered from mental illness and murdered her mother and their young daughter. She was executed as a result. His second wife, a Maltese woman named Charity, died in Holland. After marrying in Ireland in 1805, the pair initially intended to travel to Canada but during their ship's layover in England, Mary became ill and on advice from their 'friends in Christ' remained in Portsmouth until she was better or until Jea would be able to return. Soon after setting off, however, the ship Jea was travelling in was captured by French privateers. Along with the other passengers, Jea was taken to France where during his five year imprisonment he continued to spread the gospel.

On his release and after many further tribulations - including resisting demands that he fight against the English - Jea finally managed to return to Portsmouth where he found Mary alive and well amongst the port's 'brethren in Christ'. The pair settled in Portsea and with the assistance of missionary friends, Jea opened what is thought to be the first black church in Britain (likely in a flophouse or illegal inn) on Hawke Street - the same road in which Charles Dickens lived with his family a few years earlier. Jea's congregation was made up of those working in or for the maritime industry - sailors, labourers, innkeepers and prostitutes - and particularly those of black heritage.[1] The crowds that surrounded Jea during his street preaching were not always welcomed by 'respectable inhabitants', reported the press, some of whom had petitioned the local magistrate to disperse them.

On the 7 April 1817, *The Hampshire Chronical* stated the following in the extract below:

> *'We omitted last week to mention that application was made by several respectable inhabitants of this city, to Dr Newbolt, requesting that he would exercise his authority, as a magistrate, in dispersing the crowd assembled round the African Black preacher on Monday.'*

26. Blossom Alley, near Hawke Street, Portsea, 1906.
Image from *Portsmouth History in Hiding*, 1989,
courtesy of Anthony Triggs.

Around 1815, Jea went on to publish his memoirs *The life, history and unparalleled sufferings of John Jea, the African preacher.*[2] As Rodgers notes, Jea's autobiography 'reveals a life of poverty, insecurity, restless movement and spiritual obsession' and, as such, 'that any woman would struggle to maintain such a partnership over a prolonged period of time suggests deep affection, or the absence of any better prospects back home in Ireland or, possibly, some combination of both'.[3] It is interesting to note that amongst all the trauma reported in Jea's memoirs, nowhere does he express either himself or Mary experiencing any opposition to their interracial relationship.

The Jeas were likely not as uncommon a sight in the Portsmouth area as might be imagined as, like many other port cities in Britain during the late eighteenth and early nineteenth century, a small population of black sailors - many of whom served in the Royal Navy - could be found there, as well as servants, enslaved people, prostitutes and other individuals. As elsewhere, it is highly feasible that many also entered into interracial relationships.

27. Jack Tar admiring the Fair Sex, 1815.
Etching by Thomas Rowlandson.
Image © The Trustees of the British Museum,
no. 1948,0214.800.

28. Sea Stores, 1812.
Print made by Thomas Rowlandson.
Image © The Trustees of the British Museum,
no. 1872,1012.5014.

As Brooke Newman discusses, despite their grotesque caricatures of black women, Thomas Rowlandson's 1812s prints, which show a white naval officer and sailor negotiating with prostitutes, points to the everyday presence and integration of black people in British port districts such as Portsmouth.[4]

In 1796, a fleet of ships docked at Portsmouth with over 2000 prisoners of war. The prisoners - mainly soldiers from a French garrison in St. Lucia who had been captured by the British - were mostly black or mixed race men, former enslaved people or freeborn, who had enlisted in the French Revolutionary army. Initially imprisoned at

Portchester Castle, before being housed in other locations, many of the prisoners were eventually sent to France though it is also thought that some may have been recruited into the British Navy or Army.

As far as is known, the Jeas did not go on to have children, whether through infertility or infant mortality, and Mary herself likely died soon after Jea's memoirs were published as he married a fourth wife, Jemima, in 1816, with whom he did have a child - a daughter named Hephzabah who was baptised in the parish of Portsea in September 1817.[5] Jea himself died a few months after his daughter's baptism during a trip to St Helier's, Jersey, from where he had planned to travel on to preach in Guernsey. Sadly, this mission was not to occur, and the press reported that 'the poor African took his departure, not whither he intended, but to "that country from whose bourn no traveller returns"'. His funeral was 'numerously sad and most respectably attended' with 'above twenty men and as many women, in deep mourning, followed the body to the church, where the funeral service was read by the curate of the parish.' Jea's body was laid to rest in the churchyard of St Helier's. Below is an extract from the *Cheltenham Chronicle and Gloucestershire Advertiser in* 1817, commenting on the death and funeral of John Jea at St Helier's, Jersey:

> *'On Sunday evening, the 12th ult, [sic] a large congregation, or rather a multitude of auditors assembled on the parade ground at St. Helier's, Jersey, to hear the farewell sermon of the Black Preacher, Jau Jey. He told his friends that he must leave them for a time, as he was going to preach the Gospel in Guernsey; but the poor African took his departure, not whither he intended, but to "that country from whose bourn no traveller returns." He was interred in the church-yard of St. Helier's on Tuesday week. His funeral was numerously and most respectably attended. Above twenty men and as many, in deep mourning, followed the body to the church, where the funeral service was read by the curate of the parish. A long hymn was then sung by the whole of the singers from the Methodist chapel, after which the body was taken in solemn procession, and deposited in the grave, in presence of a mixed multitude of spectators.'* [6]

Tony and Julie Small

Today, the Irish parliament (Oireachtas), at Leinster House, in Kildare Street, Dubin, was formerly the home of the Duke of Leinster and his Ango-Irish aristocratic family, the Fitzgeralds. Surprisingly, in the 18th Century Leinster House was also the home of a black man called Tony Small.

In 1781, during the American Revolutionary War, an enslaved man named Tony Small managed to escape from his owners when they fled their South Carolina plantation. Wandering onto a battlefield, Small stumbled across an unconscious injured British Army soldier whom he nursed back to health. On recovery, the soldier, Edward Fitzgerald, the fifth son of the Duke of Leinster and Lady Emily Lennox, invited Small to enter into his employment, to work as his waged servant, which he accepted. Small accompanied Fitzgerald on his wide ranging travels. When Fitzgerald returned to Dublin with his French wife, Pamela, he was accompanied by Small who also resided at Leinster House, the family home. As the years passed, Small became increasingly important to Fitzgerald who wrote in 1786 that he had intended 'to send Tony to London to learn to dress hair, but when he was to go, I felt I could not do without his friendly face to look at and one that I felt to love me a little.'

In 1796, Small accompanied Fitzgerald and Pamela on a trip to London where he met Julie, the French nursemaid to Pamela's baby daughter. On returning to Fitzgerald's house in Kildare, Small began flirting with Julie who responded enthusiastically to his attentions: at some point, the couple had a child that Tillyard, Fitzgerald's biographer, remarks was named Moirico. Their relationship had bloomed in the untypical atmosphere of the Fitzgerald household. Tillyard notes that Lord Edward was a fervent supporter of the ideals of liberty, equality and fraternity espoused by the French revolutionaries and at this point in his life was fully committed to the Irish Republican cause. Fitzgerald would invite Tony, Julie and the other servants up to this parlour where the company would dance jigs as well as engage in more formal dances.[7]

In 1798, Fitzgerald died after succumbing to the wounds he sustained during his arrest on a charge of treason: Fitzgerald was a key United Ireland leader and heavily involved in plans for an insurrection against British rule, ideally with French aid. Like Pamela, Small was devastated by Fitzgerald's death. With Julie and Moirico, he accompanied her and other members of the household to England when she had been ordered to leave Ireland after Fitzgerald's arrest. Posthumously condemned for high treason, Fitzgerald's estates and assets were seized leaving Pamela with nothing. While the Fitzgerald family supported her in the initial months after her flight from Ireland they showed no inclination to provide her with a home long term and she moved to live with relations in Hamburg, once again accompanied by Small and his family. When Pamela remarried, Small and Julie moved to London where they had another child, a daughter, Harriet Pamela, and used their savings to set up a business in Piccadilly. However, Small maintained relationships with the Fitzgerald family. Falling ill in 1803, he appealed to them for financial help, asking if the family could 'make up a sum of money for me so that I might be able to keep on business for my wife and children which is my greatest trouble'. The Fitzgerald family, indignant at suggestions that 'poor Tony' wasn't being helped, insisted that this was far from the case and they had indeed come to his assistance. Nevertheless, it is reported that Small died shortly after this exchange of letters in 1893, but the details of his death and what became of his family and descendants were mostly unclear until recently (see page 50). However, the historian Audrey Dewjee has noted that there are records of the burial of an Anthony Small 'a black aged 40' in Wimbledon in 1804, along with those of a marriage between a Harriet Pamela Small and Henry Anthony Tucker at Marylebone in Middlesex on 22 June 1817.[8]

```
220        WIMBLEDON PARISH REGISTER.

1804  April  1   Mary Anne James aged 4
             7   Harriet Atkinson aged 10 [St. J.]
             8   Caroline Charlotte Bradfield aged 2
            13   Mary Anne Farr aged 4 [St. J.]
            13   Mary Gutteridge aged 8 [St. J.]
            15   Elizabeth Castle aged 9
            15   Mary Tillin aged 14 [St. J.]
            22   Mr William Arnold from Clapham aged 43
            26   Elizabeth Bussey, Infant [St. J.]
            29   William Bashford, Infant
      May   14   Anthony Small a Black aged 40
            15   Sarah Rosser, Infant
            18   John Heyley, Infant
            18   Elizabeth Allen aged 86 from the Workhouse
            30   John Anthony Rucker Esq. from Wandsworth aged 85
      June  22   Lord William Leveson Gower, Infant s. of the Mar-
                    quis Stafford
            22   Henry Leigh, Inft. from St. James
      July   1   James Griffith, Inft.
             1   Elizabeth Possy, Inft. from St. James
            23   Elizabeth wife of John Towers aged 26
      Aug.   1   Elizabeth Betteridge, Infant
             11  Richard Gordon, Infant from St. James
```

29. Burial record of 'Anthony Small, a Black aged 40'.
Reproduced with the permission of Surry History Centre.

During research for the AMRI exhibition in 2020, we uncovered church records that suggested that an Edward Small was likely another of Tony and Julie's children. Edward Small was born in Dublin in 1795, see further reading by Donal.[9]

As Julie was French and Tony American, the pair were not strictly a mixed race *Irish* couple, but their strong links to Ireland - where their relationship blossomed and Moirico was likely born - as well as their intertwined connection to the Fitzgerald family warrant their inclusion. Their story also highlights the hidden diversity of racial mixing that occurred within Ireland even where neither partner were themselves Irish. For example, William G. Allen and Mary King were an American interracial couple who left the United States in the 1850s due to the hostility their relationship had attracted.

William G. Allen was a racially mixed black American Professor of Greek Language and Literature and Mary the white daughter of a Reverend. After marrying in New York in 1853, the pair set sail for England where they resided before moving to Dublin in 1856: Allen had been well received in Dublin on initial visits to Ireland to give lectures on emancipation via the Anti-Slavery Society. During their time in Ireland, in which four of their children were born (Julia, Harriet, Richard and Mary as recorded in the UK Census 1871), it seems that the pair created a good and supportive social circle. In Allen's 1860 published narrative, he lists glowing letters of recommendation and personal testimonies from gentlemen of Dublin active in the Anti-Slavery Society, one of which also notes that Mary was 'much liked and esteemed by her numerous friends in this city'.[10] Earning money, however, was not so easy, as the lectures and private lessons William gave were unfortunately not enough to provide an adequate living. As a consequence, in 1860 the family moved to Islington in London. There, the couple attempted to eke out a living through teaching and William's lectures, though by the 1880s they largely had to depend on charity from friends and supporters to survive.[11] However, the Allen couple had three more children in London (Martha, Helen and William).

The depiction of people of colour in Ireland, as part of wealthy aristocratic families, often belies the reality of the hardship many experienced. We see this kind of lavish portrayal in the painting, on page 49, by Thomas Roberts exhibited in 1772. The finery in which the sitter is dressed in the painting, has long been misidentified as a depiction of

Tony Small. Robert's portrait was exhibited at the Society of Artists in Ireland in 1772, no.69, exhibited as *Portrait of bold Sir William (a Barb), an East Indian black, and a French dog, in the possession of Gerald Fitzgerald Esq.* The chronology of this means that the sitter cannot be Small as he had not yet met Fitzgerald at this date. All the same, the lavish outfit in which the portrait was dressed, as well as the commissioning of the painting of a black Indian servant in the Fitzgerald household, points not only to further diversity within the Fitzgerald domestic staff, but also to aspects of the type of life Small is likely to have experienced in Ireland, as well as the level of esteem in which he was held by the family.[12]

30. Bold Sir William (a Barb), an Indian Servant and French Dog, in the Possession of Gerald Fitzgerald, by Thomas Roberts (1748-1778). Private Collection.

Roberts's expertise in painting animals shines through in this painting, as can be seen in the relaxed nature of the dog and horse ('Barb') which is centre of this painting. A barb is a light medium-sized riding horse, originally from the Maghreb region of northern Africa. It is considered the horse of the Berbers, which was also thought to be used by the Moors, as a warhorse when invading Spain.[13] It is intriguing that this horse is depicted here as it suggests a play horse for either the young children of this aristocratic household or for the servants. This composition of a Barb, an East Indian Servant, and French Dog in the "possession of Gerald FitzGerald Esq. is an unorthodox picture in general, but points more emphatically than any other work by Roberts to the direct involvement of his patron. Ostensibly, the main subject of the picture is the horse belonging to Gerald FitzGerald, the fourteenth child of Emily, 1st Duchess of Leinster, and a member of Ireland's premier aristocratic family."[14] Gerald's father, the 1st Duke, died in 1773, the year after the exhibition at the Society of Artists, and was by Gerald's older brother William, who bestowed on Roberts his most celebrated commission, a set of views of Carton. His brother, Lord Edward FitzGerald, was "destined to become one of the most high-profile and venerated members of the United Irishmen. Gerald himself, the second youngest of the Duke of Leinster's children, would perish at sea in 1788 aged just twelve."[15] As Willian Laffan and Brendan Rooney note in their book *"Thomas Roberts 1748-1777. Landscape and Patronage in Eighteenth-century Ireland"* (2009):

> *"The FitzGeralds were not alone among Roberts's patrons in 'employing' servants from Asia. The Ely family of Rathfarnham, for example, could count among their staff a young Indian page who appeared in Oriental attire in Angelica Kauffman's elaborate portrait of the family of 1771."*

In researching Tony Small's descendants, Laura McKenna notes that no primary sources have yet been identified showing a record of the birth of Small's child 'Moirico', and she points to the uncertainty around claims that Small had a child with this first name. However, it is possible that 'Moirico' could simply have been another name for his son Edward. Small's grandson, also Edward, son of his daughter Harriet Pamela Small, was transported to Port Arthur in Tasmania in 1838, after being convicted for assault and larceny. He died there by drowning, six years later, at around twenty six years old. Small's own son Edward lived in London, where he had five children. His daughter Elizabeth (Tony Small's granddaughter) "emigrated to New Zealand, where she married and has many descendants. She died in 1933 at the age of 93." [16]

Sake Dean Mahomed and Jane Daly

In 1784, a twenty five year old Indian Muslim named Sake Dean Mahomed arrived in the city of Cork with his patron, Godfrey Evans Baker. An East Indian Company officer from a wealthy Irish family of landowners, Baker had taken Mahomed under his wing - and into service with the East India Company's army - when Mahomed lost his soldier father at the age of eleven. Shortly after arrival in Cork, Mahomed - sponsored by Baker - took up a place at college to advance his education where he met Jane Daly, a 'fair and beautiful' fellow student 'of a family of rank' in Cork and, in 1786, a few months after Baker's death, the couple eloped.

31. Sake Dean Mahomed,
Stipple engraving of by William Maddocks,
c. 1822. Image @ National Portrait Gallery, no.
NPG D46406.

The reasons for the elopement are not clear, nor why the couple posted a bond with the church rather than have the banns read weeks in advance as was customary, though both suggest possible concern as to how the marriage would be received. Any wedding between a Protestant - which Jane was - and a Catholic was unlawful at this time in Ireland, with the officiating clergyman held responsible. Michael Fisher, Mahomed's biographer, suggests that while Mahomed is likely to have already become a member of the Protestant Church in order to marry Jane, it may be that the bond was posted to alleviate any doubts in the mind of the priest who married the pair.[17] Whatever concerns the couple had, it appears that the pair were accepted by society on their return to Cork. Mirza Abu Talib Khan, an Indian traveller who met the Mahomeds during his time in Ireland, remarked that they had several children (likely two sons named William and Dean) and had a 'separate house and wealth' in the city. Moreover, in 1794, Mahomed's popular book *The Travels of Dean Mahomet*, detailing his voyages throughout India during his time in the army, was published with the help of the wealthy elite of Ireland.

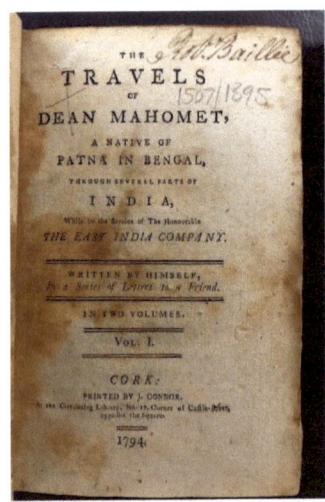

32. Frontispiece from The Travels of Dean Mahomet, 1794.
Image courtesy of The British Library Board.
Shelfmark: 1507/1395.

33. Irish baptism entry for the Mahomed's son Dean
at St Finbarr's South Parish, 1791.
Image courtesy of the National Library of Ireland.

After over two decades in Cork and approaching the age of fifty, in 1807 Mahomed and his family emigrated to London which was becoming an increasingly cosmopolitan city due to the migration occurring under the growing British Empire. There has been some speculation as to whether during this time in Britain, Mahomed entered into a bigamous marriage with another woman, also called Jane. The births of their later children, including Amelia and Henry Edwin, who were baptised at St. Marylebone Parish in 1809 and 1811 respectively, are sometimes attributed to this bigamous marriage. However, as Fisher notes, although there are discrepancies in many of the dates that the Mahomeds gave to officials over their lives, there is no conclusive evidence, as yet, that there were two Jane Mahomeds. While it is clear that at least one of the children born in Ireland, William, was part of the family in London until his death in 1833.

So, for the time being, until proved otherwise, we continue to assume that there was only one Jane Mahomed. The family lived amongst the rich and titled in the fashionable Portman Square area of London, once again suggesting their acceptance by the wealthy elite. Mahomed adopted the title 'Sake' (*Shaikh*), meaning 'venerable one', an honorific frequently used by upwardly mobile Muslims in India.

34. Sake Dean Mahomed.
Oil painting by Thomas Mann Baynes, c.1810. Image courtesy of Royal Pavilion & Museums, Brighton and Hove, no. 111980.

He found employment with the wealthy Scottish nobleman, Sir Basil Cochrane where he is said to have introduced the Indian therapeutic massage treatment of 'champi' - which he called 'shampooing' - to Cochrane's Portman Square Bathhouse clients. In 1809, Mahomed then went on to establish the Hindostanee Coffee House near Portman

Square- one of the first Indian restaurants opened in Britain,[18] which also provided a home delivery service for 'such ladies and gentlemen as may be desirous of having Indian Dinners dressed and sent to their own houses'.

35. Plaque for Mahomed's Indian restaurant. City of Westminster, George Street, Marylebone, London. Photo by Simon Harriyott on Wikimedia Commons.

36. Jane wife of S.D. Mahomed. Monochrome photographic print. Image courtesy of Royal Pavilion & Museums, Brighton & Hove, no. 50866.

Unfortunately, the restaurant was not lucrative and after filing for bankruptcy in 1812 and a stint living in the less desirable neighbourhood of Paddington, the family moved to Brighton, where Mahomed first reinvented himself as a purveyor of exotic remedies and cosmetics and bathhouse treatments before eventually opening 'Mahomed's Baths', a luxurious bathhouse on the seafront providing therapeutic baths and 'shampooing' with Indian oils.

The image below is a monochrome photographic print of a print of Mahomed's baths on Brighton seafront, just off East Street. It later became the site of the Savoy cinema.

37. Sake Dean Mahomed's Baths, Brighton, early 19th century.
Star & Garter inn can be seen on left of image. Image courtesy of the Royal Pavilion & Museums, Brighton & Hove, no. 17230.

Jane also appears to have been actively involved in the bathhouse business with her name featuring in adverts stipulating that, alongside her husband, she also possessed 'the art of shampooing' as well as 'superintended' the Ladies Baths (see the advert on page 56).

38. Mahomed's Medicated Baths.
The Sussex Weekly Advertiser, 1 May 1815.
Image @ The British Library Board.
Shelfmark: MFM.M2529.

> SAKE DEEN MAHOMED'S INDIAN, MEDICATED,
> VAPOUR, and SHAMPOOING BATHS, 7, Ryder-street, St. James's.—H.
> MAHOMED begs respectfully to recommend his Baths at this season of the year to
> Noblemen and Gentlemen as a substitute for hard exercise, which in London they
> are deprived of; and as essential to health in relieving the system and keeping the
> pores of the skin in a healthy state. To persons of a gouty habit they are peculiarly
> adapted, and for rheumatic affections, sciatica, lumbago, colds, influenza, stiff joints,
> sprains, &c., they are particularly recommended by the faculty, whom H. Mahomed
> thanks with much sincerity for the kind patronage and testimony they have given in
> favour of his baths, and his peculiar mode of administering them.—The Ladies Baths
> superintended by Mrs. Mahomed.

39. 'Ladies Baths superintended by Mrs Mahomed.'
Bell's Life in London and Sporting Chronicle, Sunday 15 May 1842.
Image @ The British Library Board.
Shelfmark: MFM.MLD14.

The enterprise was a great success, attracting a wealthy and famous clientele, with Mahomed being appointed through royal warrant as 'Shampooing Surgeon' to Kings George IV and William IV. Their family also grew during this time, seeing the births of their children Rosanna, Horatio, Frederick and Arthur.

In later years, several of the children would work in the family bathhouse business which had expanded to include several London locations, though sadly their involvement could not prevent the gradual decline of the Mahomeds' fame and fortune. By the end of the 1830s, a lack of capital saw Mahomed's Baths put up for auction and the family forced to move to more modest accommodation in Brighton. By then, Mahomed was in his eighties and Horatio and Arthur continued to run the existing offshoots of the business, with Jane also playing a main role. Advertisements of the time stated that 'The Ladies Bath is under the entire personal administration of Mrs Mahomed.' By the time Jane and Mahomed had died (in 1850 and 1851 respectively), the couple, once so prominent on the Brighton social scene, had largely fallen from public memory and attention.

In recent years, however, a renewed interest has been taken in this remarkable couple, with scholars and the media highlighting their biographies and achievements. In addition to the Mahomeds' cultural legacy, as pioneers of both Indian restaurants and 'shampooing' in Britain, their family legacy has also begun to attract attention. As Stewart and Hicks detail, their most illustrious descendant is perhaps the offspring of their son Frederick: their grandson Frederick Henry Horatio Akbar Mahomed (c. 1849–1884) who became a renowned physician at Guy's Hospital in London, playing a crucial role in the study and description of high blood pressure. Another of the couple's grandsons, James Dean Keriman Mahomed, an Oxford graduate, was appointed as a vicar for the Church of England at Ingham, Bury St Edmunds, in the late 19th century, while James's son - RAF Captain Felix Wyatt - was killed in action during World War 1, shot down whilst flying in France.[19]

> CULFORD is a parish and pleasant village on the north bank of the river Lark, 4 miles north-north-west from Bury St. Edmunds and 1 south-west from Ingham station on the Bury and Thetford section of the Great Eastern railway, which passes through the parish, in the North Western division of the county, Thingoe and Thedwastre petty sessonal division, Blackbourn hundred, Thingoe union, Bury St. Edmunds county court district, rural deanery of Thingoe, archdeaconry of Sudbury and diocese of Ely. The church of St. Mary is an edifice of stone and flint in the Early English style, consisting of chancel, nave, south porch, vestry and an embattled western tower containing one bell: the church, with the exception of the tower, which had been previously restored, was rebuilt in 1856 by the late Rev. Edward Richard Benyon M.A. rector from 1839 there are 200 sittings. The register dates from the year 1538. The living is a rectory, with those of Ingham and Timworth annexed, joint net yearly value £395, including 57 acres of glebe, in the gift of R. B. Berens esq. and held since 1898 by the Rev. James Dean Keriman Mahomed M.A. of Keble College, Oxford, who resides at Ingham. The church of St. Peter, at Culford Heath, in the neighbourhood of the Seven Hills, an out-district of this parish, erected at the cost of the late Rev. E. R. Benyon M.A. is a building of flint and stone and has stained windows: a residence was erected in 1864 for the minister who officiates, which by an exchange of glebe land, is now a part of the living and belongs to the Culford rectory. An Institute with Reading Room was erected in 1890, at the sole cost of Earl Cadogan. Culford Hall, a splendid mansion, the property and seat of Earl Cadogan K.G.,

40. James Dean Keriman Mahomed
Rector for the Parish of Ingham in the *Kelly Directory of Suffolk*, 1900, page 121.
Copyright: public domain. Image courtesy of University of Leicester, no. LUL5014.

James Dean Keriman Mahomed married Emma Louisa Black, a flower painter who exhibited work at the Royal Academy.[20] When Frederick Akbar contracted typhoid fever in 1884, he was tended for almost a month by his mentors, friends and colleagues. After his death from the illness at the age of 35, they set up a subscription to help his wife and five children.

The Mahomed's son Frederick ran a gymnasium and fencing academy at Brighton in the mid-19th century which attracted the 'nobility and gentry'. Like many other of the Mahomed lineage, Fredericks' descendants continued to marry into the respectable upper middle classes. See the notice below about the opening of Frederick's new gymnasium:

> GYMNASIUM.—Mr Frederick Mahomed, of Brighton, has recently opened the spacious building opposite the Pavilion Stables, Clench-street, as a gymnasium and fencing academy, which reminds one of the Athenian gymnasium of old, and which has been visited by many of the nobility and gentry of Brighton, some of whom have become pupils. There is a spacious gallery, which is arranged with exercises for adults, and under it are exercises for juniors; whilst the centre is occupied by that universal favourite amusement, the flying course, alias Taglioni, a name it has acquired from the grace that is displayed when properly performed. There are numerous dressing-rooms; and, in fact, the whole arrangements are so complete, that it may with truth be said to be one of the best places of the kind in the world.

41. New gymnasium opened by Mr Frederick Mahomed.
Bell's Life in London and Sporting Chronicle, 28 February 1847.
Image @ The British Library Board. Shelfmark: MFM.MLD14.

The *Fifeshire Advertiser* reported a marriage notice in 1884, for Arthur Mahomed, the Mahomeds' grandson via Frederick. The wedding was assisted by Arthur's brother, the Reverend James Mahomed, see extract below:

> At Holy Trinity, Bournemouth, on the 20th August, by the Rev. Canon Eliot, vicar, assisted by the Rev. H. W. Bull and the Rev. James Mahomed, Arthur Sulieman Mahomed, M.R.C.S., L.S.A., fourth son of Frederick Mahomed, of Brighton, and grandson of the late Sheik, Dear Mahomed, of Patna, to Mary Spicer Cruickshank Forsayth, daughter of the late Captain Forsayth, H.E.I.C., of Fifeshire.

42. Marriage of Sake Dean's grandson Arthur Mahomed.
The Fifeshire Advertiser, 30 August 1884.
Image @ The British Library Board.
Shelfmark: MFM.M25762.

Although little overt prejudice appears to have raised its head in the Mahomed family history over the generations, there are accounts of more covert manifestations. Although only their grandfather was Indian, Frederick and James were exoticised by their contemporaries who described them as 'Oriental' or 'Eastern' in appearance. Moreover, despite Frederick having been privately educated at Brighton before attending medical school in The Sussex County Hospital and then at Guy's, a student at Guy's noted that 'his teaching and his methods seemed as foreign as his name to the atmosphere of the place.' Social attitudes also shaped the family's experiences, for example, to avoid xenophobic attention during the First World War, Frederick and James's children changed their surnames to Deane and Wyatt respectively. Cameron and Hicks report Janet, the youngest of Frederick's daughters recalling that 'in the 1914 war the family thought it best to change their name as mixed marriages were in much disfavour'.

Yet, at the same time, the family, from the time of Dean and Jane themselves, were clearly firmly integrated into and accepted by first Irish and then British society. As well as Mahomed and Jane's success within gentrified social circles, his descendants all married white Britons, with some entering and achieving success within numerous traditional British professional establishments, such as medicine, the Church of England and the armed forces. The Mahomeds' family history thus vividly illustrates the racial and ethnic diversity to be found within Irish and British history, as well as points to some of the complexity of attitudes towards it.

Pablo and George Paddington

Throughout the Victorian as well as the early Edwardian period, people of colour were repeatedly visible in the highly popular circus industry as illustrated by the intriguing story of the Irish acrobat and equestrian, Pablo Paddington. In 1840, he appears in the advertisement below, for Ryan's Circus, in which he is described as 'PABLO PADDINGTION (the Man of Colour) will display his surprising Evolutions on the TIGHT ROPE':

> RYAN'S ROYAL OLYMPIC CIRCUS,
> WELLINGTON MANSION,
> *Wellington Street, Cheltenham,*
> OPENED FOR THE SEASON ON MONDAY,
> December 21, 1840,
>
> And will be continued every Evening during the present week (Christmas night excepted) with the most extensive Stud of Spotted and Party-coloured Horses and Ponies ever congregated in one Equestrian Establishment. The Gems in the art of Equitation have concentrated here, and will appear in their unrivalled Pantomimical Arena Scenes and daring acts of Horsemanship in rapid succession.
>
> THE PERFORMANCES will commence with the Grand Equestrian Spectacle and Entree, entitled ENGLAND'S QUEEN, in which Mr. Ryan's extensive Stud and Brilliant Company of Equestrian Artistes will display some rapid Evolutions and Groupings of classical Grandeur and Effect.
>
> Miss GINNETT will ride her admired Act as the ROSE MAID OF ALLANDALE.
>
> Mr. RYAN will introduce his SPANISH SPOT BEAUTY! Allowed by all judges to be the best broke Poney of the present age, which will go through a variety of extraordinary feats.
>
> The whole Company of CHINESE VAULTERS.
>
> Master C. ADAMS will appear on a Single Horse, and take a number of surprising LEAPS.
>
> PABLO PADDINGTON (the Man of Colour) will dsiplay his surprising Evolutions on the TIGHT ROPE.
>
> After a variety of other amusements, the Evening's Entertainments will conclude with GILPIN CABBAGE.
>
> By particular request of several Families of distinction,
> *A GRAND MORNING PERFORMANCE*
> will take place on SATURDAY, Dec. 26, commencing at One o'clock precisely.
> *An Entertainment in the Evening, at 7, as usual.*

43. Pablo Paddington in Wellington in 1840.
Cheltenham Examiner, 23 December 1840.
Image @ The British Library Board.
Shelfmark: 1-3593.

Paddington was a native of Cork who began to appear in advertisements for Batty's Circus tours across Ireland in the 1830s and 1840's as 'Mr Paddington', the performer of 'Herculean Feats!'. The newspaper advertisement below shows Mr Hughes, the manager of the circus, offering a grand spectacle to the 'Citizens of Cork' in 1842. He even advertised his intention to drive his horses from the Royal Stud Stables through the streets of Cork at the start of the show, as well as providing equestrian tuition. Mr Hughes also proposed to give the proceeds to the 'CORK DISPENSARY' and he would also later employ Paddington in Cork at Batty's circus.

44. Spectacle at Batty's Circus in Cork 1842.
Southern Reporter and Cork Commercial Courier on 29th December 1842 Image @ The British Library Board. Shelfmark: MFM.M20541.

In 1843, Mr Paddington was heralded as 'the Celebrated Corkonian', with the local community encouraged to attend to give public support not only on the basis of Paddington's ability 'but from being a Corkman himself.' The following Batty's Circus notice made by Mr Hughes in the *Irish Examiner* in 1843 credits Pablo as a Corkman:

45. Mr Paddington takes his benefit as a 'Corkman himself.' *Irish Examiner* on 6 February 1843. Image courtesy of the National Library of Ireland.

Prior to touring in Ireland, however, it appears that Paddington had made quite a name in England as 'the Flying African' and 'the Flying Indian', performing with a range of circus companies, including the famous Astley's and the Cooke's Olympic Circus, in the 1820s.[21]

46 Pablo Paddington, the 'Flying African'. An artist's impression. Courtesy of @AnishaBryan

However, a fascinating story about Paddington emerged in the press in 1827 which suggested that 'Mr Paddington' was in fact a woman.[22] Pregnant and destitute, a woman named Ellen Lowther was admitted to the York workhouse where she recounted that she had formerly performed alongside Paddington in the circus industry where the two had disguised themselves as men. Furthermore, Lowther said she was of Bengali ancestry, and despite both being 'women' of colour, they had stained their skins darker in order to appear more exotic. Lowther remarked that suspicions about the pair's gender gradually subsided as their smaller statures were put down to their racial backgrounds. It was noted in *The Belfast Commercial Chronicle* that Mr Cowper, a shoemaker, had recollected 'making a pair of boots for one of the black men in Mr Cooke's company, who had the smallest foot for a man.'[23]

However, it seems that generally Paddington's disguise was carried out 'so dextrously, as to have even deceived those about her' and 'by assiduous attentions gained the attentions of Miss King, who also travelled with Mr Cooke.' Pablo and Miss King's relationship carried on for some time until rumours reached Miss King's ears that Paddington was 'too much a man of the world, possessing more *female acquaintance* than was consistent with his solemn promises and plighted vows'. After a quarrel, the relationship cooled until Paddington's arm was broken in an accident and consequently 'pity again called forth the tender affections of Miss King, who, during her lover's illness, attended him with particular care.' Whether Paddington's female gender was ever revealed to Miss King is unclear, the papers stated, 'but the whole carries with it such an air of romance and of a novel story that we cannot but think the detail will be amusing to some of our readers.'

On 27th January 1827 the *Lancaster Gazette* below, included a report, from the *York Herald,* about the remarkable story of 'Two female impostors and Courtship Extraordinary [*sic*]'. Pablo Paddington was at the centre of this news story about two female imposters travelling with the Cooke's equestrian troop, who appeared as men of colour, whose feats of the most dextrous horsemanship were unsurpassed by any others in the company!

TWO FEMALE IMPOSTORS AND COURTSHIP EXTRAORDINARY.

A woman now in the York poor-house has given to the master there a strange account of herself and of another female imposter, who formerly travelled with Cooke's equestrian troop. They appeared as men of colour, and in all the feats of the most dextrous horsemanship were not to be surpassed by any others of the company. In addition to this, being dressed in male attire, and having their persons stained black, suspicion of their real sex was readily subdued by an allowance for the difference of personal appearance which opposite climates generally occasion. The real name of the woman now in the poor-house, is Ellen Lowther, but when with Cooke's company she called herself John Clifford—she is of eastern origin, though born in England; her grandfather, she says, was called Signor Rammapattan; he was brought to England from Bengal, by the late Lord Lowther, and when they arrived in London, his lordship changed his name to Lowther; he afterwards resided in the north of England, was killed by a pitman at Sunderland, when he was 106 years and nine months old. Her father, she says, lives at Tadcaster. She represents herself as being but 20 years of age, and having commenced her equestrian performances at 5 years old; she has been with the two Cookes 15 years. As might have been expected, this vagabond way of life led to vice and immorality, and the woman (alias John Clifford) was removed to the parish at St. Martin's, Coney-street, in a state of pregnancy, and thence to the work-house, where on the 2d inst. "John" was delivered of a still-born male child. The other woman, who passed for a black man, in the same company, went by the name of *Pablo Paddington*, and effected the deception so dextrously, as to have deceived even those about her, and by assiduous attentions gained the affections of a Miss King, who also travelled with Mr. Cooke. The courtship thus commenced was carried on for some time, till scandal whispered in the ears of the unsuspecting fair one, that her favourite *Pablo* was too much a man of the world, possessing more of *female acquaintance* than was consistent with his solemn promises and plighted vows. A lover's quarrel was the consequence: and slighted attachment led to some estrangement of the lady's affections. Misfortunes, however, often overtake the faithless, and the fair are sometimes, in those cases, too ready to forgive. This was the case with the parties in question. *Pablo* had his arm broken soon after, and pity again called forth the tender affections of Miss King, who, during her lover's illness, attended him with peculiar care. How the impostor rewarded her kindness, or whether she ever found out the cheat, we know not—but the whole carries with it such an air of romance and of a novel story, that we cannot but think the detail will be amusing to some of our readers.—*York Herald.*

47. Two female impostors. *The Lancaster Gazette,* 27 January 1827. Copyright Public domain. Image courtesy of The British Library Board, ref. no. Gale|R3209084374.

Meanwhile, whereas Ellen Lowther's time at Cooke's company ended tragically - she delivered a stillborn child in the workhouse - Paddington seems to have continued to work solidly in the guise of a man; before heading back to Ireland, s/he is noted as performing at other circuses in England throughout the 1830s. Vanessa Toulmin reports that as well as equestrian displays, Paddington's routines included 'dancing with skipping ropes, leaping handkerchiefs and incredible feats on the Corde Volante (Flying Rope)'.[24]

In the 1850s, Paddington worked for the famous black British circus proprietor Pablo Fanque, though he now appeared under his real name (perhaps ditching the pseudonym Pablo to avoid being confused with Fanque). Fanque had built an amphitheatre in Cork in 1850 but the pair seem to have known each other at least since appearing together at Ryan's Circus in the 1840s. Pablo Fanque placed two advertisements in *The Southern Reporter and Cork Commercial Courier* in 1851 about his Circus on Old George's Street in Cork:

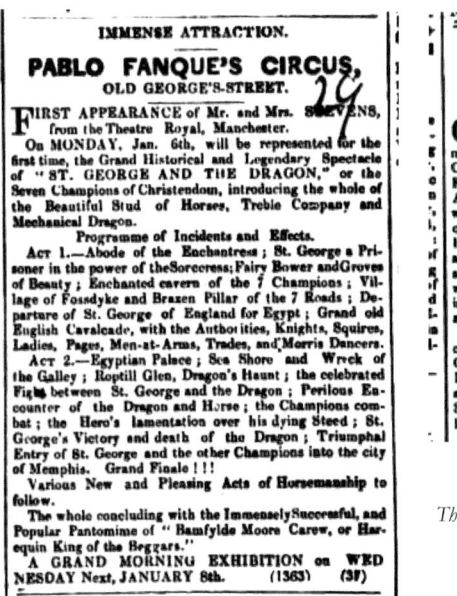

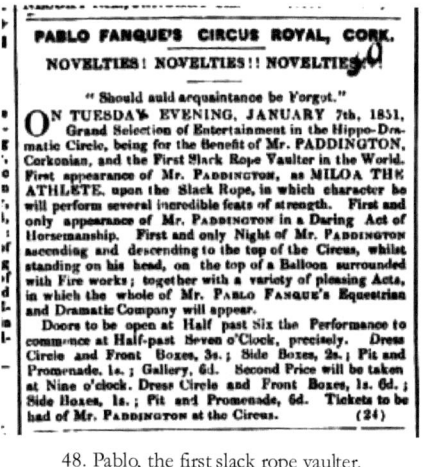

48. Pablo, the first slack rope vaulter.
Pablo Fanque's Circus in Cork.
The Southern Reporter and Cork Commercial Courier on 04 January 1851.
Image @ The British Library Board.
Shelfmark: MFM.M11333.

The Corkonian is now celebrated as the world's 'First Slack Rope Vaulter', now performing in his own home town, along with another famous black British circus proprietor, Pablo Fanque, who was Britain's first black person to own and operating a circus business. Note the

"Pablo" in Jospeh Paddington's stage name has been dropped. However, the two Pablo's knew each other for some time through their earlier work in England in the circus trade. A newspaper account in 1841 describes the men spending the night in police cells in the aftermath of a cart crash in Sandiacre, Derbyshire, in which a horse was killed. See extract below from the *Nottingham Review and General Advertiser for the Midland Counties* in 1841:

> On Sunday evening last, Mr. Radford, of Derby, was returning home from Bramcote, in a light spring cart, with some friends. In the neighbourhood of Sandiacre, a horse and gig approached, which was running at a tremendous rate, and in consequence of the darkness of the night, a collision took place. Several persons were slightly injured, and the gig shaft penetrated the body of Mr. Radford's horse, and instantaneous death was the consequence. The gig contained Signor Bernaskino, the celebrated man-monkey, Pablo Paddington, and Pablo *somebody else*, all belonging to Ryan's Circus. On perceiving what had happened, the *riders* were desirous of making a speedy exit, each individual leaving his name. But not so; two constables, "Big and Strong," were brought to the spot, and, as these functionaries are not often troubled with a "job," they seemed desirous of discharging their duty *with a vengeance*, for *monkey and men* were placed in confinement till eleven o'clock the following morning, when they were suffered to depart, on the *monkey* paying a sum of money to the owner of the animal.

49. The 'celebrated man-monkey, Pablo Paddington'.
Nottingham Review and General Advertiser for the Midland Counties, p. 4, 15 October 1841.
Image @ The British Library Board.
Shelfmark: 1060-3274.

As well as performing in Cork during the 1850's, Paddington seems to have been involved with Pablo Fanque, who was well known for his charitable generosity, in raising money for good causes. In January 1851, Fanque put on shows specifically for the benefit of charities. Adverts appeared in the *Cork Southern Reporter* thanking both Paddington and Fanque for putting on a Benefit for St. Patrick's Orphan Asylum, as well as Fanque's aid of his company to raise money for the widows and orphans of the Society of Odd Fellows and for the 'Cork Lying in Hospital'. See the extracts of two notices on page 65.

CORK LYING-IN HOSPITAL.
CIRCUS.

MR. PABLO FANQUE having generously offered the Receipts of a Performance at his Circus, for the Benefit of the CORK LYING-IN HOSPITAL, the Friends of the Charity are *earnestly requested* to attend there on FRIDAY Evening Next, the 24th inst., when a Select and most attractive performance will take place.
Cork, Jan. 18, 1851.   (135)

ST. PATRICK'S ORPHAN ASYLUM.

THE COMMITTEE of the above Institution beg to return their best thanks to Mons. PABLO FANQUE, for his kindness in giving a Benefit for the Charity. Also, to Mr. JOHNS, his Secretary, for his efforts to aid their exertions, and to Mr. PADDINGTON, for his kindness in volunteering his aid on the occasion.   (173)

50. Appreciation extended to Pablo Fanque and Mr Paddington.
The Southern Reporter and Cork Commercial Courier on 21th January 1851.
Image @ The British Library Board. Shelfmark: MFM.M11333.

Following the engagement with the Fanque Circus, Paddington was drawn into other daring firework performances in Cork on the request of another British entrepreneur and showman called Mr Van Hare.

51. George Van Hare, 1888 photographed by G. Jerrard, Regent Street, London, in *Fifty Years of a Showman's Life,* by Van Hare. Image courtesy of the British Library Board. Shelfmark: 10827.b.38.

In 1853, the celebrated British showman George Van Hare arrived in Cork, early in his career, to act as the newly appointed treasurer of a Mr Lloyd who was opening a theatre in Georges Street. Van Hare's unfortunate experience of renting the venue from the proprietor "Mr M", also known as "old cent. per cent.", resulted in him taking legal action against the proprietor for shutting the theatre just before the guests arrived for the opening show. In his autobiography *Fifty Years of a Showman's Life*,[25] published in 1888, he mentions that, while taking this legal case, he decided to pursue other activities as the Queenstown Regatta was due to start soon. This regatta required firework displays. He was asked by the organising committee if he could do the firework display and he agreed, as he had contacts in Bristol who could supply him firework materials. He knew that Pablo Paddington was in Cork at this time and writes that he was a "man of colour" and "native of Cork" whose brother, a catholic priest, had died and left him a little money.

Van Hare described how he found an old disused mansion with beautiful grounds, with a stream, close to Queen's College just outside Cork. He arranged to have this tidied up and the walkways cleared. He set about creating 'Chinese walks' with coloured oil-lamps, "à la Vauxhall 40,000 lamps". There was no platform on site, so he arranged two large rooms on the ground floor of the mansion into a dance hall and stationed the quadrille band in the entrance hall of the building. With all of this in progress, he engaged Pablo to perform for him in these gardens, as he knew him for several years as a celebrated slack-rope vaulter with Mr. Batty, of Astley's Amphitheatre in London. Van Hare created posters which read "Cremorne Gardens will open. Engagement of the Great Pablo Paddington. Grand display of aquatic and other artistic designs of fireworks".

It is not clear from archival records where Cremorne Gardens were in Cork, but it seems Van Hare made this name up after the Cremorne Gardens, along the river Thames in Chelsea, London, which were popular pleasure gardens in London at the time. An article in *The Cork Examiner* on 2 September 1853 advertised the appearance of Mr. J. Paddington at 'Castle White Gardens, Western Road, A La Cremorne', suggesting the real name was Castle White gardens, on grounds now owned by University College Cork and possibly in the area now occupied by the Castle White student apartments today.

Van Hare was keen to get the show started with the famous "Mr Pab." saying that Pablo "must do the rope first; but it's dark, and we have no lights. Oh! put some pots of coloured fire under him". Pablo dutifully went up the rope and started swinging around and doing somersaults. "Bring some more pots of fire" he called, but this caused him to start coughing and they removed the pots of fire as Van Hare feared Pablo would choke, as he was suffocating when they pulled him down. See artist's impression of "Pabs" over the fire on page 67.

52 Pablo over the fire in 1853
An artist's impression.
Courtesy of @AnishaBryan

The first night was not attended by many as Van Hare found out that the lodge-keeper had died and there was a wake taking place near the entrance and there was "howling and crying most miserably". However, the show picked up later and went on for the season, despite the imminent lawsuit against the old "Cent. per Cent." Van Hare was clear in his mind that in the last month of the season there was ample time to bring his "Cremorne season to a close and have everything prepared to get away at short notice, for I had made up my mind if I lost [the case] I would not pay".

> **THE GREATEST NOVELTIES EVER PRODUCED IN CORK.**
>
> ON MONDAY EVENING, SEPTEMBER 5TH.
>
> CASTLE WHITE GARDENS, WESTERN ROAD.—A LA CREMORNE. Under the sole Management of Mr. VAN HARE. First appearance of Mr. J. PADDINGTON, the Celebrated Slack Rope Vaulter, a la Trapeze—THE CHINESE WALK—and THE GRAND FEAST OF LANTERNS—Splendid Display of FIRE WORKS.
>
> The Gardens will be beautifully Illuminated as a Grand Promenade, a la Versailles.
>
> Brass and Quadrille Band—Leader of the Orchestra, Mr. T. C. REDDING, from the Theatre Royal, Drury-lane; Conductor, Signor BORINI. After the Fire Works, Dancing in the Large Ball Room. Gardens open at Seven o'Clock.
>
> Admission, Gentlemen, One Shilling, Ladies and Children, Sixpence.
>
> Refreshments had in the Grand Hall. No improper characters admitted. Should the weather prove unfavourable the Gala will take place the following fine evening.
>
> Tickets to be had at 14, Old George's-street. [2052]

53. Greatest Novelties ever produced in Cork by Mr. Mr Van Hare. *The Cork Examiner*, 2 Sept 1853.
Image @ The British Library Board.
Shelfmark: MFM.M7813.

Fortunately, Van Hare won his case against 'Cent. per Cent." and received damages of one hundred and seventy five pounds. He was cheered in the street by everyone who met him as nobody liked old Cent. per Cent. Shortly afterwards, he was served with a summons by Cork County Court for the agreed eight pounds due for the week's rental of the theatre, despite being awarded damages already for being locked out. Van Hare had already made up his mind that he would not pay this but told his solicitor he would pay. However, the following day he told everyone he was heading to the Exhibition in Dublin, but quickly met his friends in Cork, settled a few accounts and took steamer from Cork. People in Cork were asking his friend, Charley, what he had done with Van Hare who had disappeared. Dick Burke, a proprietor of another theatre said "Ah! Be the powers, I knew he hadn't come here with all that hair on his face without knowing his way about". Van Hare left Cork for England, leaving Pablo Paddington and his friends behind, and he then travelled on to Europe where he managed a successful show business, which later included African animals (see page 69) of Van Hare in the lion's cage, as shown in his autobiography.

54. Mr. Van Hare 'In the Lions' Cage' sketch by Irving Montagu,
in *Fifty Years of a Showman's Life* by Van Hare.
Image courtesy of British Library. Shelfmark: 10827.b.38.

It appears Van Hare's Cremorne Gardens season in Cork was the last time he saw Pablo Paddington. His exact racial heritage is difficult to determine, being variously described as 'African', 'Indian', 'Brazilian', 'Siamese' and a 'man of colour' during the course of his/her career, as well as Lowther's reports that Paddington darkened his/her skin in order to appear 'more exotic'. As Toulmin notes, tracing and identifying the histories of circus performers of colour is highly challenging due to the very nature of the circus profession - in which nom de plumes were common and biographies were frequently exaggerated - and it has been wondered whether Paddington was actually a white acrobat performing in blackface.

However, archival records we have discovered provide evidence that suggest Paddington was not only a person of colour but was part of a larger mixed race Irish family, which is supported by comments made by George Van Hare in his biography. The name of Paddington, an unusual surname in nineteenth century Ireland, is shared by Father George John Paddington, Pablo's brother, described widely in records as a black Irish priest and a 'native of Cork', who studied in Rome. Hart has since established that it was misreported in the newspapers that

Paddington went on to receive a doctorate in Theology from the University of Heidelberg. This, stated the *Irish Examiner*, was said to be the first time a 'Negro' had ever received scholastic honours at a European university. Yet this was in fact James W.C. Pennington, the African American churchman and former enslaved person who escaped from his plantation in Maryland.[26] Hart's findings now explains the initials 'J.W.' in the article below which was J. W. Pennington and not the Corkonian Rev. George J. Paddington.

> We read in one of the French papers that the University of Heidelberg is about to confer the degree of Doctor of Theology on Mr. J. W. Paddington, a black, and Catholic priest at New York. Mr. Paddington is, it is said, the first Negro who has ever received scholastic honours at a European university. He is reported to be the author of several works on Theology.—*Athenæum*. [Mr. Paddington is a native of Cork.]

55. George Paddington gains a doctorate in Theology.
Irish Examiner, 1 January 1851. Image courtesy of the
National Library of Ireland.

Arthur Jones details that Father Paddington was ordained in Haiti by an American[27] bishop and spent time in New York where he became an acquaintance of the black American Catholic philanthropist Pierre Toussaint. At the time of his award, Father Paddington was said by the *Irish Examiner* to be serving as a Catholic priest in New York, though research by Bernard Lauwyck places him in the Caribbean at the time of his awarded doctorate and his death soon later that year. The West Indian connection, is expanded on by Father Nicholas McLoughlin who states that Father Paddington was the son of a white Irish man - also called George Paddington - and his black Haitian wife. According to McLoughlin, though George Paddington Senior had met his wife in Haiti, Father Paddington had been born in Ireland.

Records have also been found[28] of Mary Anne Paddington marrying a man named Michael McCarthy in Cork in 1846, while in 1849, Father George Paddington leased a Cork property to a Michael McCarthy suggesting that McCarthy was likely his brother-in-law (see copy of rent book on the next page). The entry shows Michael McCarthy property lease at Millard Street from George Paddington, 1849.[29]

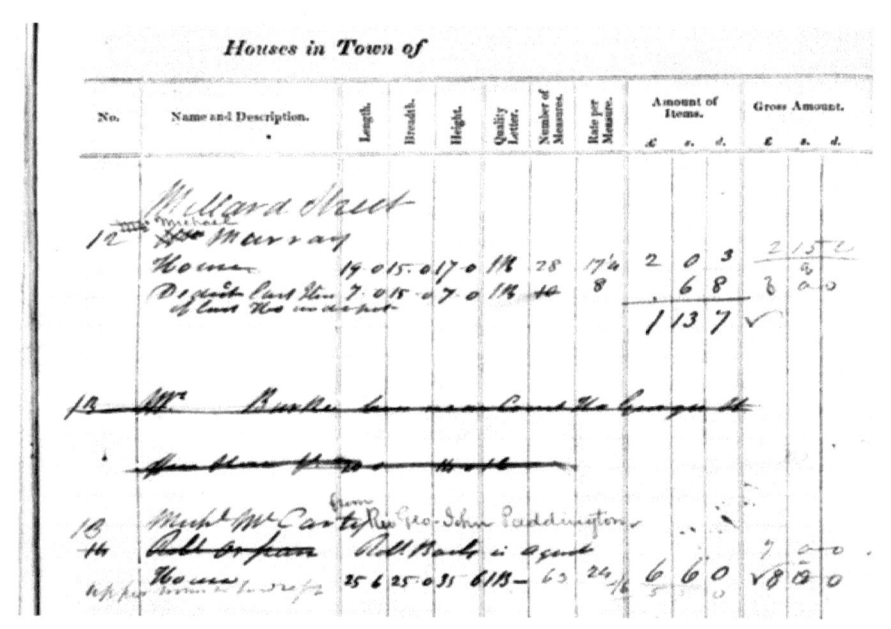

56. Michael McCarty rents from Rev. George John Paddington
Valuation Records, 1824 – 1856, Books in May 1850, Cork.
Image courtesy of the National Library of Ireland.

Most pertinently, however, Lauwyk's research also uncovered records which stated that Father Paddington not only had a sister but was 'from an acrobat family in Ireland', thus suggesting a clear link to Pablo. We have discovered that a Mr Joseph Paddington, aged 40 from Ireland, is recorded as living at Bradford Street, Birmingham in the 1841 Census with a Mr Michael McCarthy, aged 20 and a Mr James Tippen, aged 50, both also from Ireland. All three people are recorded in the 1841 Census working as equestrians. This discovery confirmed that Pablo's real first name was Jospeh and that he was not a woman. Further records show that George Paddington ran a school at Miller Street, the same address given in an advert in the *Irish Examiner* where tickets for Batty's Circus in Cork in 1843 - featuring the first night of 'the Celebrated Corkonian', Mr Paddington - could be purchased.

It is difficult to established where Joseph Paddington spent his remaining days as there are no traces of Joseph Paddington, in any Irish birth, marriage or death records in the civil or church registers in the 19th century. Towards the late 1850s, the trail for Joseph Paddington goes cold after a long and remarkable circus career in both Ireland and England. We still don't know if he had his own family or children. In

1853/54, he appeared in The Royal Amphitheatre in Fishamble Street, Dublin as the 'Flying Man' (*Saunderer's Newsletter*, 26 December 1853) and as part of the 'Timour the Tartar' act (*Freeman's Journal* 5 January 1854). He returned again to Britain and appeared in a local newspaper advertisement announcing that he would be performing as a Slack Rope Vaulter at the Bristol Zoological Gardens, for the benefit of the 'Widows and Orphans Fund'.[30] His performances in Bristol appear to be his last known circus engagement. Finally, in 1856 we see him advertise for the first time for work in a newspaper, suggesting hard times ahead. See extract below:

> *TO PROPRIETORS OF PLEASURE GARDENS AND COMMITTEES OF FETES, GALAS, etc – after Monday next, 19th May, MADAME EUGENIE, the celebrated tight rope dancer, Pablo Paddington, the renowned slack rope vaulter, and W.H. Dodd, the popular clown of Cremorne celebrity, are OPEN of engagements either for long or short duration. Sole agent Mr. Clarke, 95 Portland Street, Manchester.'*[31]

This suggests Paddington and others in his age group (he would have been in his late 50s) were struggling to find work or perhaps they faced more competition from younger up and coming acrobats. It is possible given the address of the agent that he settled in Manchester or the English midlands. So far, the only trace of a death of a Mr Joseph Paddington around the same age is in March 1871, in the Witney Union Workhouse, which records the death of a man of 69 years old with the same name. Though this is speculation, and more research is required, it is true that many circus performers and Irish emigrants to Britain died as paupers, interred without separate headstones. We may never find his final resting place.

Although there was much ambiguity around the identity and story of Pablo Paddington, when we started our research, existing records and evidence suggests that, along with his sibling George, as confirmed by Van Hare, and their Irish and Haitian parents, he was certainly part of a fascinating nineteenth century mixed race Irish family that traversed countries, boundaries and conventions. This Cork family of colour lived at a time when Ireland faced the most terrible famine and yet somehow the two brothers, George as a catholic priest and Joseph as the acrobat, managed to avoid the ravages of poverty that tragically fell upon Ireland.

William Love – Fugitive 'Slave', Lecturer and the Gold Watch

A strange story appeared in the *The Londonderry Standard* [32] newspaper in September 1857, about 'a Negro Adventurer' called William Love. He visited Derry and the surrounding area, claiming he was an escaped 'slave' and he delivered lectures and took subscriptions towards, what was described as his "own sustentation fund". He provided people with testimonials claiming to be written by highly respectable gentlemen. It was also reported he had delivered lectures at Strabane, Donagheady, Stranorlar in County Donegal, Ramelton, Moville and other places. Before going to one of his lectures in Moville he borrowed a gold watch from his landlady, Mrs. Hurst, so that he could time his appointment punctually. However, the next morning he disappeared with his landlady's gold watch, without paying for his lodgings.

William Love rented a room at Mr Edwards Hurst's home in Derry for himself, his wife and his "mulatto child". The newspaper reported that he "is married to a white woman, who says she is a native of Dublin". Love disappeared with the golden watch, leaving his Dublin wife and his child behind. However, following some news, Mr Hurst's wife went to Glasgow in search of the fugitive and traced him to several locations, but without actually finding him. Mrs. Hurst discovered from an English newspaper that a person fitting his description had been arrested by Sunderland Police. After Mrs Hurst returned home to Derry, Love's wife gave her a pawnbroker's ticket showing that the stolen watch had been pawned before her husband left Derry.

The *Newry Telegraph* also reported that "in addition to the above particulars, which appeared in yesterday's *Standard*, we have been informed that Love called upon the Rev. Sewell, Independent Minister of this City, represented that he was a fugitive 'slave' and said that he had testimonials from the Rev. Goudy, Strabane and the Rev. Mr Porter, Donagheady."[33] At this time, the 'escaped slave' narrative and associated lectures had a strong appetite amongst audiences and anti-slavery groups in Ireland, as seen earlier with the lecture tours in Ireland of Moses Roper in 1838 and Frederick Douglas in 1845. There were also several 'fugitive slave' lecturers touring Britain and Ireland during this period.[34]

When researching Mrs Hurst's trip to Scotland, for her gold watch, the only credible newspaper reports found about lecturers on tour in Scotland, in 1857, was about a John Andrew Jackson who spoke in

Aberdeen 16 February 1857[35] and a 'Mr Jackson' who spoke in Alloa in Scotland on 17 April 1857.[36] A Mr J.A Jackson spoke at Liverpool with his "Wife, a Creole" on 16th June 1857,[37] and again Mr John A Jackson appeared at Kilmarnock at Sabbath on 11 September in St Marneck's Church,[38] which stated that Jackson had arrived in Liverpool in October 1856. It is unknown if he travelled in Ireland or if William Love was an imposter, presenting himself as John A. Jackson who was well known at this time.

Finally, we tracked William Love down to 'Potter Hill Chapel' in Sheffield England, on 7 February 1857. *The Sheffield and Rotherham Independent* newspaper reported that "a man of colour, occupied the pulpit...and on Monday, there was a local tea meeting, when several eminent ministers, along with Mr Love gave addresses". The following day he gave "a very interesting lecture on American slavery...The audience were highly pleased with the lecturer and cheered him heartily several times, while he graphically showed the nature of the abominable system of slavery".[39] However, in Darlington, suspicions were raised in another article, on the same day, titled "Caution – Real Fugitive Slave! - Darlington".[40] In Darlington he spoke at the Central Hall and the Primitive Methodists in Queen Street. When he failed to turn up for his engagement at the Committee of the Darlington Temperance Society, the committee was informed that after making some false excuse that he had absconded from Mrs Johnson's Temperance Hotel without settling his account. The article described him as "not particularly dark, but remarkably tall, stout in proportion. Walks with a swagger, and so far as we can judge, is on this side of 30...we hope this notice may put the neighbourhood upon its guard against this black imposter".

At this stage it was not clear whether he really was an imposter or whether there was any truth to his 'slave' story. Or if the arrest mentioned by Mrs Hurst was simply related to the gold watch. In any case, it appears he was touring around England and Scotland like other black lecturers at the time. Meanwhile, several reports appeared in Scotland of his movements and lectures. The *Montrose Arbroath and Brechin Review*, gave extensive coverage on 6 February 1857 in an article titled 'Negro Imposter' which said "we noticed the appearance amongst us of a Mr William Love, calling himself a fugitive 'slave' from Baltimore, who electrified our citizens by his narration of stirring incidents, his powerful eloquence and inimitable humour and pleasantry...William Love was, instead of being a fugitive 'slave', was an accomplished imposter."[41] The paper goes on to say that, from documents received, he "has never been a slave, except to his own inveterate habit of lying and deception: and, though often a fugitive, his flying has only been from those he has duped and fleeced."

Apparently, he had a new story and name for every place he lectured. He has been known as Andrew Baker, Hiram Swift, Rueben Nixon, Henry Smith and lastly William Love. He was described as:

"a fine, well made, muscular man, about twenty five (now twenty eight) years of age; nearly six feet in height; dresses well, and has a remarkable easy carriage. He is a dark mulatto, nearly black, has good white teeth and bright eyes, the left having a slight obliquity. His woolly hair comes close down upon his brow, and his whiskers are large under his chin. His manners are pleasing, and his voice soft and musical. He can excite compassion by shedding tears, which he does with great facility. He affects not to be able to write; but as he has also said he could not read, which he can do, perhaps he can do both"[42]

He was arrested and sent to prison, probably shortly after his visit to Potters Hill Chapel, though the details are not clear yet. He was convicted as a rogue and a vagabond and he showed tact in rebutting the charges, with remarkable *sang froid*. After being hard pressed and believing he had silenced all accusations, he very coolly observed that *"There are more mistakes than beef-steaks in Scotland"*.

This story again provides a fascinating insight into the presence of mixed race marriages in Ireland in the 19th century. Nevertheless, as with other historical glimpses of mixed race families, there are more questions about this story than answers, such as was Love really married to the white Dublin woman? Where was he really born? In Baltimore? Or was he an Irish born person of colour who travelled throughout the British Isles, in his case, on the run?

We found an article in the *Kings County Chronicle* dated 26 November 1856,[43] about a case of a "Negro Imposter" in Ballinasloe, County Galway, which happened before William Love's Derry incident in 1857. No name is mentioned at Ballinasloe, but this could be the same person. The article described "a coloured man, representing himself as an escaped slave, from the United States", who proposed to give lectures in Ballinasloe and "raising at the same time contributions to aid (as he said) in purchasing the freedom of his sister, still a slave". It continues to say that information was received that the man's story was a fabrication and that he "is a practiced rogue and imposter".

George Henry Thompson – Belfast Riots

A contribution by Mark Doyle from his piece "Those the Empire Washed Ashore: uncovering Ireland's multiracial past".[44] *The text below is reproduced with permission of the Licensor through PLSclear (pp 76 to 82), ©Palgrave Macmillan:*

The strange story of George Henry Thompson, a black man arrested for riot in Belfast in 1872, provides an opportunity to explore questions of racial tolerance in Ireland in the nineteenth century.

57. The Riots in Belfast in 1872
Orangemen attack the procession. Front page of the *Illustrated London News*, 31 August 1872. Image courtesy of @ Illustrated London News Ltd and The British Library Board. Shelfmark: P.P.7611.

The Belfast riots of 1872 were typical of the sectarian riots that plagued that city in the latter half of the nineteenth century.

Like many others, they were sparked by a parading dispute: the Party Processions Acts, which banned sectarian marches, had just been repealed, and, although the Orangemen's marches had passed off peacefully in July, a nationalist (and mostly Catholic) parade in August was not so fortunate. Skirmishes between working-class Protestants and Catholics on 15 August, the day of the procession, evolved over the next few days into full-blown battles between rival factions. It had been eight years since the last major riot in Belfast, and in that time new neighbourhoods had developed along the Falls and Shankill roads, which were not yet fully segregated by religion. Catholics tended to live along the Falls, and Protestants tended to live along the Shankill, but these areas were far from homogenous, and many people from different faiths still lived and worked alongside each other.

One of the objectives of extremists during the riots, then, was to force outsiders in their midst to flee to their 'own' neighbourhoods. Sometimes this entailed a note slid under the door or a whispered warning from a neighbour, but sometimes it involved what in Belfast was known as a 'wrecking': a home invasion by an armed gang who would break furniture, tear clothing, and threaten (and sometimes harm) the inhabitants. It was during one such episode that George Henry Thompson was arrested. On 18 August, at the height of the riots, Thompson was part of a Protestant crowd engaged in threatening and wrecking Catholic homes along Crimea Street, off the Shankill Road. He was arrested in September and tried at the Belfast Police Court, where it was determined that he should be held over for trial at the spring Assizes. One of the key witnesses against him was Margaret Donegan (or Donaghy), who alleged that he had broken into her house at the head of a mob. She told the court that she was unsure that the man who invaded her home was Thompson, but the man in the dock certainly looked like him. To be sure that they had the right man, the presiding magistrate asked if the man who invaded her home was 'a sweep or a man of colour'. Donegan said that he may have been a sweep, 'but I am almost sure it was a black man'.

At Thompson's Assize trial the following March, Constable Andrew Doherty said that he saw Thompson shouting and cheering while waving a stick above his head. He also saw him enter several houses along the street, and shortly thereafter the inhabitants fled. Sub-Constable Gilbert Hasley corroborated Doherty's story, adding that he saw Thompson sitting atop the shoulders of another man and shouting 'Come on ye sons of William' to a crowd of about 2000 rowdies armed with bludgeons. Detective Joshua Crosswell saw Thompson in a stone-throwing mob that was chasing a man down Townsend Street, some distance away from Crimea Street. When the man fled into a house, Thompson tried to kick down the door; when Crosswell tried to stop him, Thompson hit the detective on the shoulder, incurring a charge of assault upon a police officer in addition to the charges of riot, unlawful assembly, and common assault, for which he was also booked.

A bystander named William Henry provided a slightly different picture. He said that he saw Thompson in a mob, 'but he appeared to be led on by the mob, who were making fun of him. Other members of the mob seemed to be more violent than he was'. To Henry, it seemed as if the mob was making 'a cat's-paw of him, and were urging him on. They called him "Sambo" and "Snowball", and applied other bantering epithets. If this is true, it gives the story a different flavour: instead of (or in addition to) being a mob leader, Thompson may have been an object of ridicule for the white Protestants in the crowd.

Unfortunately, no available source gives Thompson's side of the story. He spoke only twice at his Assizes trial. The first time was when the Deputy Clerk of the Crown asked if he was ready for his trial. Thompson replied, 'I don't mind at all. Is the trial ready for me?' This spirited response drew laughter in the courtroom, and it hints at a defiant personality, which is consistent with the testimony against him (he pleaded not guilty). His second utterance was more pathetic: Asked by the clerk if he had any witnesses to call after the Crown witnesses had testified, Thompson said, 'I have, but they are not here'. The jury found him guilty, and In early Apr"l he'was sentenced to two years' hard labour, the most severe sentence available for the offences of which he had been convicted.

The *Daily Examiner*, which became the *Ulster Examiner and Northern Star* in 1873, was the organ of the Catholic Church in Belfast. It had spent the week of the riots raging against the 'Orange rabble' and excusing Catholic violence as acts of self-defence, and it had little sympathy for the likes of Thompson. In two editorial leaders, one published after his Police Court trial and the other following his appearance at the Assizes, the Examiner mercilessly ridiculed Thompson both for his supposed sympathy with the Protestant mob and for the colour of his skin. The first leader, whose headline referred to Thompson as an Ethiopian (a generic term for any African), made free and inventive use of existing discourses about Africa to attack Thompson:

'How this waif from 'Afric's sunny fountains' got himself promoted to the important post of Commander-in-Chief of a mob of the 'Sons of William' … or how he picked up the phraseology in which he fired the flagging zeal of his tatterdemalion following it is difficult to guess. Yet there he was, black and glossy, like another Othello, braving dangers and encountering perils from paving stones and brick-bats to gain by their recital, on a future occasion, the warm affections of some Desdemona.'

Readers would easily have grasped the Othello references, and they would probably also have recognised 'Afric's sunny fountains' from a popular missionary hymn of the time, which urged Christians to deliver 'the heathen' and other lost souls 'from error's chain'. After twice mocking Thompson as a 'political n*****', the writer then deftly twisted the old slogan of the anti-slavery campaign ('Am I not a man and a brother?') in a way that simultaneously ridiculed both Thompson and the brethren of the Orange Order:

'It is, doubtless, all very good to suggest to one the truism that Mr. George Henry Thompson is a 'man and a brudder,' but the increase of such 'bruddern' is not desirable at the present moment, if the gentlemen can find no more befitting or profitable employment than leading on mobs even more degraded than themselves.'

The author then struck an anthropological pose, before returning to the missionary hymn:

'Black men are interesting subjects of study when they appear as keepers of elephants, or as lion-tamers, in menageries, or even as cooks on board American liners; but this interest suffers considerable abatement when we are called upon to regard them as leaders in party politics. What the complexion of the mob must have been that followed on the war trail of this amiable specimen of the race that 'calls us to deliver their land from error's chain,' it was easy to infer from that of their exalted leader, as he stood in the dock like a representation of Innocence 79odelled in black sugar.'

The writer continued In this vein "or s'me time, deriding Thompson as a 'child of nature', a 'black potentate' leading a mob of 'white coolies' and a 'blackamoor', before finally suggesting that he left a devilish whiff of sulphur in his wake.

The second leader, published at the time of Thompson's Assizes trial, adopted a similar tone and was probably written by the same person. It recommended that Thompson enrol as a 'Sir Knight of the Black Perceptory', alluding to the Protestant loyalist organisation of that name, and then, somewhat incongruously, compared him to the Modoc people, a Native American group then fighting settlers in Oregon and California:

> 'George Henry did not put on his paint and feathers, and go out upon the war trail without meaning business. Captain Jack, with his handful of Modoc warriors in their stronghold of the Lava Beds, is not more in earnest in the blood-letting line than was the Ethiopian Orangeman with his two thousand faithful followers in the lanes and alleys abutting on the Shankill Road.'

The writer spent several lines gloating that the 'two thousand braves' who had held Thompson up as an idol during the riots had now abandoned him, and he ended by affecting pity for the poor 'Ethiopian Orangeman' who had mightily tried to smite Popery in defence of the Constitution. 'Happy Constitution! Happy civil and religious liberty! That in the hour of trial can always reckon upon the strong arms and willing hearts of fighting n***** like George Henry Thompson.'

In Dublin, the nationalist newspaper The Nation picked up these reports and joined in the fun. On learning that this 'Ethiopian' had been leading a crowd of Protestants with cries of 'Come on, Sons of William', it asked facetiously, 'Was William III a negro?' and averred that 'If the sons of William are "gentlemen of colour" in the sixth generation, the parent hero must have been a deep black indeed'.

On 20 July 1873, nearly a year after the riots, *The Nation* imagined Thompson entertaining the Orangemen during their annual marches with a song set to the tune of 'Camptown Races', a popular minstrel tune.

The minstrel tune went, in part:

> De sons ob William sing dis song –
> Doo-dah! Doo-dah!
> De sons ob William might strong,
> Doo-dah, doo-dah, dah!
> We's gwine to booze all night,
> We's gwine to booze all day,
> We must uphold our ancient right
> An' dat's just what I say.
> King William was a fine ole boss,
> Doo-dah! Doo-dah!
> We lubs himself, and lubs his hoss –
> Doo-dah, doo-dah, dah!
> We'll toast dem bof all night,
> We'll tost dem bof all day,
> Till William's sons hab all got tight,
> For dat's our good ole way!

Thompson, of course, would have been in prison at this time, and so quite unable to entertain the marching Orangemen in the manner suggested. Who was George Henry Thompson, really? Did he live in Belfast? What brought him to Crimea Street on 18 August 1872, and did he really seek to defend the legacy of King William III? Who were the people following him, mocking him, or egging him on? Sadly, it seems, no evidence survives that can answer these questions. The relevant court records, from the Belfast Police Court and the Antrim Assizes, are lost, as are the prison records. These might have provided details about Thompson's places of birth and residence, his occupation, and other interesting details. Belfast street directories contain listings for several George Thompsons, but there is nothing to suggest which one, if any, was the man in question. The only local newspaper to have taken much interest in Thompson's case, the *Examiner*, did provide transcripts of his two trials but said nothing about his background.

However, in 1864, at a trial of some rioters, a policeman reported seeing a 'dark-complexioned man' drop to his knees to fire upon a group of Catholic workers. 'I recollect going up beside the black fellow', the policeman said, 'and saying he was a murdering rascal, and bidding him get up off his knees'. Was this 'black fellow' George Henry Thompson? We will probably never know as so many of the official sources that we might use for a systematic search have been lost (many in the Four Courts fire of 1922).

Even if these scraps of evidence do not tell us much about a specific individual, however, they do tell us several important things about nineteenth-century Belfast, and about Ireland generally. They remind us that there were racial minorities in Victorian Ireland, and that they, like everybody else, occasionally got swept up in the larger historical forces that buffeted the island. The attitudes of the *Examiner* and the *Nation* toward Thompson tell us that racism was certainly not absent from Ireland, despite what other sources might suggest, and they also tell us how the language of abolitionists and missionaries could be repurposed for less exalted ends, as indeed could the songs of the minstrel shows. At the same time, the testimony of William Henry at Thompson's Assizes trial, if accurate, tells us that racist taunting was not simply the sport of nationalist newspaper editors; the working-class Protestants who made a 'cat's-paw' of Thompson, calling him 'Sambo' and 'Snowball', also knew that game. Does all this suggest a shift in Irish racial attitudes after the 1840s, when Frederick Douglass was so impressed with Irish colour blindness, and from the 1790s, when Dean Mahomed and his Irish wife were accepted by the cream of Cork society? I suspect the reality is more complex.

(The above is reproduced with permission of the Licensor through PLSclear, ©Palgrave Macmillan)

=========

As Dr Mark Doyle notes, it is particularly challenging researching and finding official records of racial minorities and individuals of colour in Ireland in the eighteenth and nineteenth centuries. During our own research for the AMRI exhibition, we discovered that the *Daily Examiner Belfast* reported on 9 November 1872 that George Henry Thompson "a coloured man who had been in custody since 17th September, awaiting his trial for taking part in the recent riots on the Shankill Road, was admitted by Mr O'Donnell to bail on "his own recognisances" in the sum of £10 to appear at the next Assizes. The considerations which are said to have influenced the Bench in making the admission to bail were, that the prisoner was a foreigner, being a native of America, and consequently able to procure no bail, and that a wife and child were depending on him for support". We now know he was an American ('foreigner') and married with a child, for which he was given some leniency. However, he was later convicted by Mr Justice Lawson on Friday 4 April 1873 and finally sentenced to prison.

As reported in *Irish Times* on 5 April 1873, Mr Justice Lawson said in summing up: "You must be imprisoned for two years, with hard labour, and I hope this sentence will serve as an example to other evil doers". Others were given prison sentences of up to a maximum of ten years. Then on 6 June 1873 the *Ulster Examiner and Northern Star* reported that a Mr Hughes, previously sentenced to six months in prison, appealed his sentenced and the bail offered was measured "for a mere working man, charged with a mere assault on a police officer, as £80 for himself, and two sureties in £40 each". The reporter notes that this "was rather extraordinary, especially when we remember that the negro, George Henry Thompson, accused of a much more serious offence, was allowed out on his own recognisances".

Earlier, a Henry Thomspon was listed amongst 11 people in an article called "Illegal Procession" in *The Newry Commercial Telegraph* on 2 August 1853 as being "placed at the bar to receive sentence for taking part in a party procession on the 12th July last". It noted that from several witnesses the prisoners received a good character. However, we cannot tell if this is the same Thompson. We still have more research to do in order to find out what finally happened to George Henry Thomspon or to find out more about his family and origins.

Joseph Wilson – A Black Businessman and Town Councillor in Belfast

A contribution by Dr William Hart from his article titled "Black Joe: the life of a black man in nineteenth-century Belfast" [45]:

In March 1888 newspapers in Ireland and England began to report on a scandal involving the agents of a life assurance company in Belfast. In what became known countrywide as 'the Black Joe case', a 'coloured man' called Joe Wilson, who was reckoned not to have long to live, had a life assurance policy taken out in his name by Robert Dunlop, a Belfast businessman and town councillor, with the connivance of local agents of the Equitable Life Assurance Society of New York. The case involved a corrupt, or at any rate compliant, medical man who examined Wilson, gave him a clean bill of health and declared him to be in insurance terms 'a first class life'. When Wilson died within seven weeks Dunlop claimed on the policy, supplying medical and death certificates that, it later proved, had been tampered with to make it seem that the death was sudden and unexpected. The company's manager in London smelled a rat and began an investigation that led to the prosecution of Dunlop and his accomplices for fraud and conspiracy. The ensuing trials were reported on in exhaustive detail in Irish newspapers, and 'the Belfast Assurance Frauds' became for a time a cause celebre in England and even in the United States.

The English newspapers had little to say about the 'coloured man', except as the pawn, the 'poor oyster-room keeper', whose death was the subject of the fraud. Yet Joe Wilson, as one of the trial lawyers recognized, was a prominent figure in his own right in his home town.

> 'Joseph Wilson... was for many years living in Belfast, and had been for many years in a responsible position. He had filled the position of collector of rates for the Belfast Guardians. He was convicted some years ago of embezzlement and sent to prison, and that led to the loss of his position in Belfast as a respectable man; and when he came out of prison, he set up a sort of oyster shop or small restaurant in Commercial Court, off Donegall Street, one of the leading thoroughfares of Belfast. Now this Joseph Wilson was a remarkable man in many respects. He was as well known in Belfast perhaps as any other inhabitant of that large city. He had been there all his life

and went by that well-known name of 'Black Joe', as he was a mulatto, and there were not many of them in Belfast.' (Belfast News-Letter 30 October 1888, quoting Sergeant C. H. Hemphill)

As we will see, however, it was not his colour alone that marked Joe Wilson out from others of his fellow citizens. A man of humble origins, he worked his way upwards to become a well-known and respected member of Belfast's middle class. And even after the fall from grace that led to his conviction for embezzlement in the 1870s, he achieved in his later years a measure of rehabilitation in his local community.

Joe Wilson was born in 1836 in Newry to a black father and a white mother. His father's name was George and he was a cooper by trade. Apart from Joe there was a daughter, Ellen, and a younger son, also called George, who died in 1862 aged 21. The family were Roman Catholic and, after their move to Belfast around 1837, Joe probably went to the National School beside St. Patrick's church in Donegall Street. In later life he would reminisce about having gone to sea as a boy and been a ship's cook. Whatever the truth of this, by 1853, still only seventeen, he began work in Belfast as the employee of Samuel Teirney, a law agent and businessman with a finger in many pies. Joe was married in March 1857 to Margaret Lawson, and the couple set up house in one of Teirney's properties, 220 Conway Street in west Belfast. Over the next six years they had three children, all girls, of whom one, Agnes, died in infancy. By the beginning of the 1860s Joe had a key position in Teirney's businesses as his rental agent and confidential clerk, and, presumably with Teirney as his mentor, had begun to invest in property on his own account.

In May 1862 Joe took on a public role for the first time, when he was appointed by the Board of Guardians of the Belfast Poor Law Union as poor-rate collector for St. Anne's Ward, a post demanding ability to write legibly and keep accounts. Candidates had to nominate two persons to act as sureties and put up a large sum of money, in Joe's case £1900, as security. Teirney was a member of the Board of Guardians and had a long association with St. Anne's Ward, so he probably had a part in obtaining this position for his protégé. Collectors received a small commission on the sums paid in, normally 2%, to supplement whatever they earned from other sources. They were required to keep office-hours for the receipt of the poor-rate, to lodge sums collected with the bank, and to chase up householders for non-payment, if necessary, by obtaining decrees against them in the local police court. In the worst cases they were authorized to seize items belonging to the defaulters until the arrears were paid.

Joe earned a reputation for energy and efficiency in his new role, being "strict in his accounts, prompt in his payments, and accurate in his returns." (*Belfast Morning News*, 24 March 1879). His duties often required him to appear in court, whether to obtain decrees against householders for non-payment of the poor-rate or to respond to rate-payers disputing the claims upon them. Other cases resulted from their resistance to the collector's seizure of their goods. In one instance Joe was physically threatened with a hatchet when he attempted to execute such a warrant.

These, perhaps, were the ordinary hazards of life as a rate-collector. But on other occasions Joe himself was on the receiving end of a court summons. In November 1863 he was prosecuted by the Town Council for failing to attend to waste and stagnant water at houses he owned in Conlan Street, and in 1870 a similar complaint affecting houses for which he was responsible in Blackstaff Lane led to him being fined 40/- and the comment by the town surveyor that he was 'troublesome and very stubborn'. He could be sensitive to slights and remarks that sullied his good name. He brought an action for slander, unsuccessfully as it happened, against a Belfast shop-owner who had taunted him and Samuel Teirney with swindling one of Teirney's creditors.

Was he more sensitive because of his colour? That is hard to say. It was certainly the cause of two scuffles in which Joe was embroiled in the mid-1860s. In the first case, while walking with a companion in North Street, he was confronted by a drunk who called him 'a Papish and a n*****' and punched him in the face. The assailant was subsequently jailed for a month for the assault and fined 40/- and costs for his use of 'party expressions' ('party expressions' in question were presumably the word 'Papish' and not 'n*****'). On the second occasion a man 'newly arrived from New York' saw Joe walking in Hill Street and called after him that he was a 'bloody n*****'. When Joe asked him what objection he had to his colour, the other struck him and Joe retaliated, knocking him down. The man's companion then traded blows with Joe and the two were arrested for fighting in the street. The magistrate fined both of them 1/- but conceded that Joe had been provoked. The New Yorker, the provocateur, had fled the scene and evaded arrest. It may be of significance here that the offender was an American, or at any rate someone who had imbibed American prejudices against 'blacks'. The fact that Joe called him out on his use of the word 'n*****' and didn't let it go unchallenged suggests that this wasn't something he was used to hearing in Belfast; also, that he didn't lack for self-confidence. By all accounts he was a large strongly built man, well capable of looking after himself in a scrap.

In May 1871, following in the steps of his mentor Teirney, he made the first of several bids to be appointed a commissioner for taking Affidavits for the town of Belfast. This was a legal appointment, on an altogether different level from his local position with the Poor Law Union. His petition was forwarded to the Lord Chancellor of Ireland by a Queen's Counsel and supported by the signatures of a 'numerous and respectable' group of his fellow citizens. He was unsuccessful on this occasion but the Lord Chancellor promised to bear him in mind should a vacancy occur in the future. In November 1871 he had a second petition forwarded for the post of Commissioner for Belfast to the Court of Queen's Bench in Dublin. Again, he was told there was no current vacancy, although the Chief Justice pronounced himself satisfied that he was "a gentleman, both in point of respectability and intelligence, well qualified for the office" (Belfast News-Letter 20 November 1871). He was finally appointed one of the fourteen Commissioners for Belfast at his third attempt in June 1873.

By 1873, still only 37, Joe was on the fringes, if not indeed already a fully-fledged member, of Belfast's urban elite. No longer just a hard-working city functionary and man of property, he had begun to join in the leisure activities of the well-to-do. He was the owner of an 18 ft. yacht Ocean Terror that took part in the Greenisland Regatta on Belfast Lough in August of that year. Tragically in the course of the fourth race the yacht overturned in heavy seas and its two-man crew drowned. Joe himself was not aboard. Later, when the bodies of the men had been brought ashore, he undertook to cover the costs of their burial. One notices that, in reporting the incident, newspapers referred to him as 'Joseph Wilson of Holywood', as if he had taken an out-of-town residence in Holywood for the summer.

As for Joe's political affiliation at this time, he was the Liberal Party's personating agent for St. Anne's Ward in the 1874 election to the

Westminster Parliament. His old patron Samuel Teirney had been a pillar of the Conservative Party in Belfast, so this is one area in which Joe took an independent line.

It was in the autumn of 1874, when Joe's star seemed to be fully in the ascendant, that the life he had so painstakingly created for himself and his family came crashing about his ears. The immediate cause of his downfall was an audit of the collectors' rate-books. Joe had always been exemplary in his collection of the rate and his record-keeping, but on this occasion perusal of his rate-book showed him to have collected £465 which had not yet been lodged in the bank. At a meeting of the Board of Guardians on 13 October Joe was asked the reason for this and answered that he had not had the time to do it. Accordingly, he was required to lodge the money in the bank and produce his bank-book as evidence to the Clerk of the [Poor Law] Union by noon the following day. But Joe didn't appear at the Clerk's office as agreed. Instead, he left Belfast that night, taking the ferry to Liverpool, and straightaway caught a ship, the S.S. Spain, to New York on 14 October.

There are a couple of puzzling things about this affair. First of all, the sum of money unaccounted for doesn't seem very large relative to the amounts that routinely went through Joe's hands. One would have thought that he could have borrowed money to cover the deficit, for example from one or other of his named sureties, who in the event of his absconding had to make up the difference anyway. The second thing is that Joe wasn't alone in having collected poor-rate that hadn't yet been paid into the bank. John Holden, the collector for St. George's Ward, was owing £292. But while he and the other collectors were allowed a fortnight to settle their accounts, Joe was required to settle by the following day. Why the urgency in his case? There is evidence that Joe had become sloppy in his book-keeping and that the unexpected audit caught him by surprise. He had taken to giving out receipts on blank sheets of paper rather than on the official forms. But the pressure put on Joe in this instance suggests that there was something about him that made the Guardians less accommodating, less inclined to go easy on him. We don't know that it was his colour. Being Belfast, it could have been the fact that he was a Catholic. Or that he riled people by calling on them for the poor-rate late in the evening.

Whatever the explanation, Joe's response in leaving Belfast under cover of night and taking ship to America served to confirm the Guardians' worst suspicions as to his honesty. They took out a warrant for his arrest and frustration was expressed that there wasn't an extradition treaty with the United States that would have facilitated his being returned to Ireland to stand trial. It did nothing to sweeten their mood that they were roundly criticised for failing to exercise proper supervision of the rate-collectors, Joe in particular, in their handling of public funds. It fell to William Mussen and Thomas Crozier, Joe's sureties, to make good the sum of money estimated to be short in his returns. And there for the time being the matter rested.

Four years passed, and then word reached Belfast in February 1879 that Joseph Wilson, the defaulting poor-rate collector, had been apprehended in Liverpool. When he had come back from America and how long he had been in Liverpool are unclear, and he would probably have escaped detection but for his fatal predilection for litigating in the courts. Liverpool was then in the throes of a dock strike and there were widespread reports of intimidation by strikers of those who were continuing to work. Joe who was working as a 'machine keeper' for the Mersey Steel and Iron Company brought an action for intimidation against an 'iron planer' Thomas Camm. It caught the eye of Detective-Constable Samuel Canning of the Royal Irish Constabulary stationed in Liverpool, who recognized in the complainant the fugitive who had been pursued by the police for embezzlement four years earlier. He promptly arrested him and sent word to Belfast. Joe, who seemed to think that the case against him had been resolved by the action of his sureties in repaying the deficit in the Poor Law Union's finances, made no attempt to resist arrest and allowed himself to be brought back to Belfast.

However, the Board of Guardians, possibly still smarting from the criticism they had received at the time for the laxity of their financial controls, were determined to make an example of him. They rejected Mussen's and Crozier's intervention on Joe's behalf, that it was they and they alone who had suffered loss by his actions. The case came up in the Crown Court for the County of Antrim on 21 March. There was a good deal of confusion in the Poor Law Union's accounts as to precisely what sums of money Joe was alleged to have embezzled, so the prosecution opted to charge him with three small payments, amounting to less than £6 in total, where the evidence against him was felt to be particularly strong. It argued that these payments had been made after Joe had made his final lodgement with the bank on 30 September 1874 and that therefore he must have made off with the money.

Joe's defence lawyer appealed to his thirteen years of unblemished service as a poor-rate collector in which he had been responsible for sums upwards of £8,000 a year. Was it credible, having proved himself faithful and honest in discharge of his duties over such a long period and with respect to more than £100,000, that the accused would sacrifice his reputation for probity for the kind of paltry sums listed in the indictment? That he had fled the country in a moment of panic and fearing that his records of payments received would be subjected to a harsh scrutiny was not in itself evidence of guilt. An innocent man, perhaps more than a guilty one, might shrink from exposure to such an investigation. As for the receipts produced in evidence by the prosecution, it had not been shown beyond doubt (he argued) that the sums in question were not part of the money lodged in the bank on 30 September.

It was a robust defence, but the jury were unconvinced. They returned a verdict of guilty, with a recommendation for mercy on account of Joe's "previous good behaviour, his hitherto unimpeachable character, and his long service."[46]. Asked if he had anything to say before the judge pronounced sentence, Joe made a brief statement, which in its self-possession and absence of recrimination tells us much about the kind of man he was, and makes it worth quoting in full.

> *'My Lord, allow me to return my best thanks to the eminent counsel Mr. Weir, who pleaded my case so ably; also to my two solicitors, Mr. Macaulay and Mr. McErlean, who have discharged their duties faithfully. In reply to the question just put to me by the Clerk of the Court, I don't know that there is anything I can say that would prevent your lordship from passing sentence upon me. As I have been found guilty by the jury, I presume the unpleasant duty is cast upon you to pass the sentence of the law. As I am bound to receive it, so you are compelled to give it. But, my Lord, the jury which returned the verdict of guilty accompanied it with a strong recommendation to mercy. And I would have you bear in mind three very important considerations—*

first, my offence was committed five years ago, and since that time I have suffered as an exile and outcast from society. I will not trouble your lordship with an account of the sufferings I have undergone in the meantime; second, any money that was deficient through me, was paid by two of my friends to the Belfast Poor Law Guardians; and not one farthing of loss has been sustained by that body or the ratepayers; and third, I have a wife and family who are dependent upon my support and who are now ruined by my misfortune. I have one word to add, that, at the time I was arrested, I was honestly earning my livelihood in Liverpool and supporting my family respectably. But I have been dragged from that position by the officers of the law, and I stand here humbly awaiting your sentence, which I hope will be tempered with mercy.' [47]

Notice that, while making no attempt to justify himself, Joe doesn't anywhere in the statement admit to criminality on his part. He had been found guilty and the law must take its course. But not that there had been a betrayal of trust for which he ought to feel contrite. And whether the judge concurred or was simply responding to the jury's recommendation of mercy, he gave Joe the relatively light sentence of three months' imprisonment without hard labour from the time of his committal.

In the years following his imprisonment Joe was able to rebuild his life to some extent, renting premises in Commercial Court in the heart of Belfast and opening a billiards saloon and supper rooms that became a popular place of resort. An account of Joe's supper rooms written a quarter of a century later by someone who looked back nostalgically to their glory days was published in the Northern Whig in 1906. In it the writer recalled his youth when he and other young bucks would finish up their nights on the town by going to Black Joe's and ordering up a feast of 'oysters on the shell', or a supper of tripe or fried fish, washed down with porter (the bar was open from 11 o'clock in the evening till 4 o'clock in the morning). The speciality of the house was Cleethorpes oysters. Joe was fiercely proud of these and would hear of no witticisms at their expense. Teased by one would-be humourist that their shells seemed 'a bit too patriarchal in the way of beard', Joe snatched the oysters away from him. "Then, holding the plate aloft, and slowly addressing the low ceiling, he added, 'A plate of oysters, in soul, fit to put before the Prince of Wales; too good for a half-cocked hobbledehoy, who won't put a lip on one them if I know it, and who would be better suited with a handful of cockles or a pennyworth of tripe on a skewer.'" Joe's own impish, not to say subversive, sense of humour comes across in a series of tongue-in-cheek advertisements in Belfast's Morning News in which various enemies of empire (the Zulu king Cetshwayo, the Mahdi, and others) are quoted as praising his oysters, fish and tripe, and ordering fresh supplies for their troops. (10 September 1883, 12 February 1884, 10 March 1884).

Joe might have been unable to stand for public office himself after his conviction for embezzlement, but, curiously, it didn't prevent him nominating Robert Stewart in March 1885 for Samuel Teirney's old place as Poor Law Guardian for St. Anne's Ward; and later he was actively involved in hiring election canvassers on behalf of David Carlisle whose son was standing for the second post of Guardian for St. Anne's Ward. A few months earlier, in December 1884, Joe's wife Margaret had died of 'congestion in the lungs' at their residence 6 Trinity Street. Joe himself had been ailing for some time, and following the death of his wife his health seems to have got worse. A doctor who examined him at his request towards the end of July 1887 diagnosed chronic heart disease and a build-up of fluid in his legs. He had always been a strong and active man, albeit with a tendency to corpulence, but now people began to notice his loss of weight and difficulty in getting about. He had allowed the licence for his supper rooms to lapse and it doesn't appear that he was doing much trade there.

It was at this time, on 1 October, when Joe's personal and business affairs were at their lowest ebb, that he made an approach to a wealthy town councillor Robert Dunlop that set in train events that were to make Black Joe's name known on both sides of the Atlantic. He offered to sell Dunlop an assurance policy that he had taken out on his own life with a Scottish company. The policy was worth £150 on Joe's death, payable to his two unmarried daughters. Clearly desperate for cash in hand, he offered to sell Dunlop the policy for £50, and eventually settled for £40. However, before agreeing to the deal, Dunlop had sought the advice of two agents in Belfast of the Equitable Life Assurance Society of New York, Chestnutte Smyth and James Speers Orr, as to the policy's likely market value; and they, reckoning that Joe had not long to live, persuaded Dunlop to take out a further policy on Joe's life for the sum of £2,000 with their company. To have the policy approved by Head Office Joe needed to pass a medical examination by a qualified practitioner who would certify him as in good health. Dr. James Smyth, who just happened to be Chestnutte Smyth's brother, examined him on 2 November and found no cause for concern, giving as his professional opinion that Joe was for insurance purposes 'a first class life'. Joe himself had to fill out a form answering a number of questions about his health, stating that he was free from any disqualifying ailment or illness, and that his parents and grandparents had all lived to a ripe old age.

Why Joe went along with this scam is unclear. Since the policy was in Dunlop's name, there was no benefit to Joe's daughters. And that may be why he pressed for a third life assurance policy to be taken out in his own name, this time with the Marine and General Mutual Life Assurance Society, for £1,000, to be re-assigned to Dunlop on condition that he pay £200 of it to the two Wilson sisters. This required a further medical examination of Joe by the obliging Dr. Smyth on 3 November and he duly provided Joe, or rather the Assurance Society, with the requisite clean bill of health.

However, it was by now becoming clear to those around him that Joe was seriously ill. Margaret, Joe's older daughter, alarmed at his condition, called in her own doctor David Johnston to examine him on 6 November. Johnston found him at home sitting in a chair, his feet badly swollen, and barely able to stand up. He confirmed the earlier diagnosis of Joe's doctor in July that he was suffering from heart disease and that this was responsible for the presence of fluid in his legs and abdomen. He tried to relieve the symptoms by puncturing Joe's legs in several places to let the fluid drain away. A few days later Joe made his final visit to his premises in Commercial Court, but had to go by cab, without wearing anything on his feet, and had to be physically carried into the rooms by two of his neighbours. Shortly after he took to his bed. There he was visited by Dr. Johnston and on a number of occasions by Robert Dunlop, who professed himself taken aback at how ill he seemed. Sick as he was, Joe was able from his bed to sign over the latter two assurance policies to Dunlop, and the paper in which Dunlop guaranteed to pay Joe's two daughters Margaret and Martha £200 at his death. He died at home on 20 December 1887.

The rest of the story can be told briefly. Following Joe's death Dunlop allowed only a couple of days to elapse before claiming on the three assurance policies. Failing to persuade Dr. Johnston to change his report on Joe's medical condition on 6 November, he turned a blind eye to Speers Orr's altering the date of the examination to 16 November, and altering Johnston's statement on the death certificate that the dead man had been ill for '2 months' to 'a month', so as to make it appear that his death took everyone by surprise. But the suspicions of the London managers of the two companies had been aroused by Joe dying so soon and by discrepancies in the documentation provided to them. They launched their separate inquiries into the circumstances of the policies being taken out on Joe's life. Speers Orr caved in under the pressure of the investigation and confessed to having altered the documents in question. Chestnutte Smyth was arrested at Moville in the act of boarding a ship to America. Preliminary hearings began in the Recorder's Court in Belfast in the middle of April 1888. Other cases came to light in which Chestnutte Smyth and Speers Orr were alleged to have forged signatures and taken out policies on the lives of two other prominent citizens of Belfast without their knowledge. The accused, who by now included Dunlop and Dr. James Smyth, were returned for trial in the July Assizes on the charge of fraud and conspiracy. Almost immediately the Attorney-General of Ireland announced his intention of prosecuting the case himself as a matter of public interest. Because of irregularities in forming the Grand Jury, the trial was postponed to October and also transferred from Belfast to Wicklow. It lasted two weeks and at its end Dunlop and Orr were found guilty and sentenced to nine months' and six months' imprisonment respectively with hard labour; James Smyth to six months' imprisonment, pending an appeal; and, to most people's surprise, Chestnutte Smyth, who had pleaded guilty and given evidence against his fellow accused on behalf of the prosecution, was discharged without punishment of any kind. Coincidentally in the same month Martha Wilson, Joe's younger daughter, was granted Letters of Administration of his personal estate at death. It amounted to £18.

What can the life of 'Black Joe' tell us about the life prospects and experiences of people of African descent in mid-nineteenth-century Ireland? Clearly, he was exceptional in the place he came to occupy in his home town. No other Irish-born black man of the period figured so prominently in municipal life or was reported on so often or in such detail in the local press. Posthumously, indeed, and for extraneous reasons, he acquired a transient international notoriety. But in his lifetime, at least until 1874, he experienced few checks in his career and achieved a degree of local celebrity that was remarkable for the son of an ordinary working man. If we set aside the two episodes when he was clearly the object of racial abuse, his interactions with his fellow citizens, friendly or otherwise, seem to have been singularly free of racial slurs. Joe's colour was never alluded to in Belfast newspaper reports. It was only in Dublin newspapers such as the Dublin Daily Express that he was singled out as 'a negro rate-collector'. Of course, people in Belfast were aware of his colour. He was 'Black Joe' after all.

Ira Aldridge, Paul and Eslanda Robeson - The African Diaspora

"Up Abyssinia!" African Diaspora Politics and the Dublin Theatre Stage, 1830s-1930s.[48] *A contribution by Dr Maurice Casey:*

On 4 April 1936, the *Irish Workers' Voice,* the weekly newspaper of the Irish Communist Party, reported on a remarkable gathering that had taken place outside a well-known Dublin theatre. On 28 March of that year, a performance at the Theatre Royal by two African American musicians, Jules Bledsoe and Clarence Johnstone, was met by protestors. However, these protestors were not inspired by a racist rejection of two black performers. Quite the opposite: they were united in African diaspora solidarity.

A few days before Bledsoe and Johnstone's concert, Johnstone informed an *Irish Times* reporter that Fascist Italy's invasion of Ethiopia, then commonly referred to as Abyssinia, would "mean civilisation for the people of Abyssinia and stated that the 'millions of natives in Abyssinia will be better off if Italy wins".[49] *The Irish Workers' Voice* described how black residents of Dublin gathered outside the theatre to respond to these remarks with cries of 'Up Abyssinia!' and 'We don't want Johnstone here!'[50]

This gathering of black Dubliners was, according to the radical Irish paper, 'joined in the protest' by Irish workers.[51] Providing further detail on the event - and how it led to the end of the Bledsoe and Johnstone musical partnership - Lynette Geary describes the protestors as composed of 'about twenty West Africans' who succeeded in forcing Johnstone to leave the stage.[52] Although a small moment in the grand sweep of post-revolutionary Irish history, this Dublin protest signifies currents of culture and migration whose influence on Ireland has been under-explored.[53] Not only was there evidently a population of African residents in 1930s Dublin, there was a community sizable enough to organise political support for a cause important to the wider African diaspora: solidarity with Ethiopia against Mussolini's invasion.

Searching for the historical roots of such a community inevitably brings us through the fascinating story of the revered African American classical actor Ira Aldridge. Many decades before West Africans protested at the Theatre Royal, Aldridge performed in the Irish capital in the same theatre's predecessor.[54] Born in New York in 1807, Aldridge was raised and trained as an actor in the bustling American metropolis.[55] Aldridge first performed in Dublin in 1831.[56] Although best known for his Shakespearean performances - particularly Othello - Aldridge also performed explicitly political sketches.[57] In 1847 at Dublin's Theatre Royal, he performed in the *Black Doctor*, a tragedy personally adapted by Aldridge which tells the story of an enslaved man who falls in love with a French princess during the revolutionary events of the 1790s.[58] Hazel Waters describes the play as 'probably the first contemporary melodrama to deal seriously with issues of race'.[59]

In the early 20th century - and particularly amid the Irish revolutionary period - another theatre, Dublin's La Scala, brought African diaspora culture to the Irish capital. One of the best known jazz journeys to Ireland - notable for the tragedy that accompanied it - revolved around a performance at La Scala in late 1921. In October 1921, the Southern Syncopated Orchestra, an early jazz ensemble composed of African diaspora and African musicians, were travelling to Dublin on board the SS Rowan when the ship sank off the west coast of Scotland.[60] Nine members of the Orchestra died in the disaster. Yet the show went on: La Scala hosted the surviving members for a set of jazz concerts later that month.

On St Patrick's Day 1923, amid Ireland's Civil War, the Senegalese boxer Louis 'Battling Siki' Fall lost to the Irish boxer Mike McTigue in a fight hosted at La Scala.[61] In September of the same year, La Scala was the subject of a protest from the Irish National Association of Musicians when the theatre advertised a presumably in-house jazz group known as La Scala Rhythm Kings. The Irish musicians' organisation objected to the performances in racist terms, stating that "on moral grounds the admission to Ireland of coloured musicians is undesirable".[62]

Yet the reception of African diaspora culture in Dublin proved that there were always Irish people who did not hold such prejudices. Paul Robeson, the radical and revered bass-baritone, performed in the

Capitol cinema in February 1935. According to one report, a 'tumultuous audience' demanded 'many encores' and scores of 'autograph hunters swarmed around America's leading singer' when Robeson performed in the Capitol.[63] The Capitol was the successor theatre to La Scala, located on the same premises off O'Connell Street.

This remarkable photograph below captures a group of black students from Trinity College Dublin meeting with Robeson and his wife Eslanda on the occasion of this 1935 visit to Ireland.

Perhaps some of those same members of Ireland's African diaspora community would find themselves outside the Theatre Royal a year later, standing alongside fellow Dubliners and shouting 'Up Abyssinia!'

58. Paul Robeson and his wife Eslanda visiting Dublin in 1935.
Visiting students at the University of Dublin medical school in 1935. This image includes (back row, third from left) Dr Noel Holmes who became the Chief Medical Examiner of Jamaica and Dr Errol Thompson (back row, fifth from left).
Dr Thompson went on to become an Ear, Nose and Throat Surgeon in New York and founded the Speech and Hearing Centre at Harlem Hospital. Thanks to Professor Christine Kinealy for contributing this picture with permission from Karen Greene, daughter of Dr Errol Thompson.

========

It is worth noting here that many African students visited Ireland in the 20th century, particularly during the period of decolonisation of African nations. Many Africans visited Ireland to study subjects needed by the newly formed African nations, such as medicine, law, government and business administration, as well as military training in the Curragh military college, in Kildare. At one point in the 1960s 10% of university students in Dublin were African and Asian. Some of these overseas visitors met with Irish women who had children following these relationships. This resulted in a new but small generation of mixed race children born, in Ireland and Britain, in the 1940s to 1970s. The histories of this new generation of people of colour in Ireland are reflected in later chapters of this book.

Overview

In summary, in the 18th and 19th centuries, not all people of colour or mixed race couples who met, lived or had children in Ireland, were themselves of Irish descent. The global nature and networks of the colonial world meant that some mixed race couples were themselves both made up of 'foreigners', such as Tony and Julia Small and William G. and Mary Allen. Both couples lived in Ireland, as well having children there, before moving to Britain in the nineteenth century. In both cases, the couples' links to Ireland highlight the hidden diversity of racial mixing that occurred within the country, even where the partners were not themselves Irish. On the other hand, there were those who arrived in Ireland and had relationships with white Irish women. We note the presence of the impostor, William Love, who supposedly had a mixed race child in Ireland and travelled around both Britain and Ireland, lecturing on anti-slavery and pretending he was a former enslaved person in America; John Suttoe, who survived a shipwreck, and went on to marry Margaret Brien in county Louth in 1785; and the black American, George Henry Thompson, who was involved in the Belfast riots in 1872, and who reportedly had a child. In general, most of these stories seem to indicate the existence of a tolerant and surprisingly harmonious Irish society in relation to people of colour, who resided in Ireland in the 18th and 19th centuries.

Chapter 3

Racial and Ethnic Diversity in Britain

Multiracial Britain

The racial and ethnic diversity, that had long been a part of British life, visibly expanded from the 17th century onwards, similar to the general expansion of the Empire. Note the three black drummers in the middle of the picture below:

59. Changing the Guard at St James's Palace, 1792.
Coloured line engraving. Artist Unkown. Image provided courtesy of the
Council of the National Army Museum, London, ref. no. NAM. 1963-07-32-1.

As the British empire strengthened its grip on India and the Caribbean, as well as ramping up its slave trading of Africans, the British homeland saw an increasing number people from all parts of the world arriving and settling down. These people populated the country's largest cities and smallest hamlets, whether through force, opportunity or chance, and found Britain, temporarily or permanently, to be their home.

Like the Chinese, many Indians, commonly termed 'lascars', arrived in Britain to work as sailors, while others were brought by returning British families as nannies or domestic servants. Meanwhile, though many African and Caribbean peoples were initially forced to work in British domestic households as 'slaves', ostentatiously dressed young black boys were considered a status symbol for wealthy white British women, many also escaped and found other employment. In 1772, Lord Mansfield set a legal precedent by ruling that no 'slave' could be forcibly removed from England (see page 38).

Others meanwhile came to Britain already as free men and women, not least the several thousand former American enslaved people who had joined the British military and become mariners. Many found work as servants. However, for most of the migrants who had joined the ranks of Britain's working classes, making a living could be hard and being reduced to begging or the workhouse was a common fate.

The sketches below of Charles McGee and Joseph Johnson, a beggar, in *Vagabondiana; or, anecdotes of Mendicant Wanderers through the streets of London. L.P.* (John Thomas Smith, 1766-1833. London, 1817), is from a collection depicting and discussing beggary in nineteenth century London by John Thomas Smith in 1817:

60. Sketch of Charles McGee.
A beggar in *Vagabondiana*, by John Thomas Smith, 1817. Image courtesy of The British Library Board. Shelfmark: 134.d.6.

61. Sketch of Joseph Johnson.
A beggar in *Vagabondiana*, by John Thomas Smith, 1817. Image courtesy of The British Library Board. Shelfmark: 134.d.6.

Henry Mayhew also describes the poverty in 1815 in his report called *London Labour and the London Poor*:

> *"The Asylum for the Houseless Poor of London is opened only when the thermometer reaches freezing-point, and offers nothing but dry bread and warm shelter to such as avail themselves of its charity. To this place swarm, as the bitter winter's night comes on, some half-thousand penniless and homeless wanderers. The poverty-stricken from every quarter of the globe are found within its wards; from the haggard American seaman to the lank Polish refugee, the pale German "out-wanderer," the tearful black sea-cook, the shivering Lascar crossing-sweeper, the helpless Chinese beggar, and the half-torpid Italian organ-boy. It is, indeed, a ragged congress of nations—a convocation of squalor and misery—of destitution, degradation, and suffering, from all the corners of the earth."* [1]

However, not all were impoverished or in service, some earned a living as labourers, craftsmen and seamstresses, soldiers and sailors, musicians and performers, ministers and others.

62. John Orde, His Wife, Anne, his Eldest Son William, and a servant (between 1754 and 1756). Oil on canvas by Arthur Devis, 1712–1787, British. John Orde was a landowner in Morpeth, Northumberland. Image courtesy of the Yale Center for British Art, Paul Mellon Collection, ref. no. B2001.2.65.

During the 19th century in particular, there are numerous accounts of people of colour solidly being part of the middle classes. The painting, on page 101, of the Orde family by Arthur Devis includes a servant of colour, similar to the servant boy depicted in the painting of Ely family in Ireland by Angelica Kauffman in 1771.

Other people of colour were engaged as musicians, such as Joseph Emidy,[2] who was a former enslaved person who had been a virtuoso violinist in the Lisbon Opera before being press ganged into the Royal Navy. He worked as professional musician and teacher in Cornwall in the early 19th century, becoming the leader of the Truro Philharmonic Orchestra in 1816 for a decade.[3]

63. A musical club, Truro, 1808.
Anonymous. Held at the Royal Cornwall Museum.
Image reproduced with the kind permission of
the Royal Institution of Cornwall.

Others even became part of the British upper classes, for example Victor Duleep Singh, the son of the last Maharajah of the Sikh Empire, caused a sensation when he married Lady Anne Coventry, the daughter of the 9th Earl of Coventry in 1898.

Irish Presence in Britain

While some Irish migrants to Britain were part of the middle or upper classes, the majority had also long formed part of Britain's working classes. Britain had been a significant destination for Irish migrants since the medieval era, with poor Irish immigrants causing concern amongst local authorities in numerous cities and towns of Tudor England.[4]

From the late eighteenth century onwards, Irish emigration to Britain increased substantially due to the decline in living standards resulting from agricultural depression in the country. In the 1840s, the Great Famine, in which the potato harvests, Ireland's main crop, were repeatedly decimated by blight, led to an even greater rise of Irish men and women and families seeking to escape starvation by migrating to Britain. This population, like most of those who had left Ireland for Britain in previous centuries, worked principally as casual labourers and domestic servants. Like many of their migrant counterparts of colour, life could be very hard, though again some, like the Tierneys discussed earlier, became part of the English elite.

The wood engraving below featured in the book *From London: A Pilgrimage*, a collaboration between the French artist, Doré and the British journalist Blanchard Jerrold. The notorious Seven Dials area of London had long been home to an Irish immigrant community.

64. 'Dudley Street, Seven Dials', a wood engraving.
Illustration by Gustave Doré, 1872.
@The Trustees of the British Museum, ref. no. 1979,0407.16.46.

Multiracial Cities

London

Some areas in particular became home to longstanding multiracial populations. From the eighteenth century onwards, numerous ethnically diverse communities, including Irish migrants and those of colour, could be found across London. Along with the East End, the St. Giles area of central London - a notorious slum quarter - were well noted by contemporary sources as areas that housed a range of immigrants: St Giles was colloquially referred to as the 'Holy Land' due to the large number of Irish Catholics who resided there.[5] As Brooke Newman discusses, satirical prints in the eighteenth century drew attention to the interracial contact that occurred in Britain's ports, such as in Thomas Rowlandson's early eighteenth century depictions. The etching below, *Black Brown and Fair* (1807), shows a multi-ethnic set of prostitutes and patrons at a Wapping bathhouse. This etching was accompanied by a parody of a love letter from a Wapping bathhouse patron to his sweetheart.

65. 'Black Brown & Fair' with song sheet.
Print made by Thomas Rowlandson, 6 May 1807.
©The Trustees of the British Museum, no. 47364001.

The love letter included the following first lines, written under the *Black, Brown and Fair* print by Thomas Rowlandson, 1807[6] :

> *'You tell me dear Girl that I'm given to rove.*
> *That I sport with each lass on the green.*
> *That I join in the dance, and sing sonnets of love.*
> *And still with the fairest am seen.*
> *With my hey derry down, and my hey down derry.*
> *Around the green meadows so blithe and so merry.*
> *With Black, Brown, and Fair. I have frolick'd, tis true.*
> *But I never lov'd any, dear Mary, but you.[sic]'*

This London multiracial community is also portrayed by J. Ewing Ritchie in his book *The Night Side of London* (1857), quoted in Seed (2006):

> *'Up and down Ratcliffe-highway do the sailors of every country under heaven stroll – Greeks and Scythians, bond and free. Uncle Tom's numerous progeny are there – Lascars, Chinese, bold Britons, swarthy Italians, sharp Yankees, fair-haired Saxons, and adventurous Danes– men who worship a hundred gods, and men who worship none"*[7]

Further glimpses of the racial diversity can be seen in the report below of a burglary in Ratcliffe, East London, where a black woman was part of the gang of thieves along with four white men.

> Late on Sunday night four men and a black woman broke into the house of Mr. Datewell, near Ratcliff-highway, and carried off a pint silver mug, seventeen tea-spoons, a bag of half-pence, and other articles of value. It is hoped the gang will soon be taken, as one of them is known to be an intimate acquaintance of the Ball, the noted house-breaker lately executed at Tyburn, one of the Finchley gang.

66. Four men and a 'black woman' break into house
Kentish Gazette, 18 September 1779.
Image @ The British Library Board.
Shelfmark: 95-3554.

In the 1820s, the cartoonists George and Robert Cruickshank provided illustrations for Pierce Egan's *Life in London* series (published in 1821 in a single collection) which described the adventures of three fictional men about town, Tom, Jerry and Logic, loosely based upon themselves and their own escapades. The images accompanying the characters' visit to the 'lowest' life of the East End and the 'back slums' of St Giles clearly depict a casual multiculturalism in which black men and women are not just drawn and described as present, but as engaging in easy, friendly and intimate interactions with others in the crowd on an equal footing.

In the illustration, *Tom, Jerry and Logic among the sophisticated Sons and Daughters of Nature at "All Max"* in the East' below, a black woman, 'African Sall', is depicted jigging with an Irishman, 'Nasty Bob, the coal shipper', while her baby sits on the knee of a fellow carouser. Meanwhile, Logic is depicted as 'happy as a sand-boy', enjoying the 'jargon' and 'chaste salutes' of 'Black Sall'.

67. Lowest "life in London". by R. and G. Cruickshank (1821).
Printed in *from Life in London* (Pierce Egan, 1870). Image courtesy of
The British Library Board. Shelfmark: 2350.b.14.

In the far right hand corner of the illustration below, the Cruickshanks depict the character of 'Mahogany Bet' on the left of the fireplace, a black prostitute, 'so termed for her never-fading colour'.

68. 'Midnight' by R. and G. Cruickshank (1821).
Printed in *from Life in London* (Pierce Egan, 1870).
Image courtesy of the British Library Board. Shelfmark: 2350.b.14.

Despite the reference to her colour, however, Bet, sitting with Pretty Poll, a white prostitute, is depicted as just another member of what the book called the 'low life' of London: "Mahogany Bet has braved the winter weather, night after night, under some gateway, for succeeding winters, but quite done up as to matters of trade ... is now glad to singe a muffin ... to prevent total starvation."

> "*ALL MAX was compared by the sailors, something after the old adage of "any port in a storm." It required no patronage; - a card of admission was not necessary: - no inquiries were made; - and every cove that put in his appearance was quite welcome: colour or country considered no obstacle; and dress and ADDRESS completely out of the question. Ceremonies were not in use, and, therefore, no struggle took place at ALL MAX for the matter of them.*" [8]

> *"The parties paired off according to fancy; the eye was pleased in the choice, and nothing thought about birth and distinction. All was happiness - everybody free and easy, and freedom of expression allowed to the very echo. The group motley indeed; - Lascars, blacks, jack tars, coalheavers, dustmen, women of colour, old and young, and a sprinkling of the remnants of once fine girls, and. were all jigging together, provided the teazer of the catgut was not bilked of his duce."*[9]

Not all the Cruickshank images depicted diversity amongst the poor classes. For example, in one of his drawings called 'A Shilling Well Spent' (1821) he portrays a finely dressed black gentlemen amongst the crowds at the annual Royal Academy show.

Outside London

Outside of London, many other port cities, such as Bristol, Cardiff, Newcastle and Glasgow, were also hubs of multiracial community settlement, with migrants from around the world arriving and settling via trade routes and opportunities, as well as the slave trading economy. In particular, by the late eighteenth century, Liverpool, Britain's dominant slave trading port city, was the most cosmopolitan city outside the capital with the establishment of its free black community. The city was made up not only of servants, but also wealthy African students and the racially mixed sons and daughters of white plantation owners and enslaved women.[10] The large Irish community that was also present in Liverpool at this time expanded further during the course of the nineteenth century as a result of the Famine; by 1851 almost a quarter of Liverpool's population was Irish.[11]

During the course of the nineteenth century, the multiracial nature of the area was expanded further by growing settlement by the Chinese as well as South East Asians. As in other city locations that housed migrant communities struggling to make a living, residential housing was often low quality and detrimental to community health and welfare. Living in close proximity and increasingly sharing a local culture, many white Irish women in Liverpool entered into relationships with men of colour. Such relationships were notably described by Charles Dickens in his 1861 'Uncommercial Traveller' collection of short stories, based on his forays around Liverpool with the police as part of their nighttime dock patrol. Unlike other contemporaries, Dickens does not seem to overly castigate the white women for their intimacy with black men.

Racial and Ethnic Diversity in Britain

"LEMONADE. BAL-LOON SAY, AND SWING."

69. "Lemonade. Bal-loon say, and Swing" in Dicken's
'Uncommercial Traveller', 1876.
Engraving by Charles S. Reinhart. Image courtesy of
Philip V. Allingham at the Victorian Web.

Searching for different types of 'Jacks' - sailors - and coming across them and their '(un)lovely nans' (their girlfriends or escorts) in the story 'Poor Mercantile Jack', Dickens describes coming across a pub which contained a group of 'Dark Jacks', black men dancing with their white '(un)lovely nans'. The police superintendent noted that the men kept together in order to avoid the trouble and insults they experienced when walking the streets alone.

Extract from 'Mercantile Jack', in *The Uncommercial Traveller* by Charles Dickens, 1860:

"But we had not yet looked, Mr. Superintendent—said Trampfoot, receiving us in the street again with military salute—for Dark Jack. True, Trampfoot. Ring the wonderful stick, rub the wonderful lantern, and cause the spirits of the stick and lantern to convey us to the Darkies. There was no disappointment in the matter of Dark Jack; he was producible. The Genii set us down in the little first floor of a little public-house, and there, in a stiflingly close atmosphere, were Dark Jack, and Dark Jack's delight, his white unlovely Nan, sitting against the wall all round the room. More than that: Dark Jack's

delight was the least unlovely Nan, both morally and physically, that I saw that night.

As a fiddle and tambourine band were sitting among the company, Quickear suggested why not strike up? 'Ah, la'ads!' said a negro sitting by the door, 'gib the jebblem a darnse. Tak' yah pardlers, jebblem, for 'um Quad-rill.' This was the landlord, in a Greek cap, and a dress half Greek and half English. As master of the ceremonies, he called all the figures, and occasionally addressed himself parenthetically—after this manner. When he was very loud, I use capitals.

'Now den! Hoy! One. Right and left. (Put a steam on, gib 'um powder.) La-dies' chail. Bal-loon say. Lemonade! Two. Ad-warnse and go back (gib 'ell a breakdown, shake it out o' yerselbs, keep a movil). Swing-corners, Bal-loon say, and Lemonade! (Hoy!) Three. Gent come for'ard with a lady and go back, hoppersite come for'ard and do what yer can. (Aeiohoy!) Bal-loon say, and leetle lemonade. (Dat hair n***** by 'um fireplace 'hind a' time, shake it out o' yerselbs, gib 'ell a breakdown.) Now den! Hoy! Four! Lemonade. Bal-loon say, and swing. Four ladies meet in 'um middle, Four gents goes round 'um ladies, Four gents passes out under 'um ladies' arms, swing—and Lemonade till 'a moosic can't play no more! (Hoy, Hoy!)'

The male dancers were all blacks, and one was an unusually powerful man of six feet three or four. The sound of their flat feet on the floor was as unlike the sound of white feet as their faces were unlike white faces. They toed and heeled, shuffled, double-shuffled, double-double-shuffled, covered the buckle, and beat the time out, rarely, dancing with a great show of teeth, and with a childish good-humoured enjoyment that was very prepossessing. They generally kept together, these poor fellows, said Mr. Superintendent, because they were at a disadvantage singly, and liable to slights in the neighbouring streets. But, if I were Light Jack, I should be very slow to interfere oppressively with Dark Jack, for, whenever I have had to do with him I have found him a simple and a gentle fellow. Bearing this in mind, I asked his friendly permission to leave him restoration of beer, in wishing him good night, and thus it fell out that the last words I heard him say as I blundered down the worn stairs, were, 'Jebblem's elth! Ladies drinks fust![sic]'

Mixed Race Relationships

Sharing precarious existences, cramped living spaces and eking out a living cheek by jowl, could obviously cause tensions and resentment between working class people of colour and white Britons and Irish, but these shared circumstances also led to intimate friendships and relations. The print below, inspired by David Garrick's 1760 farce High Life Below the Stairs, shows a black footman, 'Mungo' - a stereotypical name for black male servants of the period - wooing a receptive white lady's maid.

70. High Life Below Stairs; or MUNGO addressing my Lady's Maid. William Humphrey in 1772. Held at Yale Center for British Art, Paul Mellon Fund. Image @ The British Museum, ref. no. 2010,7081.1136.

Sitting behind Mungo there is another black footman, who tilts his chair, blowing his bugle. On the floor there is a book lettered 'Ovid'. For all the satire and caricaturisation of the black male figures in the print and play, both nevertheless depict the presence and integration of black people in British life.[12]

From the outset of migration to Britain, interracial relationships were commonplace. Scholars such as Imtiaz Habib, Onyeka and Miranda Kaufmann have documented such relationships as early as the Tudor period. Moreover, most migrants of colour in Britain were men due to the gender imbalance, and interracial relationships tended to be between men of colour and white women. Though, certainly there is also clear evidence of black women partnering white men, as can be seen in the article below:

> On Monday laſt was committed to Newgate by Juſtice Berry, one James Flower, for raiſing Scepters on Shillings, &c. and then uttering them for Guineas, Half Guineas, &c. his ſuppoſed Wife and Man were taken up, and committed to Clerkenwell Bridewell, for putting them off: This has been done at ſeveral Places about Shadwell, particularly at the George, in Milk-Yard, and at a Shop next Door to the Swan, King James's Stairs. Ten or fifteen of the ſaid counterfeit Pieces were found up the Chimney, and under the Feet of ſome Drawers. They were taken by a Preſs-Gang, near the Mill-pond Bridge, Rotherhithe; ſeveral falſe Draughts for Money were found upon Flower: He goes for a Horſe-Dealer, is well known at Deptford Turnpike, and at ſome of the Inns in Blackman-ſtreet, Southwark; at Dover, Portſmouth, Pool in Dorſetſhire, Briſtol, and at Sean near the Devizes. He is a little Man with his own black Hair: His Wife, a luſty black Woman, who was to have taken her Trial for the above Faƈt, died in Newgate: He was then ſwore againſt but made his Eſcape.

71. 'a lusty black Woman' and death in Newgate Prison *Derby Mercury*, 14 March 1755. Image @ The British Library Board. Shelfmark: MFM.M11963.

Throughout the 18th and 19th centuries, the visibility of interracial relationships and families on Britain's streets was frequently commented on, particularly by white tourists or visitors to the country.

> *'You will occasionally meet in the streets of London genteel young ladies, born in England, walking with their half-brothers, or more commonly with their nephews, born in India, who possess, in a very strong degree, the black hair, small features, delicate complexion and brown complexion of the native Hindus. These young men are received into society and take the rank of their fathers. I confess the fact struck*

me rather unpleasantly. It would seem that the prejudice against colour is less strong in England than in America; for, the few negroes found in this country, are in a condition much superior to that of their countrymen anywhere else. A black footman is considered a great acquisition, and consequently, negro servants are sought for and caressed. An ill-dressed or starving negro is never seen in England, and in some instances even alliances are formed between them and white girls of the lower orders of society. A few days ago, I met in Oxford-street a well-dressed white girl, who was of a ruddy complexion, and even handsome, walking arm in arm, and conversing very sociably, with a negro man, who was as well dressed as she, and so black that his skin had a kind of ebony lustre.' [13]

Irish Women

Though the lack of archival evidence makes it difficult to know approximate, let alone exact, figures, it is likely that most mixed race Irish families that formed in the latter part of the nineteenth century were made up of men of colour and Irish women, or women of Irish descent in Britain, who often struggled to find work in traditional female occupations such as domestic service. Bronwen Waters notes that in the 1850s, Irish women were considered 'particularly undesirable' for such employment amongst the respectable English classes. Many Irish women thus found themselves settling in the ports of entry, and in the larger metropolitan areas, often alongside other migrants, many of whom were men of colour. As in the USA, where indentured Irish servants worked and lived in close proximity with Chinese servants, black free or enslaved people, they shared physical spaces and experiences could often, unsurprisingly, lead to intimate relationships.

As noted earlier, however, people of colour in Britain were not confined to the working classes and neither were their relationships. Similarly, these relationships were not confined to multiracial cities. From the Tudor era onwards, evidence of individual residents of colour can be found across a wide range of towns, villages and even hamlets across Britain, with many of these residents entering into interracial relationships.[14] Some of these were also mixed race Irish families. In 1860, for example, the *Nottinghamshire Guardian* reported that two men had been arrested for being drunk and riotous in a pub in Sneinton when 'a quarrel arose among the company' when one of the men decided to 'amuse them with his vocal powers, contrary to the wishes of a blackman and his Irish wife who were drinking there.'

> DISCORDANT HARMONY.—Two labourers named Frederick Barnett and John Leavers were charged with being drunk and riotous in a public-house at Sneinton, and refusing to quit the same when requested to do so.—On Tuesday week the prisoners went into the Duke of Wellington Inn, Manvers Street, about half-past eleven o'clock, and presently a quarrel arose among the company out of the obliging disposition of Barnett to amuse them with his vocal powers, contrary to the wishes of a blackman and his Irish wife, who were drinking there. The consequence was a general disturbance, and Mr. Fox, the landlord, was eventually compelled to call in the aid of the police to remove the defendants, who were both drunk.—Fined 5s.

72. 'Discordant Harmony' in 1860.
The Nottinghamshire Guardian, 6 December 1860.
Image @ The British Library Board.
Shelfmark: 1-6499.

Attitudes towards Racial Difference and Mixing

What would attitudes have been like in Britain towards mixed race Irish families, like the Mahomeds (see page 51), Jeas (see page 41) and Allens (see page 48)? From the outset of contact with people of colour, British attitudes had tended towards stereotypes, tropes and fantasies; attitudes that were later expanded upon to justify slavery and colonial acquisition.[15]

By the eighteenth century, racism was institutionally ingrained. Black men, women and children were sold throughout the country at 'slave' markets and, along with Indian people, were advertised for sale in newspapers. While in London, legislation was passed in 1731 to prohibit free black people from taking on apprenticeships and thus acquiring a useful skill. Black people in particular were portrayed grotesquely in cartoons and literature. Nevertheless, at this time the concept of race had not yet solidified into a strong social boundary and interracial marriages were fairly frequent, particularly amongst servants and the working classes.[16] Though the elite, particularly of the plantation class, could be sneering and vitriolic about the mixed race relationships and families that were occurring in Britain during the eighteenth century, many of these marriages and families, which were largely between men of colour and white women, seem to have been mostly accepted by the general public. This is not of course to say that racism on an individual or everyday level, did not occur, but such partnerships were certainly not received with widespread condemnation by white Britons, particularly in comparison to white American attitudes at this time.

An article, in 1798, describing a mixed race marriage in Hull, neatly highlights the contrasting attitudes that could be found towards interracial marriage throughout this period. The writer of the article below sneeringly describes the black groom and his white wife but notes the 'great cheerfulness' of the local crowd stepping in to pay the cash poor couple's marriage fee.

> On Monday last, Peter Cooper, a negro, was married to a young woman at the Neptune Inn, in this town. When the ring was wanted, it was discovered that poor Mungo had omitted bringing one; but their distress occasioned by this omission his lovely willing bride soon removed by taking from her pocket a curtain ring, which chance had luckily deposited there; this difficulty removed, the ceremony was concluded, and pleasure appeared in the eyes of Molly and her dingy dear, when a demand of the customary fees dispelled, for a moment, their happiness, which they thought complete, for their fortunes were found insufficient to answer the demand. The surrounding spectators, with great chearfulness, paid the fees, and thus relieved the lovely pair from all their present embarrassments.

73. Irish woman in a mixed race marriage in 1798.
Hull Advertiser and Exchange Gazette, 28 July 1798.
Image @ The British Library Board.
Shelfmark: MFM.M24511.

However, by the time of mass Irish migration in the nineteenth century, social attitudes across the board were starting to harden. Under the expansion of Empire, a racial and class imperialism, bolstered by pseudo-scientific viewpoints, justified British colonialism and exploitation by deeming that the white race was superior to all other races, that the English were superior to all other white groups, and that the lower classes were themselves a race apart. Thus, as Jolly Rwanyonga Mazimhaka remarks, though the British racial hierarchy placed the Irish slightly above people of colour, both were negated in English thought. The remarks of the novelist Charles Kingsley in 1860 during his visit to Ireland, which at the time was still reeling from the devastation of the Great Famine, were illustrative of the types of attitudes during the nineteenth century which viewed Irish and black people as more animal than human.

'*I am haunted by the human chimpanzees I saw along that hundred miles of horrible country. I don't believe they are our fault. I believe there are not only many more of them than of old, but they are happier, better, more comfortably fed and lodged under our rule than they ever were. But to see white chimpanzees is dreadful; if they were black, one would not feel it so much, but their skins, except where tanned by exposure, are as white as ours.*' - Charles Kingsley, letter to his wife, Fanny, 1860.

As with those in Britain's colonies further afield, the Irish experienced many of the same processes of 'othering', and both groups in Victorian Britain, were subject to deeply ingrained prejudices and stereotypes.[17] In British cartoons and caricature, the Irish were frequently portrayed as ape like grotesques, as in the periodical called *Funny Folks, a Weekly Budget of Funny Pictures – Funny Notes – Funny Jokes – Funny Stories (1874-1884),* published by James Henderson. The sketches below and on page 119 were included in the January and February 1881 editions:

THE MODERN ŒDIPUS (?) AND THE IRISH SPHINX.

74. The Irish Sphinx. Funny Folks, 13 January 1881.
Image courtesy of the British Library Board. Shelfmark: PENP.NT152.

Racial and Ethnic Diversity in Britain 117

"ANOTHER UGLY ONE!"

75. "Another Ugly One!"
While 'John Bull' stands on a picture of 'Ireland'. *Funny Folks*,
19 February 1881. Image courtesy of the British Library Board.
Shelfmark: PENP.NT152.

In 1857, an article in *The Carlow Post*, in Ireland on 14 March 1857, and in the London Weekly Investigator on 11 March 1857 reproduced a piece from the *Australian and New Zealand Gazette* commenting on the marriages between Chinese men and Irish women that had been noticed at gold diggings. The article sarcastically noted that 'we should rather suspect the Chinaman has the worst of the bargain', though went on to suggest that it was hard 'to decide between the merits of a Chinese husband and those [the women] would have been likely to obtain in the purlieus of Drury Lane or Saffron Hill' (areas of London with large Irish communities).

> CHINESE AND IRISH INTERMARRIAGES.—A few of the Chinese at the gold diggings have married wives, chiefly Irish girls—a new inducement for emigration, certainly. We should rather suspect that the Chinaman has the worst of the bargain, but we do not pretend to decide between the merits of a celestial husband and those they would have been likely to obtain in the purlieus of Drury-lane or Saffron-hill. What the future character of the offspring of such unions may be forms an interesting subject for discussion. Such as have married will, in all likelihood, remain in the country of their adoption; indeed, we suspect their Irish ladies would not be very welcome in the land of the "celestials."—*Australian and New Zealand Gazette*.

76. Irish girls marrying Chinese men in Australia, reported in English and Irish newspapers. *The Carlow Post* 14 March 1857. Image @ The British Library Board. Shelfmark: MFM.M7053.

Such attitudes were thus infused not only with racial but also with class prejudices. For many Victorians, a person's social class and standing was more important than colour alone; as such, in many circumstances, a black or Indian 'gentlemen' would be a preferable in-law to a member of the 'white underclass', whether this be English or Irish. As such, those interracial couples that were perceived as educated and of rank were for the most part viewed and engaged with differently in Britain than those in working class communities or areas. Fisher remarks that 'none of the many European descriptions and anecdotes during his sixty-six years in Britain criticized [Mahomed's] marriage'. Similarly, William Allen, who resided in London with his white American wife and Irish born children, wrote to friends in America that he was struck by the 'entire absence of prejudice against color' amongst the English people, and that his interracial marriage passed 'as a *matter of course*' in England, with no commentary, insult or sneer made directed towards them when out in public.

As Lorimer highlights, the barriers of language, culture, and social class frequently proved greater obstacles to economic security and social acceptance than colour distinctions. Even though social and scientific thought, regarding the status of people of colour, hardened towards the end of the century. David Olusoga[18] also remarks that while 'a growing sense of white superiority and British exceptionalism spread, and came to influence even how many poorer Britons viewed Africans and other racial outsiders', such perspectives were 'by no means universal'. However, as Olusoga further notes, a 'widespread disdain' for foreigners and a sense of racial superiority did increasingly become a feature of British life. Indeed, in the decade after he had initially praised the English for their lack of race prejudice, William G. Allen begun to have different thoughts when he admitted to a friend that he thought 'a spirit not usually supposed to exist among Englishmen' had been a factor in the forced closure of his London school.[19]

> *'Certain schoolmasters in this locality, not influenced by a spirit of honorable competition, but by a spirit not usually supposed to exist among Englishmen, resolved to put down my school. They could not disperse my pupils nor draw them into their own schools, but they did succeed in inducing the landlord to compel me to put the school out of the house and this after I had gone to much expense in fitting up the house for school purposes. [...] I deplore the circumstances which have placed me at this disadvantage, but I cannot change my colour to please those who have thus placed me. And I would not do so if I could'*[20]

Class, race and status thus overlapped in complex ways during the eighteenth and nineteenth centuries, meaning that attitudes towards interracial families in Britain, alongside their everyday experiences, could vary quite widely across the board and by individual cases.

> *'That which, in an American community, would startle it more than seven thunders could - I.e., the marriage (or even the surmise of it) of two respectable persons, one of whom should be white and the other colored, passes as a matter of course in England.*
>
> *In no party, whether public or private, to which we have been, in no walk which we have taken, in no hotel at which we have had occasion to put up, in no public place of amusement, gallery, museum ..., have we met the cry of "amalgamation", either outspoken, or as manifested in a well-bred sneer.[sic]'*[21]

Colonel Edward and Catherine Despard

While it was common for many Irish men in the West Indies to engage in interracial relationships with women of colour, often by brutal force or exploitation, those that developed into marriage were rare. In the late eighteenth century, however, Colonel Edward Despard, an Irish soldier in the British army, married a woman of colour named Catherine whose mother was a free black resident of Jamaica.

A war hero and later a revolutionary who believed in racial equality, Edward Despard went on to move to London with Catherine where he would eventually be accused of treason and, despite Catherine's tireless efforts to secure his release, would become the last man sentenced to be hung, drawn and quartered in Britain.

77. Edward Marcus Despard
by John Chapman, after unknown artist
stipple engraving, published 1804.
Image © National Portrait Gallery, London,
ref. no. NPG D2268.

Born in 1751 to William and Jane Despard (neé Walsh) in County Laois (formerly Queen's County), Ireland, Edward Marcus Despard was the youngest of six sons, five of whom served in the army or navy. At the age of 15, Despard himself joined the British Army, leaving in 1772 for Jamaica where he embarked on a distinguished military career. Bright, charismatic and with a talent for engineering, Despard was appointed Chief Engineer to the unsuccessful 1780 San Juan expedition led by John Polson and Horatio Nelson to take the coastal area of Nicaragua during the American War of Independence.

On his return to Jamaica, Despard was promoted first to Commander-in-Chief of the Rattan Islands and then, after regaining control of territory from the Spanish at the Battle of the Black River, Superintendent of the Bay of Honduras. It was during this period of time that he met and married his wife, Catherine, flouting social conventions that saw relationships or sexual relations between white men and black women accepted as an inevitable consequence of colonialism, as long as they were conducted in the shadows or margins of society.

As Mike Jay highlights, as part of the treaty with Spain that granted the new British enclave, British settlers along the Mosquito Shore were required to resettle in the Bay, and Despard was in charge with accommodating them. While some of the settlers were wealthy white planters, the 'Baymen' who had become wealthy on the back of mahogany logging using enslaved labour, most were 'Shoremen', a multicultural mix of former military, labourers, smugglers and freed 'slaves'.

78. Day and Son, Cutting and Trucking Mahogany in Honduras. Sketch in The Mahogany Tree, Liverpool: Rockliff & Son; London Effingham Wilson, 1851. Image courtesy of the British Library Board. Shelfmark: 7076.d.8.

In 1790, Edward Despard was summoned to London following complaints from the Baymen who had been antagonised by Despard's upholding of the law as set out in the treaty with Spain for the enclave. Under Despard, there began to be a fairer distribution of land and mahogany trading rights than approved of by the Baymen, who had previously acted as what Despard called an 'arbitrary aristocracy' dividing the land informally amongst themselves, which was land still technically under the Spanish Crown. With the overwhelming majority of inhabitants approving, Despard had replaced the Bayman system of government with a committee headed by himself as Superintendent, with all fifteen committee members to be elected by the male inhabitants of the Bay, regardless of colour or class.

The Baymen were incensed to see the new arrivals, particularly black and mixed race, being treated as equals and granted the land plots and homes the law entitled them to under Despard's new ballot system of land allocation. On one occasion, Despard was confronted at the courthouse by a group of Baymen who had gathered alongside a large group of angry Shoremen protesting the arrest of Joshua Jones, a recently arrived free black man. Jones who had infuriated the Baymen when he had knocked down the shed of a wealthy settler on the plot, he was granted in Despard's ballot, had been placed in custody for destruction of property. Entering the courthouse, Despard ended the dispute, to the infuriation of the Baymen, by putting his hand on Jones's shoulder and stating 'I declare this man free in the King's name'. By this action, Despard further indicated that he saw Jones, and all the Shoremen of colour, as equals in name as well as in law to all British subjects.

While the British authorities had initially authorised Despard's actions, Lord Sydney, the British Home Secretary, was nevertheless concerned that during the process of land distribution, no distinction was being made 'between affluent Settlers and Persons of a different description, particularly people of Colour' or Free Negroes who, from the natural Prejudices of the Inhabitants of the Colonies, are not, however valuable in point of character, considered upon an equal footing with People of a Different Complexion." Despard, however, retorted that the situation 'must be governed by the laws of England which know no distinction.'

The Baymen's continual petition to the British government against Despard's actions, including how his partiality for 'people of colour' was threatening the lucrative logging trade, finally gained traction when Lord Sydney was replaced by Lord Grenville, the cousin of the prime minister, William Pitt. Caring heavily for the mahogany trade and little for internal colonial politics, Grenville abolished the new constitution, suspended Despard from his post, and summoned him to England to face an inquiry. Before Despard returned to London in 1790 to clear his name, he decided to stand for election as a magistrate under the old system, now re-instituted by the new superintendent. He won by a landslide (over 80% of the vote), which he argued demonstrated he was not the 'petty despot of Belize' as he had been labelled by the Baymen. Despard left for England with Catherine and their son James. In London, arguments over what had occurred in the Bay were soon overshadowed by arguments over expenses. The government had refused to pay him his full wages, there was no promise of a new commission, and his lawyer's fees were stacking up. Consequently, Despard soon found himself imprisoned for two years, due to his debts.

In prison, where he read Thomas Paine's *The Rights of Man* (1791), Despard had his leanings towards political reform further awakened, in particular his identification as an Irishman and his sympathy for those fighting colonial rule. On release, he joined the United Irishmen, an organisation supporting Irish independence, and became involved with the London Corresponding Society (LBC), a group made up of artisans and tradesmen seeking political reform, including the right to vote for

79. 'London Corresponding Society, alarm'd.'
By James Gillray, 1798.
Image © National Portrait Gallery,

all British men. Due to its call for radical change as well as the perceived French revolutionary influence on the organisation, the LBC, which had links with the United Irishmen, was viewed with great anxiety by Pitt's government and, along with both groups, Despard was put under surveillance. As with portrayals of Irish nationalists, the members of the LCS were depicted by satirists as ape like beings.

In 1798, several newspapers were at pains to report that, on his arrest, the Irish Colonel Despard was found in bed with a black woman. It wasn't reported that she happened to be his wife.

> Yesterday the Privy Council met about eleven o'clock, when *Mr. Evans* and *Colonel Despard*, (who was apprehended by four Messengers on Sunday morning last, in Mead's Court, Soho, in bed with a black woman) were brought up and underwent a short examination, when they were remanded into the custody of the Messengers.

80. Colonel Despard in bed with a black woman.
Jackson's Oxford Journal, 17 May 1798.
Image @ The British Library. Shelfmark: MFM.M9782.

Pitt had nothing on Despard and most of his fellow suspects at this stage, though Father James O'Coigley was hanged for treason due to the contents of the letter on his person. However, the Irish Rebellion that occurred in the summer of 1798 allowed Pitt to suspend habeas corpus, thus allowing suspects to be detained indefinitely without trial, as well as to introduce two Acts of Parliament to make it easier to convict on charges of treason. Despard was placed in jail with no immediate prospect of trial let alone release.

The MP George Tierney, whose brother James worked in Jamaica and had two 'mustee' daughters, was highly critical of Pitt's suspension of habeas corpus; not only did he challenge Pitt to a duel, but he defended Despard in parliament. In a debate in 1799 on Pitt's new bill to 'suppress seditious societies and practices' (which would effectively ban the LDC and other societies seeking political reform), *The Times* reported Tierney as saying:

"It was contrary to humanity to expose a gentleman of rank and education to the hardships of such a place; and a man of Colonel Despard's rank in his Majesty's army must keenly feel the insulting condition to which it reduced him. He knew

nothing of Colonel Despard; he never saw him, and had never heard of him till after his committal to Cold Bath fields; yet he was a man living in the same state of society, educated on the same principles, and in the same liberal manner as the Members of that House; and for such a person to be put in a cell, a place where to be dry it was necessary to exclude the light, - was it not a painful reflection?"

Tierney's pleas were, however, fruitless; Despard spent three years in jail before finally being released, without charge. On release, Despard and Catherine went to ground, moving from location to location in London, and possibly Ireland, in an attempt to avoid the continued surveillance of the authorities. However, late in 1802, in what became known as the Despard Plot, Despard was named as part of a conspiracy to seize the Tower of London and Bank of England and assassinate King George III. Arrested at the Oakley Arms, London at a meeting with 'near 40 men labouring men and soldiers, the major part of them Irish', the police found 'unlawful oaths' on three men, though nothing on Despard. Despite the lack of evidence and receiving a character testimony from his old friend and military colleague Nelson, now the celebrated Lord Nelson, Despard was found guilty of high treason and sentenced to be hung, drawn and quartered, the last man in Britain to be sentenced by hanging.

Thanks to tireless lobbying from Catherine (alongside the fear of sparking public unrest), the gruesome act of disembowelling and dismemberment was removed from the sentence, but the plea for mercy as recommended by the jury was not accepted. Despard was still to be hung and beheaded. He accepted the sentence calmly and, likely with Catherine's help, spent his final days preparing his execution speech. See the extract below of Despard's final speech, reported in *The Times* on 22 February 1803:

> *"Fellow Citizens, I come here, as you see, after having served my country, - faithfully, honourably, and usefully served it, for thirty years and upwards, to suffer death upon a scaffold for a crime of which I protest I am not guilty. I solemnly declare that I am no more guilty of it than any of you who may be now hearing me – But, though his Majesty's Ministers know as well as I do, that I am not guilty, yet they avail themselves of a legal pretext to destroy a man, because he has been a friend to truth, to liberty, and to justice. Because he has been a friend to the poor and the oppressed. But, Citizens, I hope and*

trust, notwithstanding my fate, and fate of those who no doubt follow me, that the principles of freedom, of humanity, and of justice will finally triumph over falsehood, tyranny, and delusion, and every principle inimical to the interests of the human race."

Despard had been warned that if he used his speech to inflame the crowd then he would be hung before he finished speaking. The early nineteenth century was a time of immense political turmoil and unrest, existing in the aftermath of numerous global revolutions, uprisings and political awakenings, not least the French Revolution, the American Revolutionary War, the Irish Rebellion and the Haiti Revolution. Such egalitarian forces preoccupied the fearful English authorities who were concerned about uprisings on their own shores. The Gordon Riots still lay on people's mind, and there was concern that Despard's execution, perceived as unjust in many quarters, could be used as a spark to violence. Indeed, his death sentence was not popular with the populace. Pamphlets calling for an uprising had been circulating in London and it had been difficult to find carpenters to build the scaffold. *The Times* noted that on the delivery of parts of his speech, 'several shouts were raised by the mob nearest to the platform, and it was found necessary to admonish him of the impropriety of using such inflammatory language.'

Despite government fears that his funeral would provoke a riot, the relatively small procession went off without incident, though it attracted a crowd of 500 mourners. After Despard was laid in his coffin, Madame Tussaud, the wax modeller, requested permission to make a cast of his face; this would be the first death mask she made since her arrival in Britain and would prove a huge draw with visitors to her exhibition, featuring in what would be known as her 'Chamber of Horrors'. Edward Despard was executed on 21 February 1803.

81. The hanging of Edward Marcus Despard
Unknown artist, line engraving, 1804.
Image © National Portrait Gallery, London,
ref. no. NPG D2266.

Catherine Despard

As is frequently the case with the history of women of colour in Britain, there are many gaps missing in the story of Catherine Despard. Details of her early life are vague and there has previously been speculation as to whether she was born in Jamaica or Belize, or that her origins were Spanish Creole. However, as Mike Jay outlines, the discovery of a will dated 1799 detailed that Catherine's mother was a free black woman named Sarah Gordon, a woman of property living in St Andrews Parish, near Kingston who had left four enslaved people to her daughter.

82. Kerri McLean as Kitty Despard
in the television series Poldark.
© Mammoth Screen Limited 2018.

Catherine Gordon was baptised on 15 February 1758, at the Church of England in St. Catherine's parish, Jamaica.[22] While the parents' names are not mentioned, also recorded in St Catherine's Parish is the death record of Sarah Gordon 'a free negro' on 12 January 1805 (under the heading 'Diseases' the word 'age' is noted).

Thus, it seems likely that Catherine was born in Jamaica and, at some point, moved to Belize, though whether she met Despard there or elsewhere in the West Indies remains unclear. In Sarah Gordon's will made in May 1799, she bequeathed four 'slaves' to her "daughter Catherine Gordon Despard now in London".[23] Catherine and Edward had a son together called James. They brought him with them to London in 1790 after Edward was summoned to explain his actions while acting as the Superintendent in the Bay of Honduras.

Interracial relationships between women of colour and white men, particularly from the middle and upper classes, were not as familiar a sight in Britain as in the West Indies, not least due to Britain's much smaller multiracial population. The interracial relationships that did occur in Britain tended to be primarily between men of colour and white women, due to the migration patterns. However, relationships and marriages between women of colour and white men were not unknown in Britain, especially in London, though generally they were confined to the lower classes. It is unknown whether Edward and Catherine had much interaction with members of London's small black community, though it is not beyond the realms of possibility that they may have crossed paths with Tony and Julie Small, who were resident in London from the 1790s, given that Tony's employer, Edward Fitzgerald had been a prominent leader of the United Irishmen, the organisation which Despard also joined.

There is no record of how Catherine felt having to move from her home in the West Indies to Britain, though initially she, like Despard, likely assumed that it would only be a temporary visit whilst her husband cleared his name. Instead, Catherine spent most of her time in Britain, a foreign land to her, with either Despard in jail or avoiding the authorities. However, Catherine proved to be a formidable woman who refused to be cowed by either her race or gender in her fight to support, defend and ultimately save her husband's life.

During Despard's initial arrest and imprisonment on suspicion of treason in 1798, Catherine publicly campaigned on her husband's behalf, decrying the conditions he was subjected to in prison. Attracting the support of the prison reformist MP, Sir Francis Burdett. Catherine also petitioned the Duke of Portland (the home secretary), Sir Richard Ford (the chief magistrate of London), and William Wickham (the founder of the secret service), as well as rallying the other prisoners' wives and alerting the press to the appalling conditions Despard was subjected to. As a result, a three week debate on whether to extend the suspension of *habeas corpus* was conducted in the House of Commons, with one of Catherine's letters presented to the House. In this, Catherine had written that her husband had been 'confined near seven months in a damp cell, not seven feet square, without either fire or candle, chair, table, knife, fork, a glazed window, or even a book to read' and lamented that her previous pleas had gone unanswered by Portland and Wickham.

Catherine also appeared in person, the only woman of the twenty four witnesses questioned, before the House of Commons during the committee's inquiry into the state of Cold Bath Fields Prison where Despard was initially held. With the support of Burdett, a committee of inquiry was set up to look at the prison conditions.

Glossing over Catherine's accusations, the authorities instead attacked her testimony on the grounds of her literacy. The attorney general, Sir John Scott, and the MP George Canning, suggested that the letter presented to the House was too well-written to have been written by Catherine herself. Sir John Scott also levelled a thinly veiled threat to

Catherine, writing in his parliamentary report on the issue: 'By the way, there were some wives who had met with much indulgence, in not being taken up and confined as well as their husbands.' While Burdett's report recommendations on prison reform post the inquiry failed (by 147 votes to 6), eventually, Catherine's sterling efforts were rewarded and Despard was released in 1801. A year later, however, he would be back in jail, accused of treason once more for his role in the Despard plot.

During his subsequent arrest, Catherine petitioned as furiously and fiercely as she had previously done, proving a thorn once more in the side of the authorities. Continuing to lobby at the highest levels, she not only brought Burdett on side, but also met with Lord Nelson to ask for his support in seeking leniency for Despard. This intervention contributed to the government's dropping of disembowelment and quartering from the sentence. Visiting Despard frequently and at length in prison, she was suspected of carrying away Despard's writings for publication, though the authorities dared not search her in case of a public outcry, while it is speculated that she may have helped compose the inflammatory speech Despard gave at the gallows.

Catherine visited her husband just before his execution. However, later that night, the authorities prevented Catherine from seeing Despard again, supposedly to spare him the pain of a second parting, a decision she did not take well. Richard Ford, the chief magistrate wrote that 'Mrs Despard has been very troublesome, but at last she is gone away.' The following is an extract, on the execution of Edward Despard, from *The Morning Post* on 22 February 1803:

> *'Previous to the execution some circumstances occurred we yet must mention: Mrs Despard, after having taken leave of her husband at three o'clock yesterday afternoon, came again about five o'clock. It was thought advisable to spare the Colonel the pangs of a second parting, and she was therefore not admitted into the prison. She evinced some indignation at the refusal; and expressed a strong opinion with respect to the cause for which her husband was to suffer. Half frantic with leaving the prison, a part of the mob laughed at her agitation. This again provoked her resentment.'*

Even after Despard's death, Catherine's efforts on his behalf continued. Discovering that Despard had a hereditary right to be buried in the churchyard of St Paul's, she insisted on his right to be interred there to the vehement protestations of the Lord Mayor of London. Drawing on her network, Catherine once more lobbied furiously for her husband and, with Nelson's likely intervention, the burial plot was registered under the Hamilton family name (Lady Emma Hamilton was Nelson's mistress).

Shortly after the funeral, Lady Hamilton issued a statement in which she denied that she had ordered the internment and had only met Catherine two days before Despard's death and, moreover, that she disapproved of his conduct and had refused to see Catherine since. Regardless of whether Lady Hamilton's statement was true or simply an attempt to distance from any backlash, Catherine had yet again managed to have the necessary strings pulled to help her husband as much as his infamy would allow.

> We are authorised to contradict a report that has been industriously circulated, that Lady HAMILTON had ordered the interment of Colonel DESPARD, and protects his widow; on the contrary, she never saw Mrs. DESPARD until two days previous to the Colonel's death, and she so highly disapproved of his conduct, and the manner in which his funeral was conducted, that she has ever since refused to see Mrs. DESPARD.

83. Lady Hamilton abandons Catherine Despard.
Morning Post, 11 March 1803. Image @ The British Library.
Shelfmark: MFR 9657.

As with her life before him, the details of Catherine's life after Despard's death are hazy. It is believed that despite Nelson's efforts to obtain her a pension, Edward's perceived inflammatory speech on the scaffold, of which she is thought to have contributed to, meant that she was denied any provision.

Certainly, no help was forthcoming from Despard's family. They had never accepted the marriage, referring to Catherine as Despard's 'black housekeeper' and denying that James was Despard's son. Rather, it seems that Burdett and other friends took care of her. Lord Cloncurry, who gave Despard a character witness, claimed to have housed Catherine on his estate in Ireland for several years, though his memoirs are somewhat unreliable. Catherine also possibly had some income from her mother's will, though there is speculation that given Edward's commitment to 'universal equality' and the 'one human race', she likely freed the enslaved people left to her.

She may also have been supported by her son James who, after being expelled from the Royal East London regiment for duelling, had joined the French army; his father's funeral had been delayed for his return. James himself disappears from the record, though there are fleeting references to him from his father's family; his uncle spying him ('a flashy creole') leaving a theatre in London arm in arm with a 'flashy young woman', and his aunt putting out the rumour that he had run off with an heiress, but this is unconfirmed.

As for Catherine, she lived until her death on 18th September 1815, records stating that she died, aged 50, in Somers Town, London, the death notices of the press discreetly noting 'At Somers Town, Mrs Despard, Widow of the unfortunate Col. Despard'. Thus ended the story of the Despards, a remarkable mixed race Irish couple whose lives crossed continents, boundaries and class and whose egalitarian sentiments and belief in 'one human race' made them outsiders in their own time.

84. Widow of the 'unfortunate Colonel Despard'.
Chester Courant, Tuesday 19 Sept. 1815. Image @ The British Library Board. Shelfmark: MFM.M18913.

85. Catherine Despard's burial record, 1815.
Last residence at James's Street.
Image @London Metropolitan Archives,
with kind permission of the parish of St Pancras.

Chapter 4

Early Twentieth Century Migration

Race and prejudice in the early-mid 20th century

As the 20th century unfolded, the hardening of attitudes towards race and difference began to move out of the confined circles of specialist race thinkers and scientists and into a more widespread and pervasive public discourse. Moreover, these public discussions of racial mixing, once mostly concerned with what was happening in the colonies, started to focus on the interracial intimacy occurring in Britain.

WHITE GIRLS MARRY BLACK MEN.

Epidemic of Lightning Weddings.

LURE OF HIGH WAGES.

(Special to "People's Journal.")

WITHIN the last few months, I am told, there has been a perfect epidemic of marriages between English girls, principally munition workers, and negroes who have come to this country from the West Coast of Africa on war work. Seldom a week passes now that a dusky bridegroom does not figure in a matrimonial ceremony in some part of London. The negroes are engaged in factories and at the docks, and while thousands of white men are in the fighting line the coloured ones are winning their way into many an English home.

Already there is quite a negro colony in the East End, and the police are becoming anxious as to the future. They have no complaint to make against the coloured men, who by all accounts are on their best behaviour, and giving very little trouble.

86. 'White Girls Marry Black Men'
Dundee Peoples Journal, 14 July 1917, p1. Image @DC Thomson & Co Ltd, and courtesy of The British Library Board. Shelfmark: MFM.SP885.

While these discussions about race were not on a large scale, there were still a mix of viewpoints to be found, including acceptance of racial mixing. Nevertheless, press reports began to appear, detailing the lives, presence or occurrence of mixed race couples or families in the country. These were not simply sardonic or sneering, as had formerly tended to be the case, but instead vituperative and antagonistic, at least towards the working classes. The stereotyping of the children of these mixed marriages can also be seen in circus and "Freak shows" around the country at the time. In the extract below from the article 'The Life and Adventures of "Lord" George Sanger' in which he talks about the secrets of "the freak show" and the "intelligent mulatto children" of a "negress" and Irish father, taken from their mother in Bristol for the travelling show:

> So, also, there was a similar little juggling with the truth in regard to Tamee Ahmee and Orio Rio, the "savage cannibal pigmies." They were really two rather intelligent mulatto children, their mother being a negress and their father an Irishman. My father had got them from their mother in Bristol, and they were aged respectively ten years and nine years. Feathers, beads, and carefully-applied paint gave them the necessary savage appearance, and the "patter" did the rest.
> "Ladies and Gentlemen: These wonderful people are fully grown, being, in fact, each over thirty years of age. They were captured by Portuguese traders in the African wilds, and are incapable of ordinary human speech. Their food consists of raw meat, and if they can capture a small animal they tear it to pieces alive with their teeth, eagerly devouring its flesh and drinking its blood."
> Thus was the tale told, and the credulous country folks were mightily impressed. So successful, indeed, was the whole show that rivals on the road hated my father bitterly, complaining that when he was about he took all the money. This enmity bore very bitter fruit a little later on at Taunton in Devon, where the show had been doing unusually good business.

87. Secrets of the Freak Show
Intelligent mulatto Irish children. *Lloyd's Weekly News*, 2 Feb. 1908. Image @ The British Library Board. Shelfmark: MFM.MLD37.

The Cambrian's article of 1908, on page 135, minced no words regarding the interracial mixing that could be observed in dockland communities such as Swansea, lambasting the 'laxity' of 'white women of the lower classes' in their willingness to 'intimately associate' with black men. Throughout these dockland communities, many of the white women so castigated were Irish or of Irish descent.

> Recent events in Swansea and district bearing upon the racial problem of black and white have brought to light the facts that white women of the lower classes in this part of the world seem as prepared to marry or otherwise intimately associate with a black man as readily as with whites. A laxity of opinion prevails which no Colonial or American could understand in the slightest, and frequent incidents occur which would lead in the States to burnings at the stake and similar little ebullitions, demonstrating the large capacity of the white race for acts of savagery. In England and Wales, as we see in so many cases in our midst, no such opinion prevails even amongst women of the working class, ordinarily respectable and well-behaved. The results are seen in the occasional Mulatto children to be met with in the streets. Unnatural alliances, which would excite the strongest disgust and abhorrence in the Colonies, are not infrequent; it is earnestly to be desired that a healthier opinion upon the subject should be inculcated amongst the class concerned.

88. Racial problem of black and white.
The Cambrian, 9 October 1908. Image courtesy of the National Library of Wales. Unknown copyright owner.

As the population of colour in Britain grew larger under the labour demands of the First World War, so did a sense of concern and hostility. The visibly multiracial aspect of many dockside communities began to attract wider attention as, with issues of economic strife and politics on the continent rising, working class interraciality threatened the idea of a strong, homogenous nation. The press joined politicians, local commentators and trade unionists in vilifying minority groups who became the recipients of both projected fears about moral and racial degeneration and the requisitioning of white British jobs and women.

There was an 'epidemic of marriages' between British girls and black men 'on high wages', fumed the *People's Journal* in 1917, and while white men were on the fighting line, 'coloured ones are winning their way into many an English home.' Racial mixing between well to do Britons and people of colour at this time, particularly involving white men and women of colour, were largely reported in respectful or even gushing terms, such as the marriages of Princess Pretiva and Princess Sudhira to the Manders brothers, and the Anglo-Irish family of Beauchamp Caulfield-Stoker and Countess Oei Hui-lan 'Hoey' Stoker, the daughter of a Chinese-Indonesian sugar magnate.

ROMANTIC WEDDING.

Young Englishman and Indian Princess.

BROTHERS MARRIED TO SISTERS.

Met in a London Nursing Home.

Telegrams from Calcutta announce the wedding on Wednesday of the Princess Sudhira, youngest sister of the Maharajah of Cooch Behar, and Mr. Alan Jocelyn Mander, of Wolverhampton.

The register was signed by the Governor of Bengal and the Chief Justice.

The newly-married couple left for England last night.

Mr. Alan Mander is 21 and his bride 19. They will live in London.

It is scarcely two years ago that the beautiful young Princess Pretiva, second sister of the Maharajah, married Mr. Lionel Henry Mander, of Wightwick Manor, Wolverhampton, brother of the bridegroom of Wednesday.

The bridegroom is a son of the late Mr. Samuel Theodore Mander, a nephew of Sir Charles Tertius Mander, Bart., and a member of the family which owns the famous paint and varnish business of Mander Brothers in Wolverhampton.

LOVE AT FIRST SIGHT.

LOVE AT FIRST SIGHT.

Mr. Alan Mander met his bride in a very romantic way. A few months ago she was ill in a London nursing home. With his sister-in-law he called at the home, fell in love with her, and then and there began a friendship which blossomed into Wednesday's wedding. They had been engaged for six months.

Both Mr. Alan Mander and his brother are well known in the aeronautical world. It was only a few months ago that Mr. Alan Mander and Mr. Patrick Nolan, of the Royal Aero Club, had a most thrilling experience in the English Channel. By lighting their last match as a signal of distress they were rescued in the nick of time from a sinking balloon. It was Mr. Nolan, appropriately enough, who was Mr. Mander's best man at Wednesday's ceremony.

POPULAR IN MAYFAIR.

Both the bride and her two sisters are extremely popular in London drawing-rooms. The eldest of the sisters, Maharjhumari Sukriti, is married to Mr. Jyotsna Gosal, of the Bombay Civil Service. The two younger sisters are now wedded to Englishmen. Both the late Maharajah and Maharanee were well known and highly esteemed in Court circles. They did everything possible to secure for their children the best possible English education, their four sons having been at Eton, while the eldest went to Christ Church.

The late Maharajah was a prominent personage in the ceremonies, attending Queen Victoria's Jubilee and King Edward's Coronation, and for many years acted as A.D.C. to the late King.

The present Maharajah is married to a daughter of the Gaekwar of Baroda.

89. Romantic wedding of Indian Princesses to two English brothers.
Yorkshire Evening News, 27 February 1914.
Image @ The British Library Board. Shelfmark: 2-29424.

Countess Stoker had a son called Lionel, whom she had with Captain Beauchamp Caulfield-Stoker. On 12 January 1918 she appeared in a photo in the *Daily Mirror* at a children's party with her son. However, eight years later we find that the marriage had problems due to cultural differences and probably pressure relating to racial mixing. on 5 October 1926, it was reported in the *North Mail and Newcastle Daily Chronicle* that Countess Stoker was now the wife of the new premier of China, Dr. Wellington Koo, and was now known as Madame Wellington Koo. It was also noted that she "was first married to an Irishman, an Army Officer, and used to be known as Countess Hoey Stoker."

Her former husband, Captain Beauchamp Caulfield-Stoker, was in fact an Irishman born in Dublin, at 33 Blessington Street, on 11 March 1877. The civil birth record states his name as Forde Beauchamp Stoker, whose parents were Beauchamp Stoker, a Captain in the 2nd West Indian Regiment and Alice Leathley. Church records show that he was baptised 'Beauchamp Forde Gordon' on 24 May 1877, at the Bethseda Chapel (now demolished), also known as the Bethseda Episcopal Church, on Granby Row, just off Parnell square in central Dublin. He joined the British Army on 20 February 1915, at the Davenport Army Service Corps depot (military transport, logistics and supplies), as a Lieutenant and was promoted to Captain on 1 August 1915.[1] His appointment was for the duration of the first world war and he was released from service in 1919. In his military records at the National Archives in Kew, his former job is noted as a businessman and sugar merchant, "born in Dublin of Irish parents" and living at Graylands, Augustus Road, Wimbledon Park in London.

The pictures on page 138 shows Madame Koo in 1922 with her new second son Yu-chang Koo. Countess Stoker divorced Beauchamp Caulfield-Stoker in April 1920. In an article on the divorce in the *Western Mail* in 1920 Caulfield-Stoker was now described as an "Englishman".

90. Madame Wellington Koo
(née Hui-lan Oei) with Yu-chang Koo
by Oscar Hardee Blyfield, for H. Walter
Barnett, vintage bromide print, 1922
© National Portrait Gallery, London,
ref. no. NPG x45435.

The extract below describes the circumstances of the divorce as follows:

The Chinese wife of an Englishman, Mr Beauchamp Caulfield Stoker, formerly of Wimbledon Park, was granted a decree nisi and the custody of the children of the marriage in the Divorce Court on Monday. The marriage took place in 1909 in Dutch Java, where the respondent was representing a Manchester firm. Counsel said the lady's father, who was a wealthy Chinaman, made large and handsome settlements on the couple. After coming to London the lady had reason to complain that her husband had not introduced her to his people, who lived at Burnham, in Somerset, and was recognising her as his wife. Her father bought them Graylands, at Wimbledon, so that she could take her proper place in society. Her husband would not allow her to visit him at Devonport while he was serving in the Army, and subsequently wrote declining to return to her, as their lives and ideas were so far apart. Afterwards he supplied proof of misconduct' [2]

91. Lionel Montgomery Caulfield-Stoker with his mother Hui Oei-lan (then Mrs Beauchamp Caulfield-Stoker), 1920. Portrait by Miss Compton Colliers. Public domain image on Wikimedia Commons.

This story reveals that mixed race marriages were not only a lower class phenomenon. Like the story of Colonel Edward Despard, Captain Beauchamp Caulfield-Stoker returned to Britain with a woman of another culture and ethnicity. Both high ranking Anglo-Irish members of British society. It is unclear as to why the surname Caulfield-Stoker is recorded in the military records. As to the son Lionel Stoker, we do not know if he was taken to China with his mother or was left behind in Britain with his father's family. Little is known in public of his life after the divorce of his parents.

Mixed race Irish families in Manchester

Like many British port cities, Manchester has long been home to a widely diverse population of people from around the globe. As with London and Liverpool, the combination of Irish settlement alongside that of many people of colour meant that Manchester has a rich history of mixed race Irish families. Many of these families first formed during the late nineteenth and early twentieth centuries in the wake of the creation of the Manchester Ship Canal.

92. The Norseman ship passing Barton. Jan. 1st 1894.
The opening of the Manchester Ship Canal by the yacht Norseman. Unknown photographer.
Image from the Manchester Local Image Collection courtesy of
Manchester Libraries, Information and Archives.

The Irish Community in Manchester

While Manchester's links to Ireland go back to before the Industrial Revolution, during the mid-nineteenth century the city, alongside Liverpool and London, became a huge draw for Irish immigrants, attracted by the promise of work in Britain's industrial heartland. In the 1850s, it was estimated that over 14% of the population of Manchester had been born in Ireland, the second highest population density of Irish people in England after Liverpool. Many of the Irish that came to Manchester immediately after the Famine were heavily concentrated in an area that became known as 'Little Ireland'. At the University of Manchester in 2012, Michael D Higgins said:

> *"Liverpool [is] a city that is sometimes considered the most Irish of British cities. But the Irish connection in Manchester is no less evident than in Liverpool. And where Liverpool was a gateway for so many Irish people, Manchester tended to be for many the end of the journey, a home."* [3]

As in London and Liverpool, the poverty of the immigrants to Manchester saw them crowded into closely knit, unsanitary properties which became notorious as dangerous slum neighbourhoods. Such squalid conditions in these Irish migrant communities across Britain's cities, where families were forced to share rooms and even cellars, would lead to outbreaks of disease, low mortality rates and negative stereotyping of the Irish people as a whole.

James Philip Kay, a local doctor, reported on the Manchester Irish community in 1832 as follows:

'The rapid growth of the cotton manufacture has attracted hither operatives from every part of the kingdom, and Ireland has poured forth the most destitute of her hordes to supply the constantly increasing demand for labour."

"This immigration has been, in one important respect, a serious evil. The Irish have taught the labouring classes of this country a pernicious lesson. The system of cottier farming, the demoralisation and barbarism of the people, and the general use of the potato as the chief article of food, have encouraged the growth of population in Ireland more rapidly than the available means of subsistence have been increased."

"Debased alike by ignorance and pauperism, they have discovered, with the savage, what is the minimum of the means of life, upon which existence may be prolonged."

"The paucity of the amount of means and comforts necessary for the mere support of life, is not known by a more civilised population, and this secret has been taught the labourers of this country by the Irish [...]."

"The labouring classes have ceased to entertain a laudable pride in furnishing their houses, and in multiplying the decent comforts which minister to happiness. What is superfluous to the mere exigencies of nature is too often expended at the tavern; and for the provision of old age and infirmity, they too frequently trust either to charity, to the support of their children, or to the protection of the poor laws.' [4]

The Black Community in Manchester

Like all large British cities, archival records in Manchester also indicate an early history of black and other ethnic minority settlement, with a small black population being noted as far back as the eighteenth century. By the early twentieth century, the industrial expansion of Manchester, including the creation of Manchester Ship Canal which made the Port of Manchester become Britain's third busiest port, saw Indian, Yemeni, Chinese and African labourers and seamen, settling in the area. Many married local women, often Irish or of Irish descent.

Mary Brady, a white resident of Salford who participated in Professor Paul Thompson's ground-breaking oral history project 'Family Life and Work Experience before 1918' (University of Essex), vividly recalled four Catholic sisters from her neighbourhood with a common Irish surname ('Brennan') marrying black men towards the end of the First World War, as well as the hostility one of the men encountered when he left Greengate, a nearby neighbourhood in which black people had begun to settle, to visit his sweetheart. See extract from Thompson's oral history project below:

> *"Eeh, always remember this girl, this - the - this family it was, the Brennans and they lived just near us and I'd gone to school with 'em, they was Catholics and - they used to be - in Greengate, this - after the First World War these - these negroes started coming, blackies, you know and she come walking down this Cannon Street arm in arm with this 'ere - this 'ere blackie .... [sic]"*
>
> *"And I must have been about sixteen 'cos it was 1918 and she got in with this coloured man and down the street and they all started, 'ooh, here's Annie Brennan with a black', see, so all the women come out, all the neighbours and one thing another, not having them down Adelphi like Greengate – Greengate was the first to have 'em and they called it Dixie, you know, called Greengate Dixie - and they said, 'we're not having 'em here."*
>
> *"So all the women - and I remember this old woman that lived next door, can see her now with her sleeves roiled up – 'come on out now, you dirty old dog, come on, get her out, get her out.[sic]"*
>
> *"And the poor fellow had to run out the back road, the poor blackie and - course then there used to be fights in the street and try - trying to get 'em out of the house 'cos there - there was four daughters*

and they was all - at the finish the four 'of 'em was co-habiting you see, with - with these - and they had a - a very old father. [....].[sic]"

"Annie took the others with her to where - to down Dixie - Greengate - to where the blacks lived in all these houses and rooms, you know [...]. I think they all married them any road, all married coloured [...]. Ooh, they was a good looking lot of girls, lovely wavy hair you know[sic]"[5]

Some mixed race Irish couples in Manchester or their children came to wider attention, such as the African performer Prince Lobengula and the boxer Len Johnson.

Prince Lobengula

During the nineteenth century, 'international exhibitions' and 'world fairs' showcasing Britain's culture and industry, both domestically and throughout her colonies and dependencies, became increasingly popular attractions in the country. Growing in popularity after the success of the Great Exhibition in 1851, such events frequently featured displays of 'natives' from around the world, often in mocked up model villages. As Sadiah Qureshi notes, the British public 'flocked to see, among others, groups of Sami, Krenak, Inuit, Anishinaabe, Bakhoje, Zulus, San, Arabs, Pacific Islanders, Aboriginal people, Indians, Japanese, Ndebele, Chinese, and "Aztecs"'. While the recruitment of these 'performers' was rooted in exploitation and exoticisation, working at such events became a profession for many who took part as performers, some of whom went on to settle in Britain and marry local Britons.

As with numerous visits of colonial subjects to Britain in the late Victorian and early Edwardian era, the reaction they caused from white British women caused great consternation amongst the establishment. The 'amorous' interest provoked by the male performers starring in the 'Savage South Africa' exhibition, many appearing in kraal village sets in traditional clothing that showed bare chests and limbs, sent the press into a horrified frenzy. The *Daily Mail* relentlessly campaigned to 'close the kraal' and women were eventually banned from the replica village area.

Lobengula was billed as the show's star attraction, promotional material naming him as 'the redoubtable chieftan warrior who was taken prisoner in the Matabele war'. Handsome and charismatic, and fluent in English, Lobengula became a celebrity overnight, even reportedly sharing champagne with the Prince of Wales during his visit to the show.

93. 'The Landing of Savage South Africa at Southampton', 1899.
Rare footage of the landing can be viewed on the BFI's website.
Image courtesy of the BFI National Archive.

An advertisement below appeared in the *The Graphic* newspaper on 5 August 1899 which reveals the exotic nature of the display of African bodies in the "Savage South Africa" show at the Empress Theatre in London. Peter Lobengula performed in this exhibition:

"SAVAGE SOUTH AFRICA"
in the
EMPRESS THEATRE,
GREATER BRITAIN EXHIBITION.
Depicted by Fillis' Monster Aggregation.
Twice daily, at 3.30 and 8.30.
Thousands of Reserved Seats at 1s., 2s., 3s., 4s., and 5s.
One Thousand Matabele, Basutos, Swazis, Hottentots, Cape and Transvaal Boers, Basuto Ponies, Zebras, Wildebeests, African Lions, Leopards, Tigers, Baboons, Wild Dogs, and a Herd of Elephants.
THE ORIGINAL GWELO STAGE COACH.
WILSON'S HEROIC DEATH AT SHANGANI.
All under Cover.
SEE THE KAFFIR KRAAL, PEOPLED BY 300 NATIVES.

94. 'Savage South Africa'.
The Graphic, 5 August 1899. Image ©Illustrated London News Ltd
and courtesy of The British Library Board. Shelfmark: C.188.c.52.

Attitudes changed, however, when news of Lobengula's relationship with a young white South African woman, Florence 'Kitty' Jewel, came to public attention. This high profile interracial relationship between an African man and a white woman outside of a working-class multicultural community caused a furore.

With Jewel's South African background stirring up fears of the threat of 'Black peril', miscegenation and opposition to white settler rule in the colonies, the press unleashed a torrent of racist invective and hostility towards the couple and their initial attempts to marry were thwarted by the clergy as well as the management of Savage South Africa. After disappearing from the public eye for several months, the pair eventually married in 1900, though the relationship was heavily troubled, with Kitty accusing Lobengula of adultery and cruelty, going on to seek a divorce on these grounds in 1902.

In 1900, the Savage South Africa Show had moved to Salford, where Peter also appeared, and he was initially accompanied by Kitty. By 1901, Lobengula had entered a relationship with Lily Magowan, a redhead from Belfast. The couple married and settled in Salford, where they raised five children. As Qureshi documents, during his married life in Salford, Lobengula found work in traditional working class Mancunian roles, working in a colliery, an iron foundry and finally as a coal miner after his time performing.

In 1913, Lobengula came back into the public eye due to his appearance at Salford Revision Court, where he claimed that he was entitled to vote in local elections as a result of his birthright as Prince Peter Lobengula, the oldest son of King Lobengula of Matabeleland, whose country had been incorporated into the British domains. His vote, initially opposed, was granted, while local press interest in his background revealed that after being denied a pension by the Colonial Office, the family were subsisting on a state pension which Lobengula declared was unfitting for a man of his birth. The local clergy joined the local press in supporting the 'Prince in Poverty' and Lobengula's case was passed to the British South Africa Company, who went to great lengths to refute Lobengula's claim to African royal heritage, asserting that 'the man's story has no shadow of foundation'.

Loben's Courtship

THE old adage which says that the course of true love never did run smooth seems to be exemplified in the strange story that has been revealed bit by bit from Earl's Court. Among the natives forming part of the show called "Savage South Africa" at the Earl's Court Exhibition was the son of Lobengula, known as Peter Kushana Loben. Report said that he had become engaged to an English lady, and that he was shortly to be married. This was subsequently denied, and a letter appeared in *The Daily Graphic* signed by Loben, who, by the way, cannot read, declaring that he had no such intention. The lady to whom he was said to be engaged was Miss Florence Kate Jewell, who is of Jewish extraction and the daughter of a mining engineer of Redruth, Cornwall. She first saw Loben in full war paint at Bloemfontein, and, it is said, fell in love with him on the spot. At Bloemfontein Loben has a farm, to which it was said he was anxious to return with his bride. Loben is twenty-four and Miss Jewell twenty-one years of age. Following rapidly after the denial that there was to be any marriage

MISS FLORENCE K. JEWELL　　　PRINCE LOBENGULA

95. Peter Lobengula and Kitty Jewel.
Portraits taken by Arthur Weston, Newgate. *The Graphic*, 19 August 1899. @Illustrated London News Ltd. Image courtesy of The British Library Board.
Shelfmark: C.188.c.52.

Suffering from tuberculosis, Lobengula died in 1913, insisting to the very end that he was the son of King Lobengula. At his funeral, large crowds lined the streets, the *Manchester Courier and Lancaster General Advertiser* on 28 November 1913 noted that 'many working women followed in procession after the hearse', while 'as the cortege passed the colliery where the dead Matabele had worked, the men raised their caps.' On the morning of his funeral, it was reported that the Reverend Rees, who had performed the ceremony, had received a letter from the daughter of the British cleric, Bishop Colenso, in which she confirmed that Lobengula was indeed the son of the noted king.

Earlier, on Tuesday 25 November 1913, the *Bolton Evening News* noted that Lobengula had just recently lost a child who died of consumption and was also buried by Reverend Rees:

> **PRINCE LOBENGULA DEAD.**
>
> **SON OF MATABELE KING DIES IN POVERTY IN ENGLAND.**
>
> A man, who described himself as Prince Lobengula, a son of King Lobengula of the Matabele, died at Pendleton on Monday. The Rev. S. D. Rees, vicar of St. George's, Pendleton, who has taken a great interest in the man, and recently drew public attention to his plight, dying in abject poverty from consumption, stated on Monday that a letter which appeared last week casting doubt on the prince being a son of the King of the Matabeles evidently came as a shock to him in his weak state of health, and, in Mr. Rees' opinion, hastened the end. "He affirmed to the end to me," says Mr. Rees, "that he was a son of King Lobengula, and I have no reason to doubt the dying man's last words." Mr. Rees wishes to thank the numerous contributors to the fund he has raised on behalf of the Prince and his family. The funeral will take place at Agecroft on Thursday afternoon, and Mr. Rees says it will be one befitting one of the dead man's position. A child of Lobengula's who died from consumption was buried by Mr. Rees last Monday. There remain a widow and three children.

96. Death of Prince Lobengula.
Bolton Evening News, 25 November 1913.
Image @ The British Library Board.
Shelfmark: MFM.M77552.

Lily Lobengula and her surviving four children continued to live in Salford in destitution. Bar one child, the entire family passed away between 1916 and 1920, where they were buried next to Lobengula at Agecroft cemetery.

Len Johnson

Born in Clayton, Manchester in 1902, Len Johnson was a professional middle and light heavyweight boxer who came to prominence in the 1920s and 30s.

97. Painting of Len Johnson by Tam Joseph.
Art studio in Walthamstow, London.
Photograph: David Levene/The Guardian 1 April 2023.
Image @The Guardian. Thanks to Tam Joseph for his kind permission.

His father, William, commonly known as Billy, was a merchant seamen from Sierra Leone who had come to England in 1897, and his mother, Margaret Maher, a local Mancunian woman whose parents were both Irish (William, her father, was from Roscrea, County Tipperary) . In addition to Len, the couple had three other children whom they raised in Manchester, returning to the city at the outbreak of WW1 after a brief stint living in Leeds soon after Johnson was born.

The British artist Tam Joseph, in the picture above, was included in *The Guardian's* Cotton Capital Series in its '*Painting a new pantheon: portrait series honours Black radicals*' section on 1 April 2023. He included a defiant portrait of Len Johnson and as quoted in *The Guardian* article: "he was "thunderstruck" when he heard the story of Johnson and the racist policy that stopped him from having a title shot in Britain. "He looks like a very, very tough-looking fellow but there's a sadness about him – he's up against this thing that he cannot do anything about it." Tam Joseph was born in Dominica where Fr George Paddington from Cork, in Ireland, was its first black Catholic priest.

Spotting Len's boxing talent as a young man, his father, William, who had run a boxing booth during the family's time in Leeds, entered Johnson into local bouts in which he performed so impressively that he would turn professional while still a teenager. Johnson went on to have a successful boxing career that would see him win 92 of his 127 fights, defeating a number of British and European middleweight champions. Yet, despite his years of impressive victories, Johnson would never hold a British or world championship title, despite all the indications that his prowess and boxing record would lead to such an endpoint.

The British Boxing Board of Control (BBBC) which ran boxing, refused to allow Johnson to even enter a championship title fight. The reason? Though a British citizen, as Johnson did not have two white parents, under boxing's 'colour bar' he was excluded from a shot at any title. Fearful of what message would be sent throughout the colonies if black boxers triumphed over white fighters, many establishment figures, such as the Archbishop of Canterbury and Lord Baden-Powell, railed against interracial matches, in particular the proposed 1911 match between the black American heavyweight champion, Jack Johnson and the white British contender, Bombardier Billy Wells. While there was tremendous public appetite for the fight, under establishment pressure, the then Home Secretary Winston Churchill shut the match down. The BBBC would go on to enshrine this 'colour bar' rule in their regulations until 1947, supported by the Home Office who would advise promoters throughout the 1920s and early 1930s not to run high profile interracial matches and would intervene to close them down if necessary.

Thus, though Johnson was a popular fighter, and despite protest from many quarters and controversy, the sporting and political establishment ensured that Johnson was kept on the sidelines. Even when he won the Australian version of the British Empire middleweight title in 1926, he returned to England to discover that, due to the colour bar, the defeated boxer Tommy Milligan had been installed as Empire Champion. Barnett notes that, 'on home turf, a rigorous defence of Len was put forward by local newspapers, particularly the left-leaning *Manchester Evening Chronicle*, which denounced the "foolish" notion that "a man be barred from attaining the highest honours ... merely because he happens to be coloured." Outrage from ordinary Mancunians also led to a protest delegation being sent to the BBBC's London offices.[6]

In the early 1930s, Johnson, suffering health issues and increasingly disillusioned with the racism of the game, retired from boxing. Racism had long had a brutal and grinding effect on his family. Despite the ethnic and racial diversity that could be found in Manchester during Johnson's childhood, the family experienced much hostility and violence. Johnson recalled being called 'n***** lips' and 'Sambo' at school, while his Irish mother Margaret, a pinafore machinist, was facially disfigured after a brutal racist street attack in which she was targeted for being the wife of a black man.

After retirement, Johnson became increasingly politically active in the fight against racism and oppression. Serving in the Civil Defence Corps during the Second World War, he joined the Communist Party of Great Britain in 1944, and acting as a local delegate to the Fifth Pan-African Congress which was held in Manchester. In 1926, Johnson married Annie Forshaw in 1926. Sadly, while he was in the US trying to launch his career, one of their two children became ill and died. The marriage eventually fell apart and Johnson remarried, to a woman called Maria Reid, whose three white children he adopted. Later, when Maria's sister died, the pair would go on to adopt her three children.

After some years in ill health and increasing poverty, Johnson died in 1974. While he was mourned by many sporting fans, as a result of the institutional racism that blighted his career, his legacy as one of Britain's most popular boxing greats has been sadly obscured, though in recent years historians Dr Shirin Hirsch and Geoff Brown have worked hard to restore Johnson to the sporting record. In recent years, the poet SuAndi has worked to preserve the history of the pre and post-World War 2 African community in Manchester, many of whom married white women, including those of Irish descent. The moving memories and histories of these families have been collected into the works *Afro Solo UK* and *Strength of our Mothers*.

Black presence in London - John Archer

In November 1913, John Richard Archer, the son of Richard Archer, a black Barbadian, and Mary Theresa Burns, a white Irish Catholic, was elected mayor of the south London borough of Battersea. Archer was the second black mayor elected in Britain, the first being Allen Glaser Minns, a Bahamian doctor who was elected in Thetford, Norfolk in 1904.[7] Born in Liverpool in 1863, Archer grew up a Catholic and spent much time when a young man travelling the world, finally returning to England in the 1890s with Bertha, his black Canadian wife.

98. John Archer in his mayoral robes c.1913. History and Art Collection. Image @Alamy.

Settling in Battersea, London, he began to take an interest in local politics and established himself in left-wing circles. In 1906, Archer became one of six Battersea borough councillors before making national headlines in 1913 when he was elected mayor of Battersea. A socialist and Pan-Africanist, Archer was also a key player in the black activist movement, working towards a common bond between all people of black origin and the fight for the independence of African nations and racial equality worldwide.

Archer's election to mayor was lauded by many, including Archer, as a progressive moment in British racial relations. Nevertheless, Archer faced racism and prejudice during and after his election. An anonymous letter that had appeared in the *South Western Star* during his campaign expressed concerns 'that the white man should be governed and controlled by a man of colour.' Archer similarly faced opposition from fellow councillors, being elected by a majority of one. Archer's racial background was also the subject of intense interest and his wife Bertha was also reported in several newspapers as the "Coloured Mayoress".

99. Mrs. Archer, a 'Coloured Mayoress'.
Leeds Mercury, 13 November 1913.
Image @ The British Library Board.
Shelfmark: 21714.

The Birmingham Daily Mail reported on 11 November 1913, that, on his selection as Mayor, Archer "declared he was proud to be a man of colour, but having been born at Liverpool he claimed all an Englishman's privileges. His father was born in the West Indies; his mother was Irish. Mr Archer's wife is a coloured lady, and will be the first coloured Mayoress." Earlier, on 7 November 1913 on his nomination, *The Evening News* described Archer as "Burmese with a Canadian-born wife, also coloured" such was the confusion about his ethnicity and about his wife that he commented that photographers "have been particularly troublesome, they have waylaid us at every turn, but I am a photographer myself and well up in the tricks of the trade…I have managed to evade them by climbing the roofs at the back of my garden and stealing over the back garden walls into my own house...I would not be photographed, nor would my wife." The press, and fellow councillors, seemed unaware of the longstanding Liverpool-born black community. Furthermore, there was wild speculation about his racial background, with reports claiming that he was 'Burmese by birth' and likening him to a 'Hindu' or 'Parsee' in appearance. During his election victory speech, a councillor heckled Archer, demanding to know where he was born. Requesting that the councillor show him the same respect that he would show a white man, Archer, employing a good dose of sarcasm regarding his birthplace, firmly set the record straight:

> *'I am the son of a man born in the West Indian Islands. I was born in England, in a little obscure village probably never heard of until now - the city of Liverpool. I am a Lancastrian born and bred. My mother - well, she was my mother. My mother was not born in Rangoon. She was not Burmese. She belonged to one of the grandest races on the face of the earth. My mother was an Irishwoman. So there is not so much of the foreigner about me at all. They have said I am a man of colour. I am. I am proud to be. I would not change my colour if I could.'*

Reporting on Archer's election victory on 11 November 1913, the *Daily Express* front page headline put Archer's race in quotation brackets, reinforcing the questioning of Archer's racial background which he addressed in his speech. The headline read:

"'BLACK' MAYOR OF BATTERSEA

SPEECH IN DEFENCE OF HIS COLOUR AND RACE

WORLD'S RECORD"

Below is an Extract from John Archer's speech, *The Globe*, in 1913. Archer's speech was covered by many leading newspapers.

> 'A remarkable speech was made by Mr. John Richard Archer, the coloured new Mayor of Battersea, after he had been elected by the Progressive vote, which numbers 30 to the Municipal Reformers' 29. Mr. Archer said:—
>
> "It is a victory such as has never been gained before. I am the proud victor. I am a man of colour. Many of the things that have been said about me, however, are absolutely untrue. I have a brother, but I should have to have several for us to be born in as many places as we have been said to have been born in."
>
> "Where were you born?" interjected a councillor.
>
> "I think," said the Mayor, "that at least you ought to show me, after my election, the same respect as you would show a white man. I have been charged with not being of the superior race, and it behoves you now to show that you do belong to the superior race.
>
> ### BORN IN LIVERPOOL.
>
> "I am the son of a man born in the West Indian Islands. I was born in England, in a little obscure village probably never heard of until now—the city of Liverpool. I am a Lancastrian bred and born. My mother—well, she was my mother. My mother was not born in Rangoon. She was not Burmese. She belonged to one of the grandest races on the face of the earth. My mother was an Irishwoman. So there is not so much of the foreigner about me after all.
>
> "They have said I am a man of colour. I am. I am proud to be. I would not change my colour if I could.
>
> "There appeared, however, in the 'South-Western Star' a letter written by a gentleman who claims to represent the majority of the people of Battersea, yet has not the courage to sign his own name. He adopts the nom de guerre of 'True Progressive.' 'It is not meet,' he says, 'that white men should be governed and controlled by a man of colour.'"
>
> "Hear, hear," interjected a councillor.

100. John Archer's speech.
The Globe, 11 November 1913.
Image @ The British Library Board.
Shelfmark: MFM.MC143.

The news about England's 'first' black mayor (a Bahamian doctor was elected mayor of Thetford in 1904!) was widely reported in other newspapers such as the *Yorkshire Telegraph and Star*, which stated that the public gallery of the council chamber was crowded with visitors and a crowd had also gathered outside the building to hear the decision.

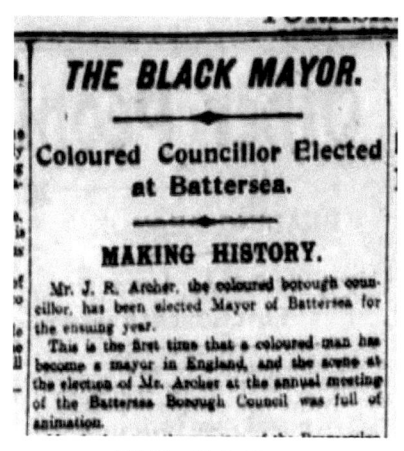

> **THE BLACK MAYOR.**
>
> **Coloured Councillor Elected at Battersea.**
>
> **MAKING HISTORY.**
>
> Mr. J. R. Archer, the coloured borough councillor, has been elected Mayor of Battersea for the ensuing year.
>
> This is the first time that a coloured man has become a mayor in England, and the scene at the election of Mr. Archer at the annual meeting of the Battersea Borough Council was full of animation.

101. The Black Mayor.
Yorkshire Telegraph and Star, 11 November 1913.
Image @ The British Library Board:
Shelfmark: MFM.M5965-8.

At a meeting at Battersea Town Hall one month after his election, Archer spoke of receiving vicious letters attacking his mother 'because she married a man of colour'.

> *"Do you know that I have had letters since I have been Mayor calling my mother some of the foulest names that it is possible for a mother to be called. ("Shame"). Before I was Mayor, I received no opposition on the Council. I have been made to feel my position more than any man who has ever occupied this chair, not because I am a member of the Council, but because I am a man of colour. My dead mother has been called in question because she married a coloured man. ("Shame") Am I not a man, the same as any other man? Have I not got feelings the same as any other? I may be wrong when I come here and meet this opposition, but would not any other man in my position think the opposition was because of his colour? If it's not then I say, as a man, I apologise to you."* - Archer speaking at Battersea Town Hall, Dec. 1913.

Such hostility towards Archer and his mother were very different responses than those received by elite mixed race families, such as the Manders and Stokers. However, racial prejudice did not deter Archer. He served his term as mayor and went on to become a significant figure in the Battersea Labour Party movement until his death in 1932.[8]

James Clarke – a celebrated swimmer in Liverpool

In comparison with official accounts, so many details of the very many personal histories of ordinary mixed race Irish families during the first decades of the twentieth century have been lost or obscured. Efforts to recover such histories, however, reveal fascinating narratives. Ray Costello's work on black history uncovered the account of James Clarke.

102. James Clarke.
Courtesy of Beverley Clarke,
granddaughter.

Clarke was a black Guyanese man who, aged fourteen, stowed away on a ship to Liverpool at the end of the nineteenth century where, after a spell in a Catholic orphanage, he was adopted by an Irish couple.[9]

> *In 1900, the 14 year old boy stowed away on a cargo ship travelling from what was then British Guiana to Liverpool. Arriving in the city, knowing nobody, he soon found himself wandering the streets - until priests from St. Augustine's Church on Great Howard Street came across the hungry and cold teenager and took him in. Soon he was adopted by an Irish family and made his home in the Scottie Road area of Liverpool, an area where today he has a street named after him.*'[10]

James Clarke was born in Georgetown, British Guiana (now

Guyana) in 1886[11] and after landing in Liverpool he was adopted in Liverpool to an Irish family. According to baptism records which we have examined, a Mrs Margaret Lacy accompanied a group of children from 'Shaw Street' in Liverpool to the Church for baptisms at the Holy Cross Church on 24 May 1893 and she is recorded in Latin as the 'Matrina Fuit' (godmother or witness). Clarke appears amongst this group and the adoptive parents are noted as James and Mary Clarke. According to a report by the *Nugent Care Society*, Mrs Lacy was matron of a boy's hostel, she rented on 99 Shaw Street, and she took two parties of destitute children, in her care, to Canada per year. When she died in 1894 it was reported that she had taken 1,911 children out of England and on to other institutions in Canada. In the 1891 census, Margaret Lacy is recorded as being a widow of 40 years and from Ireland. In the census, her employment was reported as a Superintendent of a children's institution at 99 Shaw Street in St Augustine's parish, Everton.

The Liverpool Catholic Children Protection Society was founded in 1881 by Bishop O'Reilly to save the children's "faith by emigrating them under Catholic auspices, as a number were being sent to Canada by Non-Catholic agencies."[12] It would appear Clarke was lucky to have escaped this forced transportation arranged by Mrs Lacy and her Catholic associates. In February 2010, the UK Prime Minister Gordon Brown apologised on behalf of the State for its role in forcibly transporting children in the 1960's to Commonwealth countries.[13] Ironically, Clarke possibly avoided forced transportation due to a colour bar. Nevertheless, he would go on to make an extraordinary contribution to his community in Liverpool.

Clarke became a great swimmer and athlete, and he gave lessons to local children and saved numerous local people from drowning. Liverpudlian author, Billy Woods, who recalled Clarke rescuing a child from the canal remembers him saying in his Liverpudlian accent, 'Luk, a'l av teh ger -on back 'ome an get some dry clobber on. Dis is der second time dis as 'appened to me - dis week. - Deh missus will go bonkers.' In a newspaper article in 1910 it was reported, from the Galal at Runcorn Baths, that 'James Clarke, a Negro, from British Guiana, swam two lengths by means of the peculiar "African crawl" stroke, and received loud applause.'[14]

Clarke married Elizabeth Murphy, who, like his adoptive family, was from a family of Irish descent. The pair had several children, the eldest two, Elizabeth and James, being born in the years before and after the 1919 riots. As a dock labourer, Clarke would likely have been acutely aware of the tensions of the time, but it is unknown to what extent, if any, he and his family were caught up in or affected by the violence. Costello notes that Clarke died just after the Second World War, and his popularity in the community was such that people lined the street leading to the church.

The 1919 riots and their aftermath

As a dock worker working in Liverpool after the First World War, James Clarke, would have felt rising racial tensions among British workers occurring at ports around the country. The article below shows the scale of the riots reported in the news:

WILD SCENES IN WALES.

TWO MEN KILLED IN CARDIFF RIOT.

Baton Charges Against Mob At Newport.

Two Deaths In Conflict With Police At Genoa.

A further outbreak of the racial riots at Cardiff resulted in two more deaths and a large number of people being injured.

The riots are the outcome of the association of European women of a low type with negroes, and the belief held by demobilised service men that the negroes are holding jobs which they should fill.

Melees occurred in the Bute Street district and at the Great Western Railway Station, and in Millicent Street a coloured man's boarding-house was set on fire.

Jack Donovan, aged forty, a Mons veteran, was killed, shot through the heart. Another white man, Robert Hooks (47) had his skull fractured, and is reported dying.

Four Arabs were also admitted to hospital, one with such severe injuries that he died after an operation.

MONS HERO SHOT DEAD

IN SIEGE OF COLOURED MAN'S HOUSE.

Woman With Razor for a Weapon.

Scenes resembling the famous siege of Sidney Street occurred in Cardiff, when rioting arising out of antipathy to the coloured men was renewed.

Two more deaths, making four during the two days' outbreak, resulted from the fighting. One of the victims was a white man, an ex-soldier, and the other an Arab.

Shot Through the Heart.

Jack Donovan, aged 40, of Union Street, a veteran of Mons, was killed. Another white man, Robert Hooks (47), was admitted to hospital with a fractured skull, and is reported dying. Four Arabs were also admitted, one with severe head injuries. He died after an operation. The police made numerous arrests.

Donovan was shot through the heart, and died after removal to hospital. The police came up and entered the house, one receiving a shot through the helmet and another a bullet through his cape, while others sustained slight injuries from stones. They arrested the occupants, one of whom in the melée received a severe blow on the head.

Siege of a House.

Another account states:—

For three hours the riots raged in the Bute Street area. In all fifteen people are now lying in hospital, two of these being cases of fractured skulls.

103. Wild Scenes in Wales in 1919
The Courier and Argus, 14 June 1919.
Image @ DC Thomson Co. Ltd and courtesy of
The British Library Board. Shelfmark: BLL01013909380.

The growing apprehensions about racial mixing that had occurred during the years of the First World War escalated even further during peacetime. In 1919, in the wake of the demobilisation of First World War service personnel, a series of violent disturbances targeting black, Arab and other minorities occurred in nine of Britain's main ports leaving five dead, four of whom were black men, and homes and properties vandalised.

See the artist's impression below, of the race riots in Cardiff. The final panel depicts police 'searching for n******s' in a bedroom of half dressed women, drawing on the now ingrained imagery suggesting a link between men of colour and immoral white women.

104. Racial Riots in Cardiff. Sensational Scenes.
Illustrated Police News, 19 June 1919.
Courtesy of the British Library Board, successor rightsholder unknown.

The riots were blamed not only on anger and resentment at 'coloured' men 'taking' white men's jobs but also 'their' women, some of whom were also targeted.[15] In East London, the white wife of a Chinese man and her white friend were 'badly mauled by the infuriated crowd' who 'assailed the premises' she was hiding in on learning that they had been rented to her and her husband. In Newport, a woman named Martiniaz gave evidence that another woman had 'shouted at her, "You ought to be burned", because she was a black's wife', while Jacqueline Jenkinson notes that one of the white female rioters arrested in Liverpool was reported to have screamed: 'now's the time to finish the n*****s'[16] wives.

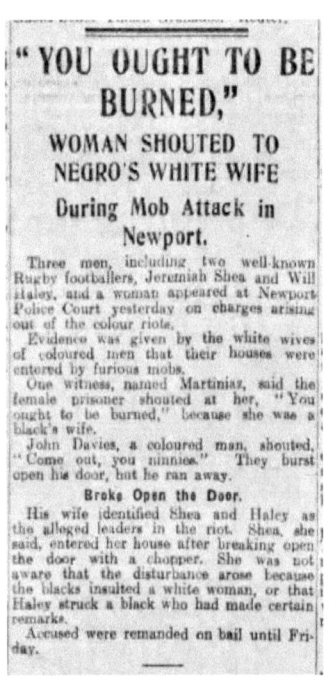

105. 'You Ought to be Burned'
Dundee Courier, 17 June 1919.
Image @ DC Thomson & Co Ltd, and courtesy of The British Library Board.
Shelfmark: 013909380.

The media, police officials and other dignitaries, such as the former British colonial administrator, Sir Ralph Williams, blamed these interracial relationships for causing the violence, with Williams writing to *The Times* on 14 June 1919, in the Letters to the Editor, that "sexual relations between white women and coloured men revolt our very nature…What blame…to those white men who, seeing the conditions and loathing them, resort to violence?" He ended his letter by stating:

> *We cannot forcibly repatriate British subjects of good character, but we can provide that every black or coloured unit is forthwith sent back to its own country, and we can take such steps as will prevent the employment of an unusually large number of men of colour in our great shipping centres…I know that I am expressing the views of the vast majority of British white men and women who have passed much of their lives in association with coloured and black races. The evil should be ended.*
> *Yours faithfully, Ralph Williams.*
> *St James Club, London, June 12.'*

In the aftermath of the violence, the repatriation scheme previously initiated by the government to deal with the high unemployment levels of black colonials who had worked or served in the forces during the war was now extended to black workers and their families, regardless of their longevity in Britain.

Interested by the promise of costs covered to leave an increasingly angry and impoverished Britain, some black seamen applied for the scheme. However, those with white wives came up against government fears about the implications of white women visibly married or partnered to black men in the colonies and in numerous cases such applications were blocked. Jenkinson notes that one such family were Norton James, a Saint Lucian, and his partner, later wife, Sarah Battersby from County Down, Ireland. The pair, who met in Cardiff and had a child together and another on the way, were refused permission to relocate to St. Lucia via the repatriation scheme:

> *'His Lordship [the Colonial Secretary] considers it would be useless to consult the Colonial Government regarding the question of her admission to St. Lucia: and I am to suggest that her application for a passage should be refused forthwith.'* - In Jenkinson, J. (1987). [17]

Racial tensions persisted throughout the 1920s in cities across Britain, with sporadic flares of violence as well as a widespread, deeply hostile tone to the racial mixing that was occurring in the country. The shoots of concern and condemnation that had been glimpsed in public debate in the late nineteenth and early twentieth centuries. This condemnation rapidly grew under economic stresses as well as growing social concerns, including the visible presence of men of colour in Britain and the degeneracy and immorality of the young, particularly young white women. National and local newspapers railed against the racial mixing that was occurring not just in dockland communities but across the country under lurid headlines such as 'SOCIAL CANKER'…. 'SPREADING COLONY OF NEGROES' …. 'THE PREY OF BLACK MEN'. In response to this perceived outrage, the police and courts cracked down heavily on clubs, cafés and other establishments, which were felt to facilitate interracial mixing drawing on a range of laws to issue fines and even deport men of colour. Yet as no laws existed against interracial relationships in Britain, such acts were virtually meaningless in preventing racial mixing and couples continued to cross the racial boundary, despite the increasing social opprobrium towards them.

Given the patterns of mixing in portside communities, it is likely that many of the couples or families caught up in the riots or reported on by the press during the 1920s were made up of men of colour and women who were Irish or of Irish descent. This was certainly the case in Liverpool. One newspaper article, dismissively reporting on the effect of seeing their black husbands being taken into police custody for their own protection. See the extract below from *The Yorkshire Evening Post* in 1919 tilted 'Black and White Tragedies' which refers to an Irish wife of a black man:

> '*Undoubtedly many of the white wives of black men in Liverpool are eminently contented with their marital choice, and the "rounding up" the negros by the police for their own protection led to some emotional scenes. A typical case was that of a dejected little family party. A well dressed negro was being led away by a policeman. He was carrying in his arms a little white child, and his English wife followed, evidently much concerned. In another case tow negros had been detained at a bridewell without their white wives' knowledge, and the two women – one unquestionably Irish – made a scene in the street in their anxiety, threatening to do personal violence to themselves if their husbands had come to any harm.*' [18]

In his autobiography *Liverpool Slummy*, Pat O'Mara, who was born in Liverpool in 1901 to an Irish family, recalls growing up in a community in which mixing, particularly between West African or Chinese men and Irish women, was the norm.[19] He remarks that many mixed race Liverpudlians he knew were 'one of the many offshoots of West African Negro-Irish wife combinations' that were commonplace in the area, such as Mary Ellen Grant, who O'Mara describes as a 'tough', 'shrewd' moneylender known as 'the Connaught N****r'.

O'Mara also remarks that not only were West African and Chinese men, the majority of whom were sailors, accepted by white women as equals but 'many times they were considered the white man's superior', a sentiment O'Mara puts down to economics: 'much better,' he said the women reasoned, 'to put up with a Negro three months in the year (while drawing his steady salary), than to marry a young dock walloper and be continually starved and beaten.' Local attitudes towards such families, O'Mara notes, varied. 'Some families, like my mother's, abhorred the practice of inter-marriage, but it was so prevalent that they had to keep their beliefs to themselves. There were others who had great pride in our coloured neighbours.'

O'Mara includes several anecdotes about mixed race Irish couples or people. These include the story of 'Galley Johnson', who O'Mara calls a 'repulsive-looking old Negro' who had had two Irish wives: Mollie McGuire, his wife of twenty years with whom he had seven children, and after her death, a much younger woman named Maggie McCoy who left Johnson when he decided to abandon his life at sea and open a boarding house. Another tale involves Bridgett Hylands, newly migrated from Connaught who defied her father to marry Joe 'Black' Diamond and then moved to Cardiff to open 'a Negro boarding house'.

Irish-Chinese families in Britain

Concerns about racial mixing in Britain in the early decades of the twentieth century were not confined to black men and white women. Despite its small number, there also emerged a feverish fascination with the Chinese population in Britain during this time, particularly the dangers that Chinese men were felt to present to white women.[20]

Although there had been a handful of Chinese visitors to Britain from the seventeenth century onwards, it was not until the nineteenth century that Chinese seafarers, employed and accommodated by the

East India Company, were firstly a familiar sight and then residents of British port areas. Similarly, in Liverpool, the small settled Chinese community was bolstered from the 1890s through the employment and boarding of Chinese seamen by Alfred Holt and Company's large shipping subsidiary, the Blue Funnel Line. In both London and Liverpool, numerous Chinese seamen jumped ship and settled in the dockland areas, setting up shops, cafés and boarding houses catering to Chinese sailors.[21] By the 1890s, the Chinese-born population of London was thought to be around 300, with most settling in the streets within the Limehouse and Pennywell vicinity, while in Liverpool, the Chinese population, also estimated in the low hundreds in the 1890s, was mostly settled around Cleveland Square, Pitt Street and Frederick Street. Although these areas came to be known as 'Chinatown', in reality they were multiracial enclaves with Chinese populations living alongside other people of colour as well as white people. Like other men of colour, many Chinese also started relationships with white women.[22] The escapades and eventual marriage of opium den owners Achi and 'Canton Kitty', herself quite possibly of Irish background given her first name, can be seen from the extract from the *Penny Illustrated Paper* below:

> On Certain Occasions East End girls who have tried opium and succumbed have gone into partnership with owners of these places, and have earned such names as "Canton Kitty," "Lascar Sally," or "Chinese Emma."—A refreshing incident is related how on one occasion the owner of the name of "Canton Kitty," who had for a long time shared a den with a Chinaman named "Achi," decided to reform, so had the banns put up and married the Celestial. They then said good-bye to all their old associates, and left England as steward and stewardess on board a steamer running to New York.   D. C.

106. "Canton Kitty" and "Lascar Sally"
The Penny Illustrated Paper, 22 August 1896.
Image @ The British Library Board,
Shelfmark: MFM.M40510.

From the outset, relationships between Chinese men and white women attracted attention. In 1817, a parliamentary committee disapprovingly noted the presence of foreign seamen, such as 'Lascars, Chinese, Greek and other filthy people of that description', in Shadwell, in the East End of London. The committee also noted 'that the women of that Town never cohabit with any other than that description of people.' With very few Chinese women in Britain throughout the nineteenth century, unsurprisingly relationships between Chinese men and white women were commonplace, as many Victorian commentators noted. The lives of the Chinese men and the women they partnered were highlighted in the accounts of social investigators, journalists and novelists. They reported an exotic, alien world of gambling and opium dealing, inhabited by numerous white women. Some of these women, as *The Penny Illustrated Paper* remarked on page 166, had 'succumbed' to opium and ran the trade with Chinese men.

The marriage of Canton Kitty and Achi was first reported by the missionary Joseph Salter in his book *The East in the West; or, Work among the Asiatics and Africans in London*, and was also covered widely by the press, see below:

AMONG EAST END ASIATICS AND AFRICANS.
LIFE IN OPIUM DENS AND GAMBLING HOUSES.

Mr. Henry Morris, late of the Madras Civil Service, contributes a preface to a little book by Mr. J. Salter, a London City Missionary, entitled "The East in the West; or, Work among the Asiatics and Africans in London" (Partridge). For a number of years Mr. Salter has laboured among the Orientals who visit the Thames, and in the book he gives an interesting account of his experiences.

"Canton Kitty" and Achi.

Although of late years a great improvement has taken place, opium dens still exist in the East End. One of the most important houses of this kind at one time in the neighbourhood of Tiger Bay was Achi's. The first floor was reserved for opium-smokers; the room above was the gambler's resort; and it was also well known that spurious coins were issued from the establishment. Associated with Achi in the management of the house was Mrs. Achi:—

Mrs. Achi bore the sobriquet of "Canton Kitty," and was the rival of the notorious Chinese Emma, who aided Apoo in a business of the same nature. Kitty was manageable when sober, but when under the influence of drink she became a perfect fury. Her life was often in danger from her own misconduct and passion. If a Celestial was robbed in the opium-smoking room or cheated in the gambling room, Kitty would enter into the tumult like a storm-bird. Then knives would be drawn, blood made to flow, and even life has been taken.

Kitty used to tell the missionary that "the devil was not so black as he is painted," by which she meant that she was better than these paroxysms of passion suggested. And so it turned out.

A New Leaf.

One day the word went like wildfire round the locality that "Canton Kitty" and Achi had put up the banns, and were going to be married in regular form! It was averred, moreover, that "Kitty" now talked "like a saint," and had been heard to declare that she and Achi were determined to quit their old mode of life; and so it proved:—

The unusual marriage caused no small sensation, and was duly celebrated by all the rough melody the locality could provide. But, what was most surprising, Kitty was not drunk on this important occasion, nor did she in any way provoke the discordant noises; she had ceased to be the petrel in the storm. The scene, in all the circumstances, was most impressive. Prayer was offered in the now quiet gambling room for a blessing on the newly-married pair. The thoroughness of the change that had come over these two was proved by the total collapse of the opium-smoking and gambling dens. "Take these things away," said Kitty, as she handed over the cards, dice, and other such implements of her late calling. "They have been a curse to me, and I'll have no more to do with them."

Later Kitty and Achi left England as steward and stewardess on a steamer for New York. What their subsequent history has been does not appear.

107. 'Among East End Asiatics and Africans'. *Westminster Gazette*, 21 April 1896. Image @ The British Library. Shelfmark: MFM.MLD31.

The Westminster Gazette was one of several outlets that reported amusedly in 1896 on the notorious Kitty, said to be 'a perfect fury' under the influence of drink, and her sudden abandonment of violence and opium dealing for a new life with Achi in New York.

'The Wedding Procession of Canton Kitty and Achi' is depicted below in the illustration from *The East in the West; or, Work among the Asiatics and Africans in London* by Joseph Salter, 1895.

108. Wedding Procession of Canton Kitty.
The East in the West; or, Work among the Asiatics and Africans in London' by Joseph Salter, 1895.
Courtesy of the British Library Board.
Shelfmark: 4192.bbb.48.

For the most part, attitudes towards the relationships between white women and Chinese men in the years leading up to and just after the turn of the twentieth century were relatively benign. Even the somewhat smirking and patronising attitudes towards the Chinese community and the white wives of Limehouse, and other portside areas, belied a level of nonchalance about the racial mixing occurring there. George Wade's 1900 article 'Cockney John Chinaman' for the *English Illustrated Magazine*, greatly cited by the national and local press, contains no open hostility to such liaisons. Indeed, while 'John Chinaman' was perceived as a curious oddity, and the 'ladies' who married him were considered of dubious morality, Wade and other commentators often conceded that he was nevertheless renowned as making a good husband and father.

As more widely with racial mixing in Britain, many of the white wives discussed during this time were Irish or of Irish descent. In his observations of Limehouse, Wade noted:

> *"I had the pleasure of seeing, while pursuing my researches in this neighbourhood, a voluble Irishwoman who had, in the first case, had for her husband a son of Erin, and then, on his decease, had taken, "for better or worse," a Chinaman. She assured me that she much preferred the second husband to the first; and, indeed, as she still keeps about the locality, though again a widow, there is once more an opportunity for any Celestial who desires to make Ireland have one injustice the less!"*

However, as the twentieth century unfolded, attitudes began to change. In many quarters, the Chinese were increasingly seen as part of a sinister 'Yellow Peril', a looming threat of swarming East Asian hordes gearing up to engulf and destroy the 'civilized' West, militarily, economically, morally and socially. In the lead up to the First World War, their touted propensity for and appeal to white British women began more and more to be viewed in these terms. The earlier nonchalant tolerance of the press towards 'John Chinaman' was replaced by a growing vilification. 'Yellow Peril' imagery was furiously invoked in the increasing warnings to the public of the dangers of the Oriental, particularly in relation to white women. *The London Magazine* published an excoriating 'exposé' in 1911 entitled 'The Chinese in Britain: A Growing National Problem', in which it was claimed that Oriental dominion of the West was being plotted in the Chinese 'lairs' of London, Liverpool and Cardiff, where young white women were tempted into unsavoury unions, the 'exotic charm' of the Chinese overcoming 'their instinctive repugnance to a race of alien blood and colour', and thus threatening 'the purity of the Anglo-Saxon blood.'[23]

The arts too reflected these growing concerns, with lurid depictions of Limehouse, in particular, as portrayed in the fiction of Sax Rohmer's *The Mystery of Fu Manchu* (1913) and Thomas Burke's *Limehouse Nights* (1916), or D.W. Griffiths' silent film *Broken Blossoms* (1919), as a multiracial, vice-ridden den of iniquity where white working-class women were corrupted, exploited or leered over by Chinese men.

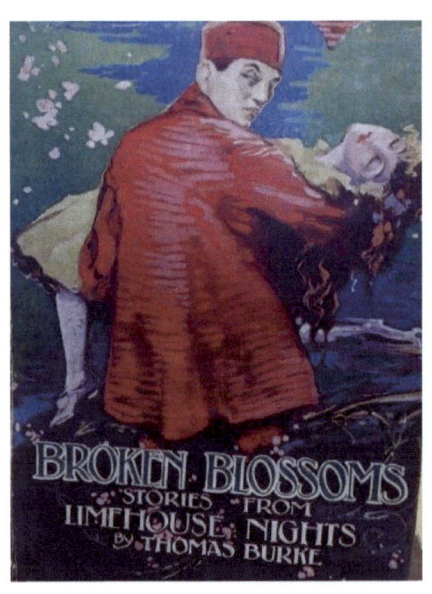

109. Cover of *Limehouse Nights* (1920).
Image courtesy of London Fictions and The British Library. Shelfmark: 012603.f.5.

Post the 1919 race riots, such depictions became even more entrenched. In the early 1920s, the Metropolitan Magistrate at the Thames Police Court, Mr J.A.R. Cairns, habitually condemned the racial mixing between white women and Chinese and other men of colour in Limehouse as the 'greatest problem' he had to face at the court. Meanwhile, drawn by its exotic and dangerous reputation, the white middle classes, including 'respectable' women, were increasingly finding their way to Limehouse seeking gambling, drugs and thrills, with the press frequently putting the blame for this sign of the physical and moral decline of young Britons firmly at the feet of people of colour, not least the Chinese.

'What is the "Yellow Lure?"' shrieked the *Western Daily Press* in a feverish article in 1922 excoriating the moral decay caused by the Chinese quarters of Liverpool, Glasgow and Cardiff but most of all the 'canker' of Limehouse.[24] See the extract below:

> *'SOCIAL CANKER. The Limehouse "Chinatown" is to-day not only a canker in our own social life but an ulcerous plague-spot the very heart of the Empire. The cheapening of white women amongst the Asiatics must have its inevitable results in the far-flung corners of our vast dominions, results which those who have lived the East shudder to contemplate.*
>
> *This state of affairs must be stopped! It must be stopped, and stopped at once, not only for the sake of those white girls who are being led into ways of unspeakable depravity by black and yellow men, but for the sake of the wives and mothers of our Imperial outposts whose honour and lives are being horribly threatened by the undermining of the respect the Asiatic has hitherto had for the white woman.*
>
> *To a lesser degree the Chinese quarters of Liverpool, Glasgow, and Cardiff share in the blame; but they are but as grey smudges beside the blackness London's Chinatown.*
>
> *If the aspect of the sorry business with which this exposure opened was only side of it, the canker might easily be eradicated. If it were only that a few girls were choosing to live as the unmarried wives of more or less respectable Chinamen the police and social workers would not despair as they are.*
>
> *A very short time spent in Pennyfields, Limehouse Causeway, and the neighbourhood, fills the investigator with horror and disgust. He sees girls, white girls, of all ages, but most of them pitifully young, consorting with Chinamen, Japanese, and men of colour. Many of these girls look though they belong to the "typist" class, and others are obviously factory workers. One and all seem devoid of shame.'*

-- 'London's Dark Side: Dangers of Its East End Chinatown', *Western Daily Press*, 21 August 1922.

Limehouse, and the racial mixing in Britain the area had come to represent, was becoming increasingly exoticised in the popular imagination. Earlier depictions of the Chinese as good working-class husbands and fathers, with normalised working class families, were now the exception. Yet, there was some challenge to these exoticised stereotypes. In 1920, The *Daily Telegraph* rebutted the lurid portrayals of Limehouse degeneracy and opium dens as stemming from 'vivid imagination and kinema [sic] pictures' rather than actual knowledge, while in the same year, the *Daily Graphic* gave voice to infuriated Chinese residents of Pennyfields, one of whom stated bluntly that there was 'a great deal of nonsense talked about yellow men and white women. The facts are very simple. Some of our men, steady and hard-working people, have married white women, and have been very happy and contented with them.' There were even measured counter voices to be found in fiction - such as Lao She's 1929 novel *Mr Ma and Son* which Anne Witchard describes as directly confronting the popular Sinophobia endemic in British society at the time, not least 'the pernicious effects' of the media on the lives of the Chinese.

Particularly striking, given the author's tendency to stereotyping and exoticisation elsewhere, is a 1924 short story 'Chingie'. Part of a collection called *Pong Ho* by the Australian-born author Dorota Flatau, a prolific and popular novelist during the 1920s and 1930s, the story recounts the adventures of 'Chingie', a Chinese-Irish boy in the East End of London who tries to evade the school bully by invoking stereotypes of Chinese mysticism and martial arts powers to keep his abuser at bay. Eventually caught out in his lies and exposing his lack of superpowers, 'Chingie' prepares himself to take a beating when a sudden turn of events sees him saving his bully's little brother and thus becoming his previous tormentor's firm friend. Unusual in its depiction of the ordinariness of its mixed race character, the story also stands out for its non-demeaning focus on the Irish, as well as the Chinese, heritage of its protagonist. See extract from the book 'Chingie', 1924 below:

> *"'What's the matter wid yer, Patsy; are ye feelin' ill now?" asked Chingie's Irish mother of whom he had spoken, on the following morning, for she had never known her son so silent.*
>
> *"Nothin' ain't the matter wiv me; but I wished I'd a-killed Screamy's mover," he sighed wistfully.*

"Whist now, ye murderin' villain you! For why would you be wantin' to harrum the poor woman?"

"She 'it me." Chingie looked up as he spoke; in his slant eyes was hope that perhaps his fond parent would be indignant at the treatment her son had received, her fighting blood might be roused, and then she could kill the Italian woman for him, and so save his reputation among his schoolfellows.

But alas for Chingie's hopes!

"Sure now, oi don't doubt ye deserved it," said the callous Mrs. Ching Hi; *"and think black shame to yerself, Patrick, havin' such a thought about a woman. If iver oi hear of ye liftin' yer hand agin a woman oi'll larn ye, so you just watch out, me foine feller!"* she added warmly.

Then she hustled him off to school; but now Chingie had gained an inspiration from his mother's words. He no longer feared to meet his schoolfellows; he had an answer ready for them if they asked pertinent questions, which they did as soon as he turned into Dingle Lane.'

Moral concern over mixed race children in the 1930s

In the early twentieth century, negative attitudes towards those of mixed race began to crystallise and harden into a pathological approach. Such attitudes were given credence by a slew of official, media and 'scientific' reports and investigations that disparaged the 'rise' of mixed race children in portside communities, including those with Irish mothers. On 18 March 1930 the *Daily Express* newspaper included an article with the following headline:

> "THE STREET OF HOPELESS
> CHILDREN
> ---------------
> NO PROSPECT OF
> HONEST
> WORK"
> --------

The *Daily Express* article painted a bleak portrait of the mixed race children living in Canning Town, East London:

> *"Poor little half-castes, looked down and jeered at from their childhood upwards [...] launched while still in their teens upon a life barren of almost everything but dirt, disease and despair, without race, with no country that they can call their own."*

110. Image of Crown Street children, 1930.
Copyright and reproduced under licence from
Mary Evans Picture Library.

The above photo is the original of that which appeared in the *Daily Express*'s 'The Street of Hopeless Children' article. In the article, the white children, who had clearly been socialising with the others, had mostly been cropped out of the photo that appeared in the newspaper. This was a group of working class children, black and white, playing together on Crown Street in Canning Town, London, E16.

Prior to the twentieth century, stereotyping and prejudice towards mixed race people in British thought was already firmly in place. While in the eighteenth century, the presence of 'Eurasians', those of mixed race descent in South Asia, had initially been seen as a positive way to unite British and Indian cultures, such populations were increasingly disparaged as attitudes towards racial difference hardened during the nineteenth century.

The subject of 'race mixture' was of great interest to nineteenth century scholars who argued vociferously over whether the races were one species or separate species. Some in the latter group proclaimed that, like mules, racially mixed people ('mulattoes') were inherently infertile. Others argued that though racial mixing was possible, it was not sustainable or desirable. It was mostly held that racially mixed people displayed 'hybrid degeneration', rather than 'hybrid vigour', where they combined the best physical and mental features of both parent groups. Instead, they were viewed as being physically weaker than their minority parent group and less intelligent than their white parent group.

The mixed race populations to be found across Britain's colonies were also considered highly problematic from a societal perspective. Often conceived through coercion, the children - usually born to white fathers and women of colour - were seen as unwelcome evidence of the crossing of racial boundaries and thus a problematic challenge to notions of whiteness, nation, citizenship and Empire. Viewed frequently as 'neither fish nor fowl', they were increasingly stigmatised as simultaneously problematic and tragic on numerous levels, including mentally, physically and socially. Depictions of the beautiful and sexually alluring but weak, unstable and marginalised 'tragic Eurasian' and 'tragic mulatto' were a common feature in late Victorian exotic romance novels as well as in the press.

By the end of the 1920s, however, the growing visibility of racial mixing in Britain began to turn attention to the 'issue' of mixed race children within the country, with endless newspaper articles decrying the presence of 'half-castes' in Britain's cities. 'Hundreds of half-caste children with vicious tendencies' were 'growing up in Cardiff as the result of black men mating with white women' declared the *Daily Herald* in 1929, whilst in 1930 the *Evening News* agonised over the plight of the Anglo/Irish-Chinese 'half-castes' of London's East End: "...the boys find work hard to get, and the girls drift about the streets ostracised by white girls of their own age. They, and not the white wives, are the broken blossoms." That same year, the *Daily Express* ran the article entitled 'The Street of Hopeless Children' referred to on page 171 and 172.

See the extract below from an article discussing the merits of the 'half-caste wives' of English, Irish and Scottish soldiers in India, drawing on growing stereotypes as mixed race women as 'pretty', but 'passionate' and 'vindictive'.

> **SOLDIERS WIVES IN INDIA.**
>
> The only European troops at Sukkur, besides our corps, was a company of horse artillery, who were as dissolute a body of men as I ever met with, and nearly an eqitable mixture of English, Irish, and Scotch. A few of them had very pretty half-caste wives, whom they got out of the Byculla Orphan school at Bombay, where any soldier of good character and possessed of capital to commence house-keeping, may obtain a helpmate.— These girls are tolerably well-educated, and would make grateful and affectionate wives, were it not that soldiers in general make such husbands. For a while after marriage they may get on pretty well, but they soon become negligent, and return to their berths. Half-caste women are almost invariably passionate and vindictive, readily offended, especially if they think that it is offered in consequence of their colour; and hence they view the indifference of their European husbands in the worst possible light—neglect their household duties, as a matter of course; and will soon learn to drink, and smoke the hookah all day long if they can; becoming slatterns in every sense of the word. It must, however, be admitted

111. Soldiers Wives in India.
The Cork Examiner, 27 September 1847.
Image @ The British Library Board. Shelfmark: MFM.M400.

Studies and Investigations – The Fletcher Report

Such attitudes were given credence by a slew of academic and local official investigations into racial mixing and other issues resulting from the country's 'colour problem'. On the urging of the Eugenics Society in 1924 to help 'investigate families of mated Chinese and English (or Irish)', Herbert Fleure and Rachel Fleming from University College, Aberystwyth conducted a series of anthropometric studies on children with Chinese and then later black fathers in Liverpool, Cardiff and East London, measuring skulls and recording head, nose, ear and eye shapes as well as observing skin and eye colour and hair texture.[25] Though their work shied away from investigating the psychology of the children, Fleure and Fleming's findings reinforced ideas that the children were 'foreign', noting that 5 per cent 'might have passed as English'.

In response to Fleming and Fleure's findings, the Liverpool Association for the Welfare of Half-Caste Children was founded to conduct research into this 'serious problem' and Muriel Fletcher, a social work graduate from the University of Liverpool, was commissioned to undertake the investigation. Fletcher did not concern herself with the biological effects of race mixing but was outspoken on its social consequences, particularly for what she termed the 'Anglo-Negroid Cross'. Her report, published in 1930, was damning. In addition to its salacious and judgemental commentary about the relationships between black men and white women, many of whom were Irish or of Irish descent, it concluded that the offspring of such alliances not only suffered from inherent physical and mental defects and an antipathy to work, but were also socially outcast. Therefore, she concluded:

> *'The children find their lives full of conflict both within themselves and within the family, and all the circumstances of their lives tend to give undue prominence to sex. These families have a low standard of life, morally and economically, and there appears to be little future for the children'.*

A measure of Fletcher's derogatory language can be discerned from the words she used, including multiple references to 'aliens', 'brothels', 'illegitimacy', 'infectious diseases', 'prostitutes', 'skin colour', 'syphilis', 'unemployment' and 'venereal disease' as well as descriptors such as 'immoral', 'lazy', 'presumptuous' and 'promiscuous', amongst others.

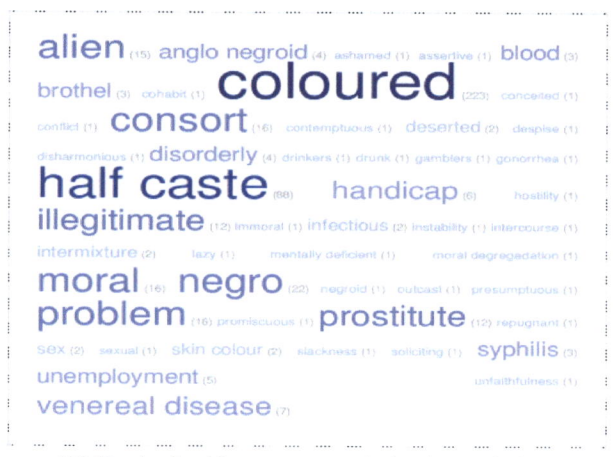

112. Tag cloud and frequency count of pejorative terminology used in the 1930 Fletcher Report, from Caballero and Aspinall, 2018.

This perspective was reinforced further by a 1934 report by Captain Richardson, commissioned by the Joint Committee of the British Social Hygiene Council, which castigated the poor hygiene and morality of the 'coloured men' and white women that had brought a 'tragic' 'half-caste population' into the world. Richardson's report was widely circulated and covered in the press. As with Fletcher's and other local reports into 'the colour problem' and 'half-caste' children in Britain's ports, it contributed to ingraining of the term 'half-caste' as a synonym for an excluded and outcast racialised group associated with immoral behaviour, psychological issues and of low socio-economic worth. Moreover, with the endless focus on 'children', there was no recognition that mixed race people had been present in Britain for centuries, such works also contributed to the infantilisation of this group who were presented as an exotic problem, rather than as ordinary British citizens.

The reports by Fletcher and Richardson did not go unchallenged; Mark Christian notes that Fletcher was 'stabbed' and driven out of Liverpool by a furious community,[26] while men of colour and their white wives in Cardiff firmly rebutted Richardson's report which 'distorted facts to make a sensation.' An article called 'Coloured Folk Attack Official Report' in *The Western Daily Mail on 9 July 1935* reported the following:

> *'Nothing was more freely discussed, especially among coloured folk, in the Docks area of Cardiff ... than the report published ... by Captain F. A. Richardson, R.N. on "Social Conditions in Ports," in which he made allegations against coloured people in the city.*
> *White women many of them the wives of coloured men, attacked the report and stoutly challenged its conclusions. Mr. C.R. Phillips, secretary to the Cardiff branch of the League of Coloured Peoples, told a Western Mail and South news reporter that no action had yet been contemplated. He added, however, that the branch took exception to the report. "As in most things," he said, "the report is true in parts. But among the white population of the city there are similar problems. Captain Richardson is talking non-sense when he asserts that coloured men prefer to remain at home on the dole than working. We like life too much to fritter it away in idleness. I do not want to add fuel to the flames of controversy, but I must state firmly that Captain Richardson has distorted facts to make a sensation."*
> *Loyal Citizens – insulted- "He has insulted men loyal to the empire.*

I cannot believe that his views are those of responsible people, or I should despair of my fellow-citizens of the Empire, whatever their colour. Asked whether immorality was rife among women in the wards, he replied: no more than anywhere else. The coloured women here are in much the same position as white women in Africa or the East. They are the centres of attraction by men of their race, but to impugn their morality is a senseless and insulting misconstruction of an obvious fact." [27]

Retrospective accounts in oral histories also challenge the official accounts of racial mixing in 1920s and 1930s dockland communities. Amongst those who had been part of Fleming's 'race crossing' study in the interwar years, was Connie Hoe, the daughter of a Chinese father and a white British mother who, along with her husband, Leslie Hoe, of mixed Chinese and Irish heritage, has spoken extensively about her experiences growing up in London's Limehouse in the 1930s. The Hoes' recollections highlight an everyday world far removed from the picture of their communities painted by eugenicists and other officials.

"LESLIE: [Limehouse] was a place where there was cobblers, hairdressers, all Chinese restaurants. Eventually, these men must have married English women…and we are the result. [28]

LESLIE: [Connie] used to read these sordid accounts in these two-penny magazines…and this is the thing—she used to look for all this and couldn't find it! [Laughs] We used to think there must be something going on here, why don't they let us in on it?" [29]

South Asian Presence in Early 20th Century Britain

The history of Indians in Britain, alongside other groups from South Asia, is also one with longstanding roots. As was also the case in Ireland, the presence of the East India Company in India provoked patterns of migration not only from Britain to India but also vice versa. In the eighteenth century, 'lascars', the term given to sailors from the Indian subcontinent as well as other parts of Asia and Arabian states, were frequently employed to work on East India Company ships. Sometimes stranded after journeys or simply jumping ship, many ended up settling in Britain. Similarly, a number of domestic servants who accompanied wealthy families back to Britain and Ireland also ended up staying, either through other employment options or, again, abandonment. Furthermore, as with the West Indian planter class, the 'Eurasian' children of Irish and British soldiers were occasionally sent to Britain to be educated, as too were those from wealthy Indian families.[30] See below the article, 'A Warning to English Girls', opposing marriage between Indian men and English women, which appeared in the *Soulby's Ulverston Advertiser and General Intelligencer* in 1900:

A WARNING TO ENGLISH GIRLS.

Again and again have we protested against mixed marriages, especially finding fault with natives of India who go over to England and marry a girl who is ignorant of the lot that awaits her out in India as the wife of a native. It is cruelly unfair to the girl. The man himself knows all about it; and he knows, too, that in her Indian home, cut off—by prejudice if you like—from her own kind in India, she will have an unhappy awakening; and he has no right to subject her to such a fate. Of course, there is no accounting for love's young dream; and it is quite likely that a young Indian in England may fall head over ears in love with an English girl and find himself loved in return. Who shall forbid the banns? Well, it is at least the man's duty in such a case to explain conditions and circumstance as vividly as he can to the girl and to her parents or guardians; and even then if he is as wise as he is amorous, he will even then try to rescue the girl from himself; for he must know that no explanations can explain real life. Woman is weak, and in the love's dream condition no tales of the future will hold her back.

113. A Warning to English Girls.
Soulby's Ulverston Advertiser and General Intelligencer, 19 July 1900.
Image @ The British Library Board. Shelfmark: MFM.M26019.

By the early twentieth century, students from India were a familiar sight in British and Irish universities, particularly in the fields of medicine and law. While lascars in the nineteenth and early twentieth centuries tended to live alongside other people of colour in multicultural portside communities, there were no tangible 'Indian' geographical neighbourhoods in the way that there were for black, Chinese and Arab communities in Britain. The many middle class Indians coming to Britain to study often lodged in university halls or boarding houses. As was the case for men of colour in boarding houses more widely, this latter accommodation facilitated contact between Indian students and young white women who were also either lodgers or family members of the landlord or lady. In some cases, relationships blossomed, much to the distaste of many in the British establishment, who were concerned that young white women were having their heads turned by Indian students.

Popular romance novels in the early decades of the twentieth century, 'Raj Romances', in which Indian men and women were highly exoticised through tales of high-caste Indian aristocrats having love affairs with white Britons, undoubtedly played a role in shaping how Indian men were seen by young British women. There were fears, therefore, that women, particularly from the lower classes, were keen to associate with Indian students because they falsely assumed them to be wealthy princes. The resulting relationships, it was feared, would destabilise notions of race and Empire. In 1913, the India Office issued a circular for registry offices in Britain to explain the risks, including loss of nationality, to British women considering marriage with 'Hindus, Mohamedans and other subjects or citizens of countries where polygamy is legal'.

Some novels reflected the relationships between white women and Indian men that had begun in Britain, either through Oxbridge family connections or boarding house interactions, such as *The Englishwoman* (1912), *Abdullah and His Two Strings* (1927) and *Mr Ram* (1929). For the most part, these works followed set tropes of fictional interracial relationship patterns.

"'But I am an English girl,' she murmured—'an Englishwoman. There is the width of a world between us!'" (see page 17).

114. Book illustration from *The Englishwoman*, 1912 by Alice and Claude Askew. Image courtesy of the British Library Board. Shelfmark: NN.5.

The most common tropes consisted of a romance that was doomed to fail, either through death or breakdown. Usually, when the couple moved to India, the Indian man reverted to 'savage' ways brought on by being back in his homeland, or was revealed to already be married. The picture in the book *The English Woman* above is an example of how books portrayed racial mixing.

In reality, such relationships were not inherently doomed, nor did all couples end up in India. Lahiri notes that many Indian doctors in early twentieth century Britain settled and married white women. Some of these women were also Irish or of Irish descent, such as the families of Aubrey Menen and Pat Cross.

Irish-Indian Families in Britain

Aubrey Menen
Born in London in 1912, the writer Aubrey Menen was the son of Narayana Menen, an Indian from Malabar, and Alice Villet, an Englishwoman of Irish descent.[31]

Early Twentieth Century Migration

115. Aubrey Menen. The Irish-Indian author of the highy sucessful novel, *The Duke of Gallodoro*. Taken In Eremita, in Amalfi, 15 January 1960. Image @Alamy.

At University College London, where he studied philosophy and formed a drama group, he developed connections with members of the Bloomsbury Group, such as Virgina Woolf and John Maynard Keynes. After his graduation in 1932, Menen worked as a drama critic and a playwright before moving to Bombay in 1939 where he worked in broadcasting. Moving to Italy in 1948, he became a full time writer, publishing almost a dozen novels as well as wide-ranging non-fiction works and journalistic articles and reviews. Raised a Catholic, his outsider perspective on culture and nationhood was further influenced by his homosexuality during a time when being a gay man was taboo. In 1980, Menen returned to India, residing in Kerala where he lived until his death in 1989.

Menen's work, which frequently satirically explored and unpicked the concept of nationalism, was heavily informed by his Indian-Irish ancestry and his experiences as a man of colour in England and as a foreigner in India.

In his 1954 work, *Dead Man in a Silver Market: An Autobiographical Essay on National Prides*, Menen remarked on the rolling reactions his mixed ancestry provoked from the English during and after the First

World War, depending on rolling attitudes towards race and ethnicity:

> '*I (my dark looks) was made much of by the English and even given pennies by old gentlemen on the street since some Indians fighting on the western front were cutting off German necks with their kukris. But towards the end of the war I was mistaken for a Turk and I earned unkind looks since the Turks were reported to be cutting off testicles of their English prisoners. But by the end of the war which was won, the Indians who cut the necks were to be seen in Britain and soon gentlemen were again giving me pennies in the street.*' [32]

During his time at UCL, Menen found his mixed heritage could also be viewed negatively; he was rejected for a bursary on the grounds that he was not of 'pure' English descent. Unfavourable attitudes towards his mixed race family were not just to be found in England. In his 1953 essay for *The New Yorker* 'My Grandmother and the Dirty English', Menen recalled his Indian grandmother's opposition to his father marrying his mother, whom he met after completing his degree in medicine in England.[33]

Having initially shown no interest in her grandson, the family matriarch suddenly summoned her twelve year old grandson to meet her in India. Menen's mother decided to accompany her son and husband on the trip. However, as a foreigner, she was considered 'ritually unclean' and so was accommodated in an outhouse on the family property. During the trip Menen wrote, that much to his mother's infuriation, his grandmother never referred to her by name 'but always as "the Englishwoman", and only deigned to meet with his mother in person once, for a couple of minutes on an outside veranda. By the end of the visit, Menen himself, however, had received his grandmother's blessing as well as an education from her on his caste background ('Nayar'), and the importance of maintaining pride in this part of his heritage, particularly 'when moving among the English'. Reflecting on the fact that his English headmaster had given him similar if reverse advice before his trip on letting Indians see he 'had been trained in an *English* school,'

Menen remarked on the importance of his Irish grandmother on his sense of belonging and identity as a young man. From Killarney, his grandmother had died before he was born but her ancestry provided him with an anchoring point when he felt caught between two worlds:

> *'I told my mother that whenever I found the English were what my Indian grandmother said they were, I would copy my other grandmother. I would close my eyes and remember that I wasn't really Indian, and I wasn't English. I would remember that I was descended from the Irish, and do my best to stay out of the quarrel.'*

Pat Cross

Indian or British? Memoirs of a Rajah's Daughter is the memoir of Pat Cross (née Rikh), the daughter of an Indian father and an Irish mother. The memoir, edited by her daughter Fenella J. Miller, is produced from the journal that Cross kept during the three years she spent living with her father and his extended family in Kushalpur, India. This provides a fascinating insight into Anglo-Indian life prior to the outbreak of the Second World War.

Born in Cork in 1920, Cross had a very European upbringing, being educated in France and Belgium and spending much of her childhood moving around Western Europe. Growing up, Cross had known that her father was an Indian prince and landowner but little else. Strained relationships with her mother and brothers led to a sudden decision to contact her father who sent her money for a First Class single flight to India. At the age of 17, Cross, with her mother's encouragement, headed out to meet him and her extended Indian family for the first time. In India, Cross discovered that she came from a long lineage of 'Anglo-Indians'. Her Rajput family, who had remained loyal to the British, had frequently incorporated English, Scottish and Irish wives.

After the death of his first Hindu wife, Cross's own grandfather had married a fiercely Catholic Scottish woman, Cross's grandmother, whom he had met in Darjeeling. The pair were outsiders in their respective ways: a ruling rajah who, due to his race, could never truly penetrate Victorian colonial British society, and a Catholic woman who also was never truly part of a rigidly Church of England society.

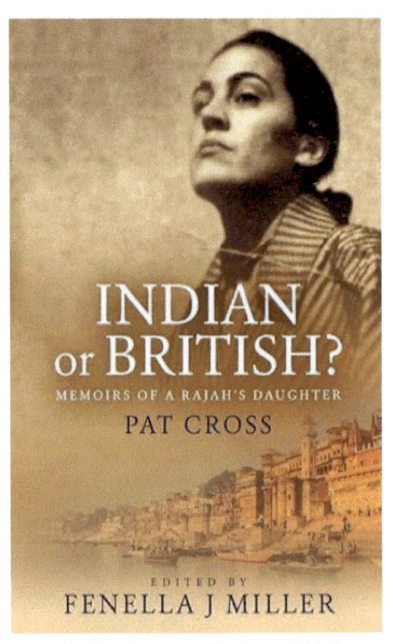

116. Book cover of *Indian or British? Memoir of a Rajah's Daughter* by Pat Cross (2015). Courtesy of Fenella J Miller.

The marriage rocked the community, not least because Cross's grandmother insisted that her future husband converted to her religion. The government, outraged at the idea of an Indian Catholic ruler, opposed the wedding; it took place finally under the condition that Cross's grandfather's younger brother became the rajah. The couple moved to Tajpur and part of Cross's grandfather's wedding gift to his new bride was to build her a Catholic church on the estate grounds, with an Italian priest brought over to officiate. In gratitude for his tactful abdication, the British government awarded Cross's grandfather a KBE, while the Catholic Church in Rome, delighted by such a high profile convert, gave him a Papal Knighthood. The couple went on to have nine children, the eldest of whom was Cross's grandfather, and lived in great opulence for many years.

Family tradition was for sons to be sent to England to be educated. Cross's father had attended Cambridge, where he had been awarded a half blue, before being called to the English Bar. A practicing barrister in London for some years, her father also held a commission in the Indian Army and was, Cross describes, the very model of an English Edwardian gentleman. During his studies in England, when Cross's father was married to her Irish mother and Cross's brother, their eldest son, was three years old son, the family had visited India. Relations between her mother and her Scottish grandmother did not go well and on discovering she was pregnant, the three returned to London. Despising the caste, class and race divisions which saw herself allowed entry to colonial social spaces while her husband was barred, Cross's mother vowed never to return.

> *"Pop told me with wry resignation, how she [Cross's mother] once made a fool of herself" by insisting that he should join her at an official reception where his fellow rajahs were politely but firmly kept at a distance by a silken cord."*

After Cross's birth, during a holiday in Ireland, the death of her grandfather saw her father recalled back to India to take up his duties as the eldest son. With her mother refusing to return, the pair divorced, though to do so required Cross's mother to make a final trip to India where another child was conceived. Neither of the pair ever remarried. Cross speculated that the pair retained their feelings for each other and that if her father had been able to establish himself in India independently of his family before her mother's disastrous visit, the relationship may have lasted.

As the Irish-born, European educated daughter of a Scottish-Indian prince, Cross possessed a fluid identity that did not fit neatly into the boxes demanded by others. On her outward journey to India, in hearing the British colonial passengers aboard the P & O liner gossip about her mixed race heritage, whispers about her as having 'a touch of the tar brush' and being a 'half chat', she remarks that: "It had always given me a special individuality to be able to announce that "Je suis Hindoo"; with that self-assumed label no particular group could claim to me as one of them. Clearly that situation no longer obtained. I would have to reassess my sense of values. I determined to switch from being an exotic mystery to becoming a proper Britain [sic]."

Outside the milieu of British colonials, things were different. Cross noted that "in the Europe of the Thirties, particularly in the capitals and resorts, nobody had seemed to bother very much about such things; I called myself English, Irish or Indian according to circumstances and my mood. Even frontier officials had never really pressed the point." However, during her time in India, with Indian nationalism on the rise,

Cross reflected that such fluid identities were likely to become more difficult to claim and that people like her and her father would increasingly be required to make choices that expressed allegiances. Cross notes that in response to asking her father what nationality she should put on the hotel register on her arrival in India, he clearly noted, in clear, clipped English tones, that she should 'put down Indian.'

Cross lived in India for two years, developing a close relationship with her powerful father all while negotiating her position as his daughter within the wider, complex family and social politics of an India that was increasingly rejecting the British Raj in favour of independent rule. She eventually made the decision to return to England in May 1939, concerned not only about the increasing likelihood of war in Europe but also the ways in which 'the insidious atmosphere of feudal India had entered [her] spirit', causing her to embrace too unthinkingly the prejudices and privileges of the landowning Indian class. War would break out five months later and Cross joined the WAAF where she served, until she became pregnant with her daughter, Fenella.

Chapter 5

Racial Mixing During and Post – WW2

British Mixed Race Families

The moral panic around racial mixing in portside communities that had been so dominant throughout the 1920s and 1930s was initially drowned out with the arrival of the Second World War. Newspaper articles, official reports and fictional accounts no longer displayed an intense prurient fascination with mixed race families, particularly those of dockside areas. The discrediting of eugenics that emerged during the war also dampened enthusiasm for research into 'race mixing'.[1]

117. The Satar family, Butetown in Cardiff, 1943.
Image courtesy of the Imperial War Museum, © IWM D 15279.

Some longstanding multiracial communities, such as Canning Town in East London, were badly affected by the Blitz, in which London and other British cities were heavily bombed. One of the worst incidents to involve civilians happened in 1940, when South Hallsville School on Agate Street in Canning Town took a direct hit. Though the official death toll was put at 77, eyewitness accounts, later reinforced by papers in the National Archives, put the true total closer to 400 dead, with many others severely injured.[2] South Hallsville School was only a few streets away from Crown Street, Catherine Street and other roads that were the homes of numerous interracial families.[3] Perhaps some were victims of the explosion, possibly being a factor in why Canning Town's multiracial community diminished after the war.

The image below is a map of Canning Town, from Maps of London,[4] where a diverse and ethnically mixed community resided. These communities were the subject of much media scrutiny in the 1930s and 1940s:

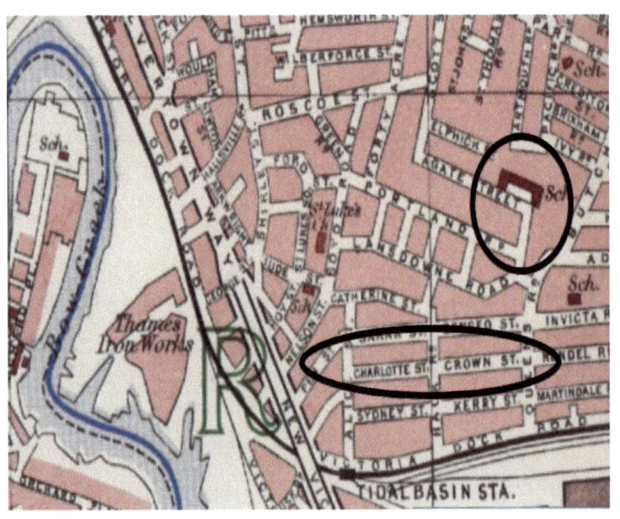

118. Map of Canning Town, 1940.
South Hallsville School, Crown Street and Charlotte Street marked.
Courtesy of Maps of London.

"There were lots of black kids. We used to play together, no animosity between any of us. There were white women married black, you know, West Indians, they were working on the boats. Got on ever so well together. Played in the street, great big skipping rope right across the road. And we had a factory down the street so we used to have quite a bit of traffic, just drop the rope and let the lorry go over it. Everybody in the street used to speak to each other, and all the children used to play together. Sometimes when me and my sister's talking, we say, "I wonder what happened to so and so," you know. During the war a lot of them went.' - Memories of Doris, who was born in 1922 in Canning Town and lived there until 1948. [5]

Children of WW2 - the 'Brown Babies'

As the war continued, the focus on racial mixing in portside communities was gradually replaced by new concerns about interracial relationships in the country. During the period 1942–1945, around one million US servicemen were based in England as part of the preparations for the invasion of Europe, with around 130,000 of these being African American servicemen.[6] Many of the black American servicemen were based in military camps in predominantly rural areas where the local population had experienced little contact with members of black and minority ethnic communities. The 'Tan Yanks', as they were dubbed by the press, provoked substantial interest and curiosity as a result. This was particularly the case amongst young local women for whom the arrival of American servicemen represented a glamorous, exciting and exotic male presence in the midst of gloomy wartime Britain. Everything was in short supply, including eligible British men. Inevitably, relationships between black GIs and white British women were formed, with some of these resulting in children.[7]

On 23rd August 1948, *Life* magazine published a feature entitled 'The Babies They Left Behind Them', which highlighted what was commonly referred to as the 'brown baby problem'. It is estimated that there were between 1,000-2,000 children, referred to as 'brown babies', from the relationships between black GIs and white British women. The relationships and subsequent visibility of mixed race children caused much consternation amongst the British authorities. Interracial marriage was illegal in most of America at this time and U.S. Army policy was to refuse permission for its black soldiers to marry their white British sweethearts. As a result, most of the children were illegitimate and between this stigma and that of having a 'brown baby', many of the mothers gave their children up for adoption.

The British authorities discussed 'shipping' these children off to America to be raised with their black fathers or adopted by black families. However, such a move was considered discriminatory and illegal, as the children were all British citizens. In the end, it was felt that to be seen to be 'exporting' the children would cause anger in Britain's colonies, where many British subjects of colour had fought for Britain in the war. So, most of the children remained in Britain, many into state care where 'their colour made adoption unlikely.' Somerset County Council used a former National Trust property, Holnicote House, to house the 'brown babies' in area. The Ministry of Health declined to get involved in the direct provision of homes and hostels, arguing that they should be integrated into existing homes if they could not be cared for by a parent. However, some local homes, including Barnardos, refused to admit 'coloured children' and it was often left to local organisations and individuals to fill that gap. For example, Pastor G Daniel Ekarte, Minister and Founder of the African Churches Mission, took many 'brown babies' into his children's home between 1945 and 1949.[8]

As with other mixed race families in Britain, some of the 'brown babies' included those born to Irish mothers, or those of Irish descent. While some were given up for adoption, others were raised with their mothers. In some cases, some even stayed with their mothers, even though they were the product of a wartime affair and their mother's husband was still on the scene.

Pauline Nevins

Born in 1944, Pauline Nevins (neé Behan) grew up in Wellingborough, a small market town in the English midlands. The product of her mother's affair with a black GI, Pauline, the fourth of eight children, was nevertheless raised by her mother's husband as one of his own. Her memoir *'Fudge': The Downs and Ups of a Biracial, Half-Irish British War Baby* gives a unique insight into the life of a mixed race Irish 'brown baby' who was raised in England.[9]

Like several other 'brown baby' accounts, Pauline's memoir details a childhood in which her racial identity was variously seen and experienced as ordinary as well as problematic, including by members of her own family. She had a closer relationship with some siblings than others, with one sibling, Doris, being particularly cruel and ashamed about Pauline's colour growing up, though acting with more kindness later in life. Meanwhile, her stepfather, 'the Old Man', who was quick to level physical punishment at all the children, including Pauline, was also capable of more intimate moments too. She remembers him taking her hand in public, unconcerned with the stares directed at them. However, when Pauline's mother had another affair and left the home in fear of what 'the Old Man' might do to her, he often berated Pauline as a 'little black bastard' in drunken rages. 'The Old Man' would finally leave for Ireland, never to return after a six month stint in prison for attacking the lover of Pauline's mother.

Growing up, Pauline wasn't the only mixed race child in

Wellingborough. In fact, she recalls knowing five other 'brown babies' of black GIs personally, as well as seeing a number of other children. In fact, her best friend, Dawn, was also the child of a black GI and a white mother, who later remarried a white man. It was with Dawn that Pauline came across the word 'mulatto' in a dictionary, the pair feeling excitedly that they had a special word to describe them. This was one word better than the cruel taunts of 'Blackie' and 'N*****' that would be levelled at them, along with stone throwing, by unfamiliar children in the streets. While the local children who she grew up with never treated her unkindly or called her names, the racial taunts and slurs that marked her early years were very painful. In addition, the frequent experiences of being an outsider, even within her immediate family, was also painful. As she notes, as was common with many 'brown babies', they 'had nobody to turn to for comfort, or empathy. How could our white mothers and siblings understand the depth of our pain, and our confusion for being singled out for abuse?'

While Pauline's experiences growing up were peppered with racial taunts, slights and prejudice, her racial identity was not a singular, defining aspect of her childhood. She also recounts many other experiences that are familiar to other white, working class memoirs of the immediate English postwar period. This included the ups and downs of being part of a large, poor family and navigating family, friends, romantic and work relationships. Amongst these recollections are being part of an Irish family. Her mother, who was born in Castlebar and her stepfather in Kildare, both retained their Irish accents and Pauline notes being aware of the different phrases her parents used to those of her friends' parents growing up, such as 'will ye whisht' for 'will you be quiet' and 'eejits' or 'amadans' instead of 'idiots'. However, her mother and stepfather only returned together to Ireland once during Pauline's childhood and only a few Irish relatives visited their home. Although, she recalls the house frequently playing host to Irish lodgers, including a couple of young men who would sing Irish songs with her stepfather in the evenings.

Although her mother could not provide any details of Pauline's father, a chance connection through a DNA ancestry testing site meant that later in life, happily married with children and living in America, Pauline discovered a part of her history that had been missing for so long: the name of her black American father. Though her father had sadly passed away, he had left behind a large family of thirteen children, as well as two remaining sisters, who welcomed Pauline and her own family with love and enthusiasm.

Beyond 'Brown Babies'

As well as soldiers and sailors serving in the British Armed forces during and post-war time, students from around the world continued to enter British educational establishments with relationships with local women often flourishing. The architect Robin Mandal was born to an Irish mother and an Indian father, the pair meeting during the war when Mandal's father, a lawyer, moved to London during his time in the RAF where he met his mother who was working as a nurse.[10]

Professor Dame Elizabeth Nneka Anionwu

Professor Dame Elizabeth Nneka Anionwu's autobiographical account, *Dreams From My Mother (2021)*, shines a spotlight on such overlooked but familiar pattern of racial mixing at this time, ones that are often overshadowed by the 'brown babies' history.

119. Elizabeth Nneka Anionwu with her mother.
Courtesy of Elizabeth Anionwu.

A brilliant student at Cambridge, Elizabeth's mother, Mary, a white English woman of Irish descent, became pregnant in 1947. Like numerous other women who became pregnant outside marriage in the mid-twentieth century, she was sent to a Mother and Baby home to deliver the child in secret. In order for Mary to continue her studies, it was planned that her parents would raise the child as their own, in their home in Stafford. The revelation, however, that as the nun delivering the news put it, 'the baby's a little dark', changed the situation dramatically. Elizabeth's father, Lawrence Anionwu, was in fact a Nigerian man and fellow Cambridge student, with whom Mary had developed a relationship. A mixed race baby could not be passed off as her parents' own. If Mary were to return to Cambridge, on which her parents were keen, this would mean placing Elizabeth up for adoption. Though Mary did not want to leave her studies, she refused to abandon her daughter.

Mary never returned to Cambridge, instead taking an office job. Although she had hoped this job would provide her with the financial means to raise her daughter, Elizabeth was placed into care where she remained for nine years. During this time, her mother worked tirelessly against social convention and disapproval to be reunited with her daughter. The older Elizabeth illustrates how the correspondence shows that her mother's plan, as agreed by Elizabeth's grandparents, was to take Elizabeth to live with her and Lawrence in Nigeria where he had returned; the two had become engaged and hoped to marry once he was in a better financial position. In the meantime, it appears the pair had visited Elizabeth together when she was 16 months old, possibly her father's first sight of her.

The marriage, however, did not occur. Lawrence married a Nigerian woman which Elizabeth suspects caused her mother great pain. Years later, her mother married a white British man who agreed to take responsibility for Elizabeth's care. 'I cannot adequately express my gratitude to you and the sisters for your care of Elizabeth during the past nine years', her mother wrote to the care home, 'but as you know, it has always been my wish to have her with me as soon as circumstances permitted'. Elizabeth grew up initially with her mother, stepfather and half-siblings in Wolverhampton. Her stepfather could not cope with the presence of a mixed race child at home. He drank and was prone to violent outbursts and could not cope with the taunts at work about having "a half-cast child" in his home. As a result, she was subjected to physical violence and had to be rescued by her grandparents in Wallasey. Yet, Elizabeth states that 'despite its rocky start plus a few unpleasant episodes along the way', she sees her life as having been 'extremely fulfilling' and 'a vindication of all that my mother had to endure'. As an adult, Elizabeth would also go on to meet and develop a close relationship with her father, Lawrence, and her wider Nigerian family. She was later awarded a CBE and Damehood in recognition of her services to nursing in Britain and the successful Mary Seacole Statue Appeal.

Lilian Bader

During the Second World War, many people of colour, including those from mixed race Irish families, fought for Britain or supported the war effort through factory work. One such woman was Lillian Bader.[11] Bader, (neé Bailey) was born in Toxteth, Liverpool in 1917. Her mother, Lilian McGowan, was a British woman of Irish parentage and her father, Marcus Bailey, was a Barbadian who served as a merchant seamen during the First World War. Despite her mother being a Catholic, the couple had married in the Church of England and, as a consequence, her mother was rejected by her own Catholic family.

120. Lililan Bader
Image courtesy of the Imperial
War Museum,
© IWM HU 53753.

Initially raised in Liverpool, Lilian moved with her family just prior to the race riots of 1919, first to Fleetwood and then to Hull.[12] Unfortunately, her parents' volatile marriage came to an end in 1924 when Lilian's mother abruptly returned to Fleetwood, abandoning her children and husband. Initially looked after by a neighbour when their father returned to sea, the children were later placed in care after he had a nervous breakdown, with Lilian separated from her brothers, Francis and James. In 1927, her father died, followed two years later by her mother, who drowned in the wake of flooding at Fleetwood. With no contact with her siblings for many years, Lilian was brought up in a Catholic Girls' Home in Middlesborough where she remained until the age of 20, prejudice against her racial background preventing employers from hiring her.

The outbreak of the war saw Lilian seeking to contribute to the war effort. She managed to find a job as an assistant in a NAAFI (Navy, Army and Air Force Institutes) canteen at Catterick Camp. However, after only seven weeks, Lilian was sacked from her role when it was discovered that her father was a West Indian. The District Manager apparently toyed with the decision for several weeks as, being an Irish Catholic, he sympathised with Bader's own Irish and Roman Catholic background.[13] Finding work first on a farm and then in domestic service, a radio broadcast provided Bader with the inspiration for her next role. Listening to an interview with West Indian men, who had been accepted by the RAF, after being turned down by the Army, Bader applied to be part of the Women's Auxiliary Air Force (WAAF). Successfully enlisting in 1941, Bader was sent to York.

'I was the only coloured person in this sea of white faces but somebody told me I looked smart in my uniform which cheered me no end.'

In the WAAF, Bader studied for exams, graduating from a First-Class Airwoman, then to Leading Aircraftwoman and then finally to the rank of Acting Corporal. During her time in the WAAF, Bader thus became one of the first group of women to be allowed on planes to run routine repairs.

In 1943, Lilian married Ramsay Bader, a British mixed race soldier that she initially met as a pen friend through a former landlady. Ramsay, a tank driver, served with the 147th (Essex Yeomanry) Field Regiment, Royal Artillery and would form part of the D-Day landings in 1944. Lilian's chances of further promotion in the WAAF were curtailed when she discovered she was expecting a baby, her first son. As a consequence of the pregnancy, she was discharged from the WAAF in February 1944 and nervously prayed that Ramsay would survive deployment which he did.[14] The couple would go on to have another son. Once her boys were older, Lilian returned to education, becoming a language teacher. She died in 2015, aged 97, having worked tirelessly to inform audiences of the participation of black Britons and people of colour in the British Forces during World War 2.

Compulsory repatriation of Chinese Seamen in Liverpool

The accounts of racial mixing in Britain during the Second World War tended to focus on black GIs, white women and the 'brown babies'. However, the longstanding patterns of mixing involving African, West Indian, Indian, Chinese and Arab men and white women (British and Irish) continued. In the early 1940s, an estimated 20,000 Chinese merchant sailors were recruited into the British Merchant Navy and, almost entirely based in Liverpool, around 300 of these married or cohabitated with local women, many of whom were Irish or of Irish descent.

Although the Chinese sailors played a vital role in Britain's warfare, their demands for the same pay and equal treatment as local sailors in 1942, which led to strike action, saw them labelled as troublemakers. Post-war, the government, in collusion with the shipping companies, were keen to rid Liverpool of what they saw as an 'undesirable element'. Hence, in October 1945, the Home Office opened a file on 'the compulsory repatriation of undesirable Chinese seamen at Liverpool'.[15]

As has been identified through recently released records, some of the Chinese men, who had families in Liverpool, were not given an opportunity to stay, as the law prescribed. Though, due to the hostile conditions in Liverpool, many sailors were willing to return to China. Although we do not know exactly how many Chinese seamen were deported, including those who had relationships and families with local women, it is estimated that more than 200 men with dependents were suddenly and forcefully repatriated, leaving behind distraught families who believed themselves abandoned.[16]

The British wives of the Chinese seamen who had been repatriated, formed a defence association in Liverpool to campaign for the rights of Chinese seamen's families, though to little avail. As far as records show, there were no reviews of individual cases, or appeals. During the last half century, those left fatherless have grown into adults and (as with the children of black GIs and British women have sought to identify and track down their fathers. Their testimony is brought to life by photographs assembled by one of them, Yvonne Foley, who has remembered these fathers and their families in her website: https://dragonsandlions.co.uk/, formerly called Half and Half.

> '*He just went out to the shop, and my mum was waiting for him to come home, and he never came.*' — Linda Davis, whose Chinese father was forcibly repatriated by British government authorities.

Mixed race adults from Irish families

As well as overshadowing other narratives of racial mixing during and immediately post the Second World War period, the national fascination, in Britain, with the 'brown babies' obscured the fact that there had been a long history of racial mixing in the country. There were similar concerns around identity, nationhood, citizenship and race in relation to other racial groupings and their experiences. Mostly forgotten in public debates, by the 1940s and early 1950s, the mixed race children of portside communities and elsewhere, once so decried in the 1920s and 1930s, had now grown up and were living lives as British citizens. As ever, many of these families had Irish heritage.

A 1943 account in the *Daily Herald* and other media shines a rare light on one such family. The article 'Girl He Hid in a Ship Locker' tells the tale of Domillie Jones, a 23 year old from Bristol with a West Indian father and an Irish mother. Quarrelling with her mother, Domillie ran away from home where she met an American sailor who suggested she sneak on to his ship and sail with him to the USA. However, midway through the journey, the ship was torpedoed and Domillie spent six hours in a lifeboat before she was rescued in Nova Scotia. Sent back to Britain, she was then charged with leaving the country without permission and, after apologising to the magistrate and promising never to do anything similar again, she was bound over. See the *Dundee Evening Telegraph* extract, on page 198, about this story.

GIRL STOWED AWAY—SHIP WAS TORPEDOED

A 23-year-old coloured girl, who stowed away on an American ship which was afterwards torpedoed, was, at Bristol to-day bound over for twelve months charged with leaving the country without the permission of the immigration authorities.

She was Domillie Lucia James, of Exford Street, Kingsdown, Bristol.

Mr Caffin, prosecuting, described how the girl became friendly with an American seaman. He proposed she should go back to America with him, and she agreed.

He suggested she should steal on board the ship in his clothes, but he could not smuggle the clothes to her. She got on board unchallenged, and hid in a small locker. The seaman brought her food, and later she went to his cabin.

When the ship was in mid-Atlantic it was torpedoed. The girl spent six hours in a lifeboat, and was eventually picked up and landed at Halifax, Nova Scotia.

121. Stow-Away Girl.
Dundee Evening Telegraph, 26 November 1943. Image @ DC Thomson Co Ltd and courtesy of The British Library Board. Shelfmark: 015113134.

Chapter 6

Racial Mixing in the Era of Mass Migration

Mixed Race Irish Families in Post-war Britain

While the mass migration of Irish citizens in the immediate post-war decades didn't attract the same level of hostile attention in the media as did migrant people of colour, entrenched anti-Irish sentiment, in Britain, was in frequent display on the ground. In some areas, Irish migrants lived in close proximity with migrants of colour and there was overt social hostility towards both groups, with many landlords and landladies refusing to house black or Irish people, their prejudice overtly displayed through the notorious 'No Blacks, No Irish, No Dogs' signs. As with white British families, Irish family members also held a range of views towards racial mixing, including within their family unit.

Phil Lynott

In her autobiography, Philomena Lynott, the mother of the singer Phil Lynott, wrote extensively about the prejudice she encountered as an Irish mother of a mixed race child in early post-war Britain. Leaving her home in Dublin in 1947 to train as a nurse in Birmingham, Lynott entered into a relationship with Cecil Parris, a Guyanese man she met in a night club. Shortly after, she became pregnant. Accommodation became almost impossible to find. Her landlords (a married couple) at the time of her pregnancy had agreed to care for her child while she went back to work. However, they kicked her out when they discovered the colour of her baby. Parris had initially not known about his son's birth due to working in London. He struggled to find lodgings for the three of them when he returned to Birmingham and reunited with Lynott. When Lynott's relationship with Parris fizzled out she moved with her son Phil to Manchester. The same pattern was repeated and the pair were only able to find lodgings in the poorer areas of town, mostly with black or mixed race people or couples.

In her autobiography, Lynott describes her reunion with Parris after Phil's birth and his attempt to secure housing in Birmingham:

> *To his eternal credit, despite the fact that winter was coming on and the weather was awful, he went out searching for lodgings. Unfortunately, the evils of racial prejudice were rooted far deeper in English society than I could possibly have imagined and, try as he might, nobody wanted us. Much later, John Lydon, the singer with the Sex Pistols, wrote a book about his life called* **No Irish, No Blacks, No Dogs**. *I know only too well what he was talking about. Those offensive words frequently appeared on signs placed in the windows of houses that had vacancies.*'[1]

Craig Charles
As such, mixed race Irish families were frequently on the receiving end of multiple prejudices. The actor Craig Charles has said that family narratives have his Guyanese father and his Liverpool Irish mother meeting outside a boarding house in Liverpool that said "No Irish, no n*****, no dogs". They left together 'hand-in-hand'.[2] Employment bars that had specifically grouped the Irish in with people of colour in Britain had a long history. Jacqueline Jenkinson[3] notes that post-WW1, when unemployment was high and there was fierce resentment at the idea of demobbed resident black or colonial workers 'taking' white British men's jobs, such barriers had appeared in Liverpool. The manager of the Liverpool employment exchange reported in 1919 that "farmers will not employ Chinese and Negroes on account of the bitter feeling that at present exists, and in the Ormskirk District, Irishmen are also unacceptable." [4]

Gus Nwanokwu
Similarly, in Gus Nwanokwu's 'Black Shamrocks',[5] his autobiographical account of growing up in the 1950s as the child of a Nigerian father and a white Irish mother in London and Kent, he notes: 'I think being a black and Irish family put us pretty firmly at the bottom of the social hierarchy in the minds of our working class brothers and sisters.' Accounts from this period also highlight that prejudice was frequent from within the family unit itself. Nwanokwu recalls how on hearing the news that his mother planned to marry a black non-Catholic, her Irish father told her never to visit again. Though her mother did receive a warm visit from his Irish grandmother when his sister Chi-chi

Nwanoku, the founder of the Chinkeke! Orchestra, was born. That would be the last time the pair would ever meet.

However, though rejection by white Irish family members was often common, it was not inevitable. Elaine Bauer's research recounts the family life of Dusty, a black Jamaican and Dawn, an Irish woman he met in London in 1950. Approaching Dawn's mother back in Ireland for permission to marry, her mother replied, 'He could be a white man, green man, black man, coloured man, he could be any kind of man as long as he's Catholic!' When the couple were thrown out of their rented accommodation for running foul of their landlord's no children policy following the birth of their first child, Polly, Dawn's mother and uncles cared for the baby at the family home in Ireland. Polly remained in Ireland with her grandmother and uncles until she was four. Her grandmother eventually moved to London. Similarly, when Philomena Lynott was unable to cope with the pressures and racism directed at her as the single mother of a mixed race child in England, her parents took Phil to Dublin where they raised him until adulthood.

Kit de Waal

Like a number of other mixed race Irish people born during this period, such as Phil Lynott, the novelist Kit de Waal has spoken about the importance of her Irish heritage in her life. One of five children of an Irish mother and a father from Saint Kitts, de Waal was brought up in Birmingham in amongst the Irish community. She remarks that from an early age she could distinguish between Irish accents. On Sundays, the family would visit her grandparents, who ran a boarding house for Irish labourers. Initially, her grandmother was horrified at the news that her daughter started a relationship with a black man. Yet, as highlighted earlier, as with many white grandparents who were initially hostile or even just generally opposed to having mixed race grandchildren, her grandmother's attitude changed after the children were born, and de Waal and her siblings would go on to have a close and loving relationships with their grandparents.

> *"As I've got older, my Irish heritage has become increasingly important to me. Every time I visit Ireland there is a sense of coming home which is strange as I've never lived there. But my childhood was lived to the soundtrack of my grandfather's rebel songs, to the sing-song lilt of all the Irish counties, to the smell of bacon and cabbage and good strong tea. On*

my childhood street, neighbours on either side and opposite were all Irish, half of the children at school were called O'Connor, Dempsey, Byrne, Whelan, MacNamara, and when I got my Irish citizenship a few years ago, there was a real sense of being complete." - Kit de Waal, interviewed in writing.ie.[6]

Mixed Race Irish Adults in the Post-war Public Eye

As with the moral panic around the 'brown babies' narrative of the 1940s, the cry of 'what about the children?' that was used to underscore opposition to mixed marriages in the 1950s and 1960s hid the reality that many people of mixed racial background during this period weren't the products of recent migration. The children of the 1920s and 1930s, including those from mixed race Irish families, were now adults, with some becoming public figures.

Dolores Mantez

Dolores Mantez, for example, was born in Liverpool in 1936 to a Ghanaian father and an Irish mother.

122. Dolores Mantez as Nina Barry character in the TV Series 'Ufo' (1974). Image courtesy @Alamy and ITC Cinematic.

Originally on a path to work in a factory or as a seamstress, Mantez had started to sing semi-professionally. An agent spotted her and suggested she would be ideal for the role of a student in *Sapphire* (1959),

Basil Dearden's film about racial passing and the racism faced by West Indian immigrants in London. Her appearance in the film led to a career in acting, with a succession of parts in television series such as *Shadow Squad* and *The Avengers*. Her best known role, however, was the part of Lieutenant Nina Barry in Gerry and Sylvia Anderson's 1970s sci-fi drama series *UFO*.

Kenny Lynch

Some had Irish roots that went back generations. Kenny Lynch was a singer, songwriter and entertainer who had several hit singles in the early 1960s. These included the Top Ten numbers 'Up on the Roof' and 'You Can Never Stop Loving Me', as well as becoming the first singer to record a version of a Lennon and McCartney composition (Misery). He also appeared in numerous television programmes over the following decades, becoming a regular face in light entertainment broadcasting in the 1970s.

123. Singer and Comedian Kenny Lynch with his latest record to gain entry into the top thirty July 1963. Image @ Alamy.

Lynch was the descendant of a mixed race Irish family dating back to the Victorian era. In 1811, James Spring, a seaman from the Caribbean, settled in London. His son, Robert, married an Irish woman and the pair had a daughter, Amelia, (née Spring), in 1895. Amelia would go on to marry Oscar, a Barbadian seaman who served in the merchant navy during the First World War. He later become a stoker at Beckton gas works. Oscar and Amelia would go on to have 11 children, one of whom was Kenny. The family initially lived at Crown Street in Canning

Town before moving to Cornwall Street in Stepney. One of Kenny's sisters, Gladys, also became well known as a successful jazz and ballad singer under the stage name Maxine Daniels. Lynch passed away in 2018. In an interview for the 1000 Londoners project, Lynch remarked:

> *"No, well my father here because he was in the Merchant Navy. Yeh my dad come over from Barbados in the late 1890's ... And my mum's from an Irish background and all that... It was just a very fun family [...] We never had any problems, like racial problems with people in Cornwall Street because, they ... basically we were probably a novelty. People would probably say, oh, we've got some black people living next door to us and all that, you should come round and see them, they're almost the same as us. You know what I mean, that sort of thing must have been going on. But basically, didn't see loads of [racism]...until I was about twenty. Basically. And then you noticed that more immigrants were coming in and all that sort of thing."* [7]

Mixed Race Irish Families and Adoption

In the years after the 'Brown Babies' scandal, the issue of mixed race children in care would continue to become a topic of public debate in Britain. Due to the continuing moral condemnation of illegitimacy and racial mixing that carried into the post-war years, a disproportionate number of mixed race children, including those born to Irish mothers or those of Irish descent in Britain, began to enter the care system. Their presence raised critical questions around race, fostering and adoption that continue to resonate in the care system today. The *Irish Independent* included the following under the heading "Reluctant to adopt babies":

> *'A Liverpool priest, son of Irish parents and head of Liverpool's Catholic Children's Protection Society, last night admitted that it was proposed to allow non-Catholics adopt Catholic babies – because Catholics in the city, most of whom are Irish-descended, were reluctant to do so.*
>
> *Father James Dunne, whose parents came from Arklow, said: "The position is so serious that we are prepared to let non-Catholics have these unwanted, illegitimate, coloured or mixed race babies born to Catholic women.*

> *Father Dunne is to travel to the U.S next month as the representative of Catholic adoption societies in Britain to study methods of encouraging white people to adopt black babies.'* [8]

In an article by Norman Longmate, in the *Daily Mirror* in 1957, about the difficulty of placing a mixed race by called Peter, he reported that the National Council for the Unmarried Mother and her Child had said:

> *"The parents of an unmarried mother often become reconciled to her when the white child is born and help her to keep it.*
> *But if she has a coloured baby, they tell her: 'get rid of it - or never come near us again.'* [9]

With the stigma around illegitimacy being highly acute in Irish families, it is unsurprising that many mixed race children who were in care during this period, were of Irish descent. In her autobiography, Philomena Lynott, the mother of the Thin Lizzy front man Phil Lynott, recalls how during her brief spell at a Catholic home for unmarried mothers in Selly Oak run by nuns, she was under immense pressure to give her baby up for adoption. The plan was she would give up her baby to a waiting married couple so that she could return to Ireland 'to start a new life'. The married couple found by the Selly Oak nuns, who were willing to adopt Philomena Lynott's mixed race child were not typical of the post-war years. Prevailing social attitudes in Britain, meant that mixed race children were not only disproportionately placed in care, but were likely to remain there. Many white adopters were reluctant to take a child they could not pass off as their own and so make themselves the target of racial prejudice.

In his biography, the Irish footballer, Paul McGrath, recounts his story about living in the Smyly Trust orphanages in Dublin. He mentions that the board of trustees were solicitors and that type of professional person and "even the deputy governor of the Central bank lent his name to the charity." He goes on to say that the Smyly Trust Homes did not have a policy of reintegrating families. See further about his story in chapter seven.

In his book, his mother Betty talks about losing her son and mentions that:

"Paul was ten weeks old when I handed him over and – though we are extremely close today – I have, I suppose, four and a half decades trying to get him back." [10]

By the 1960s, things were hardly any better. 'It is almost impossible to place a child of African blood', one social worker remarked to *The Times* in 1963, '[though] a child with Asian blood is easier.' As noted above, by 1970, Liverpool's Catholic Children's Protection Society had proposed to let non-Catholics adopt Catholic babies due to the high numbers of mixed race children born to Catholic women that were languishing in care in the city.

Black adopters were rarely considered as viable prospective adopters at this time, ingrained racial prejudice contributing to the commonly held belief in social work that black families did not have the material means to act as carers. It would not be until the 1980s that such attitudes began to shift, in part due to protestations and lobbying by the Association of Black Social Workers and Allied Professionals in Britain. John Small, who founded this association, wrote a seminal paper in 1984 in which he stated that:

"There is a crisis in adoptions caused by the shortage of available white Anglo-Saxon babies. Applications to adopt white infants exceed the supply of such children. The waiting period could be as long as between five and eight years. At the same time, there is a chronic shortage of black homes for black children because of the conscious efforts of white-controlled agencies not to involve the black community more fully in attempting to reach potential black foster and adoptive parents." [11]

Chapter 7

Racism and Daily Life

The emergence of a large post-war population of 'coloured' people in the 1950s and 1960s, and the widespread worries around race, citizenship and domestic racial mixing, dominated media discourse in Britain. The effect of these concerns, and the negative focus on racial mixing, was that frequently the scenes of 'ordinariness' in the everyday lives of mixed race people were scrubbed out of media coverage. Rather, the problem narrative continued to dominate thinking on interracial relationships, fuelled by fears about 'half-caste' children.

As well as migrants of colour, the new influx of migration to Britain also contained those from Ireland, who were propelled to seek work abroad due to the economic depression in the country. Kathleen Paul notes that in the post-war period from 1946 to the early 1960s, between fifty and sixty thousand Irish citizens entered the British work force each year. By 1951, Britain was home to almost three-quarters of a million Irish-born, this figure increased in the next decade to approximately one million making the Irish the largest national group to enter post-war Britain.[1]

Racism, Prejudice and Empowerment in the 1970s and 1980s

The black and Asian presence in Britain at this time saw a feverish debate emerge over race and citizenship. In 1968, the Conservative Shadow Defence Secretary Enoch Powell gave what would become known as the 'Rivers of Blood' speech,[2] on 20 April 1968. In this speech he drew on vivid imagery of inevitable violence and conflict on the streets of Britain. In his opposition to Commonwealth immigration to the UK, and the proposed Race Relations Bill, he said: 'like the Roman, I seem to see "the river Tiber foaming with much blood"'.

Meanwhile, Irish people in Britain also faced acute institutional and everyday prejudice. For mixed race Irish families in Britain, like other families of colour during this period, encountering prejudice was an all too common occurrence.

While Powell was immediately sacked from his frontbench post, his sentiments were wildly shared by much of the public. A Gallup opinion found that 74% were in agreement with Powell and newspapers were inundated with letters of support for Powell's viewpoints and calls for his reinstatement. Spilling over into the 1970s, this groundswell of hostility created a climate of disillusionment and fear for visible ethnic minorities in Britain. The National Front emerged as a far-right 'racialist' group in the late sixties, whose doctrine furiously opposed racial mixing. Its support grew steadily and the violence that spiked after Powell's speech became an increasing threat that would often manifest in brutal ways.

124. Enoch Powell and the Race Bill.
Evening Express, 20 April 1968.
Image © D. C. Thomson & Co. Ltd.
Courtesy of The British Library Board.
Shelfmark: NEWS178.

The historian David Olusoga,[3] who grew up in Britain in the 1970s and 1980s, notes that 'almost every black or mixed-race person of my generation has a story of racial violence to tell...from humiliation to hospitalization'. Homes and property belonging to 'coloured' people were often vandalised, and 'Paki' bashing gangs roamed the streets specifically targeting Asians but happy to assault any person of colour who crossed their path, such violence ending numerous times in murder. Overlaying the physical violence was the common regularity of verbal assault, the popular racist epithets of the day, such as 'wog', 'Paki', 'chink', 'coon', 'half-breed', 'n*****', hurled viciously or casually at passers-by. Craig Charles recalls being in fights:

> *"every day of my life, defending myself, defending my mum.... You would get on the bus and people would move as they didn't want to sit next to you and kids would shout, "N***** n*****, pull the trigger, bang bang bang!"*[4]

A key underlying flaw in the 'Keep Britain White' plan, however, was the extent to which Britain's non-white population was so genealogically as well as socially rooted, as disturbances between black youths and police in the Toxteth area of Liverpool in 1975 - a precursor to the more well-known riots of the 1980s - highlighted. Citing a report into race relations in the region, the *Daily Mail* reported the frustrations of the community, such as being repeatedly refused work, refused entry to entertainment spaces and forced into squalid housing. These were 'not the problems of recent immigrants, but the problems of third and fourth and fifth generations of children. Similarly, outside of Britain's oldest black community of Liverpool, many people of colour were not only British citizens but British born: an estimated 40% by the mid-1970s. Where, therefore, was repatriation to take place to? As Charlie Williams would quip in his comedy routine 'when Enoch Powell said, 'Go home, black man,' I said, 'I've got a hell of a long wait for a bus to Barnsley.'

Peter Aspinall notes that the 1971 Census shows that amongst the 793,390 residents in the UK with a mother born in Ireland, around half (50.4%) had a father born in the UK and 46.655 with a father born in the Irish Republic. Relatively small proportions had a father from a racialized minority group, e.g., 0.45% with a father born in India, 0.1% with a father born in Pakistan, and 0.1% with a father born in Africa. However, caution should be exercised in the interpretation of this data as country of birth is not necessarily an accurate proxy for ethnic group. For example, not all fathers born in the UK were necessarily white, and some fathers born in India may have been white (who served in the colonial administration).

During this period, Irish people in Britain also faced acute institutional and everyday prejudice. In the wake of bombings by the Provisional IRA on the British mainland in the early 1970s, the Irish community in Britain faced heavy discrimination and were strongly policed. However, anti-Irish sentiment had deep roots in Britain long before the 1970s. The ways in which longstanding prejudice towards the Irish and black communities manifested itself could be glimpsed in attitudes towards the Toxteth Riots of 1981. Tensions in the Toxteth community of Liverpool had been fuelled for years not only by inadequate housing, social segregation, and discrimination in employment and education, but also police brutality. However, in the lead up to the broadcast of a television programme on the Merseyside Police in 1978, the BBC's *Listener* magazine published an article that swept these issues aside.

Drawing uncritically on the comments of the Chief Constable of Merseyside, Kenneth Oxford, the article stated that the 'main social problem' the police faced in the area was identified as mixed race youth, who were discussed in terms that plugged directly into the prejudiced and defamatory legacy of Muriel Fletcher. Captain Richardson, and other officials who had castigated 'feckless' white women, including those of Irish descent, for mixing with men of colour to produce 'half-caste' children of a 'vicious tendency':

> *"Policemen in general and detectives in particular, are not racialist, despite what many Black groups believe.... Yet they are the first to define the problem of half-castes in Liverpool. Many are the products of liaisons between Black seamen and white prostitutes in Liverpool 8, the red light district. Naturally they grow up without any kind of recognisable home life. Worse still, after they have done the rounds of homes and institutions, they gradually realise that they are nothing. The Negroes will not accept them as Blacks, and whites just assume they are coloureds. As a result, the half-caste community of Merseyside—or more particularly Liverpool—is well outside recognised society."*[5]

As in the wake of Fletcher's report, the community was incensed. A large protest march to the BBC offices was organised, forcing an apology from the magazine's editors (as well as feeding into a new mobilisation of a political consciousness that, as throughout the country generally, coalesced around and celebrated a strong 'Black' identity, including for those of mixed black and white racial parentage.

The long history of organised black resistance and protest during the twentieth century often centred around a 'Pan-African' perspective. This history also included those from mixed racial backgrounds and those in interracial relationships, such as Samuel Coleridge-Taylor, Harold Moody, George Padmore and the Mayor of Battersea, John Archer, who was of Barbadian and Irish heritage. From the 1960s onwards, this foundation was built upon by the Black Power Movement emanating from the USA which emphasised black pride and self-empowerment, both in terms of identity and organisation. For many black and minority ethnic people in Britain, including those from racially mixed backgrounds, this message was affirming and empowering. It was particularly embraced by this younger black generation, overwhelmingly British-born citizens, who increasingly challenged the racist practices and structures that the previous generation had endured. Identifying with the strong 'Black Is Beautiful' message of the Black Power Movement provided a sense of empowerment for many of those who were labelled as doubly problematic, being firstly frequently rejected from white society for being 'coloured', as well as then specifically castigated for being seen as biologically and psychologically 'mixed'.

Racism and Daily Life – 1970 to 1989

During the period between 1970 and 1990 we saw several programmes on British television playing on racial stereotypes, with extensive use of pejorative language which caused significant offense and a rise in complaints from audiences and commentators. One example of this can be seen in the *Curry and Chips* TV series in 1969.

Kevin O'Grady

The character Kevin O Grady was created by Johnny Speight from an idea by the British-Irish comedian, Spike Milligan. The sitcoms *Curry and Chips*[6] (1969) and *Til Death Us Do Part* (1974) featured a blacked up Milligan as Kevin O'Grady, an Irishman of Pakistani heritage frequently referred to in the show as 'Paki-Paddy'.

Originally aired on ITV in November 1969, *Curry and Chips* was the first London Weekend Television (LWT) sitcom to be broadcast entirely in colour. Set on the factory floor of 'Lillicrap Ltd', a cheap novelty goods manufacturer, the six part series revolved around the workers' intolerant and hostile reactions to Milligan's newly hired Kevin O'Grady character, a recent immigrant from Pakistan who, due to his Irish father, describes himself as an Irishman.

Ostensibly a comedy aiming to skewer racial discrimination, the show featured a blacked up Milligan adopting a caricatured accent alongside an endless parade of racist abuse and epithets hurled at the O'Grady character, not least his nickname 'Paki-Paddy'. Much of the humour was clearly supposed to lie in the incongruity of O'Grady's heritage and identity to the audience, despite the existence of Irish-South Asian families in real life. While the O'Grady character was frequently portrayed as more intelligent than his fellow workers, and Eric Sykes played Arthur, a liberally-minded but ineffectual foreman who often came to O'Grady's defence, the show's comedy heavily drew on the endless racial abuse directed at O'Grady (and black, Asian and Irish people generally) from the white 'I'm with Enoch' characters played by Norman Rossington and Geoffrey Hughes.

125. Kenny Lynch, Spike Milligan and Eric Sykes in 'Curry and Chips' TV programme 1969.
Image courtesy of Alamy and Mirrorpix.

Meanwhile, though Kenny Lynch's black British character was also frequently on the receiving end of their jibes, he also taunts Kevin for being a foreigner, and Kevin himself complains about 'wogs', saying 'I may be a bit brown but I'm not a wog like him'. He also complains in this extract below:

"There are far too many wogs in this country. I leave Pakistan because there are far too many wogs there. So I come to England. And there are still too many wogs.' On Arthur incredulously pointing out that he is himself one, O'Grady retorts, 'oh no, I'm Irish. Mick, red-faced Mick. Begorrah, Bejesus' while making the sign of the cross."[7]

The combination of relentless racist language (e.g. 'Micks', 'piccannies', 'coons', 'wogs', 'sambo', 'paki', 'blackie') alongside the copious use of expletives led to a shocked reaction from both viewers and commentators. Complaints were made to the Race Relations Board and the Independent Broadcasting Authority forcing LTW to pull the series after only six episodes. However, Milligan and Speight would revive the O'Grady character in 1974 for an episode of Speight's hit series for the BBC Till Death Us Do Part entitled 'Paki-Paddy'. In the episode, the main character, Alf Garnett, well-known for his prejudice towards immigrants, is taken aback to discover that O'Grady, who he had been racially abusing, is to be his new neighbour.

Again, while Speight always insisted that the joke is on the ignorance of the Garnett character, the laughter of the studio audience that greets the tirade of racism levelled at O'Grady (and black and Asian people generally) suggests that viewers found as much, if not more, humour in the racist abuse and stereotyping portrayed.[8] Similarly, the 1970's British sitcom, *Love Thy Neighbour*, was viewed as racist. See the extract from *The Guardian* below:

'Love Thy Neighbour, in the 70s, was the most highly rated programme on television, it was peak-time viewing. The basic premise was a black couple living next door to a white couple. The white neighbour was a bigot, and the dialogue was peppered with terms such as "honkies" and "nig-nogs". Here we are in 2001, and a lot of people still think that show was racist. But that was the 70s.'[9]

Mixed Race Irish Families in Britain in the 1970s and 80s

Despite the stigmatisation and racism many mixed race families, including those of Irish descent, faced in Britain during this time, life was not inevitably and constantly filled with marginalisation, rejection and confusion. Several accounts from those growing up mixed race

Irish during the 1970s and 1980s portray how the experiences and effects of racism run in tandem with the ordinariness of British and Irish life.

Gabriel Gbadamosi

The poet Gabriel Gbadamosi's debut novel *Vauxhall* (2013)[10] draws on his experiences growing up in an Irish-Nigerian family in the late 1960s and 1970s.

126. The Gbadamosi family, Vauxhall, c.1965.
Courtesy of Lambeth Archives and
Gabriel Gbadamosi (left).

Told through the eyes of Michael, a young boy growing up with his Irish mother, Yoruba father and siblings in Lambeth, the novel documents the ordinary multiculturalism of London during this time, alongside the ingrained, casual racism of the period.

Racial taunts and tensions are detailed but so is the everyday mixedness of Irish and Nigerian cultures in family life, with Guinness and fish and chips a staple of mealtimes along with yams and ewedu. Catechism classes with nuns are interspersed with parties and ceremonies with men in agbadas and women in gele headwraps.

Discussing an extract from Vauxhall, Gbadamosi remarks how as a child he failed to recognise:

> *"that my father had sixteen tribal scars on his cheeks until my friends all kind of mobbed me and said, 'he has, look, look - it's like a tiger's*

scratched him!' We can't see necessarily these things about our parents. I couldn't for much the same reason hear that my mother had an Irish accent; her voice was completely neutral for me, I thought she's without the trace of an accent. These two details about one's parents - and the people who stand behind them - are details that do go in the book. And lots of people are saying, 'well, perhaps it's really autobiographical. And what I would say about that is that indeed it probably is. I'm the writer. But on the other hand, I'm not the only writer. I'm one of six children. And I went to all of my brothers and sisters. I went to our friends. There was another Irish-Yoruba family in the area, the Akinyeles, there were ten of them. I went to the now elderly parents of that time, back in the late 60s and 70s when we were growing up. And I asked everyone to give me their stories of that time and that place. So assembled in this novel, Vauxhall, are the memories - and in many ways the dreams - of lots of people. We are legion." [11]

Jenneba Sie-Jalloh

In 1988, three Irish women who had emigrated to Britain, Mary Lennon, Marie McAdam and Joanne O'Brien, published a book called *Across the Water*, detailing the contemporary experiences of Irish women in the story of Irish immigration. Within these accounts was an interview with the writer and actor Jenneba Sie-Jalloh, a mixed race Irish woman. Born in West London in 1964, Sie-Jalloh's mother was from Limerick and her father from Sierra Leone. Her account within a collection of Irish women's voices highlighted, perhaps for the first time for many contemporary readers interested in Irish identity, how the Irish diaspora included those who weren't white.

"I call myself an African woman with an Irish mother, and a Londoner. I want to pass on whatever I've got to my children, so I've got to work it out for myself. So, for those people who want to deny me, well, I think it's them who've got the problem, not me." [12]

Second Generation Mixed Race Irish

While those of mixed race Irish backgrounds are often not visible within contemporary discussions of the second generation Irish, the ESRC project 'The Second-Generation Irish: A Hidden Population in Multi-ethnic Britain'[13] highlighted the presence of such voices. Discussing the importance of summer holidays in Ireland for the British-born children of Irish immigrants in the 1970s and 80s, Bronwen Walter notes how such holidays could be complex for those of mixed race Irish heritage.

While those who took part in the project each had a distinctive set of parental backgrounds, Walter discusses how, due to elements of conflict in each case, none had kept up the family contacts in adulthood, although each had later revisited Ireland by choice. This is not to say that the participants had bad experiences during their visits when they were young. Like second generation white Irish, most enjoyed being with relatives and the freedoms generated by a more rural life. Nevertheless, later connections to Ireland were more to a sense of the country than to extended family members.

> "It was great, it was wonderful I don't know if you know [town in County Cork], then it was a small little town, it has changed immensely, and my grandmother's home was in a place called –, it was beautiful countryside, a river running behind the house. I was 10–11 and started going when I was much younger. For me it was a great time, get out of London, beautiful countryside, the weather was good if you were lucky, and surrounded by family. It was quite a big family then, it was my grandmother, my uncle who is still there, and another brother of my mother's who has since passed away. There were cousins and friends, so it was a wonderful time, how Irish it was for me at that age, it was just visiting relatives. I was told not to walk too near the pigs by my father […] I think we were quite happy there. I was very happy there I think, as far as I know my parents were happy there together. There was some rift between my mother and her family after she married, because of whom she married, but I think which is often the case, after the grandchildren come along, and they realize that you are serious and your partner is serious, it brings most people around. [But] I guess I am not eager to go back. I have no burning desire to go back, why that is I am not sure. Ireland for me has been a place where my mother is from, and my mother hasn't been back

often in the recent past. I think the only reason why I'd go back to Ireland is if I was going with friends, or if I had the opportunity to see the country and travel. I have heard it is a stunningly beautiful country with much to do and see. So whether I would go back to [Cork] or whether I would go back to Ireland, are two slightly different questions."[14] - Tariq, son of an Indian Muslim father and a white Irish Muslim convert mother.

Phil Lynott

The son of an Irish mother and a Guyanese father, Phil Lynott was a musician who came to prominence as a founding member, principal songwriter and frontman of the rock band Thin Lizzy.[15]

127. Phil Lynott of Thin Lizzy during a recording session for the group's new album. Picture taken 27th September 1982. Image @ Alamy.

Born in 1947, Lynott[16] was initially raised by his Irish teenage mother Philomena in a Catholic home for unmarried mothers in Selly Oak, Birmingham. Struggling to find lodgings and childcare as the mother of a mixed race child, Philomena and Lynott subsequently moved to Manchester. While her relationship with Lynott's father, Cecil Parris, had ended when Lynott was an infant, Parris initially helped pay towards his son's support, though as he lived in London there was little contact between father and son and, in due course, his payments and contact would stop.

When Lynott was three, he met his Irish grandparents for the first time. Though the couple had initially been shocked at having an illegitimate mixed race grandchild, they would go on to have a close and loving relationship with Lynott. Indeed, after Philomena felt increasingly unable to cope trying to work and raise a child on her own in Manchester, his grandparents agreed to care for him in Dublin, despite the social stigma attached in Ireland to illegitimate children, not least those who were black.

In order to try and ease the stigma for the family, Lynott's grandparents pretended to neighbours that Lynott was the son of Philomena's friend, though the secret was mostly seen through. Lynott was sent to them at the age four; he would not return to England again until he moved to London in 1971 when his band, Thin Lizzy, signed a record detail. Thin Lizzy would go on to have international hits throughout the 1970s and 1980s.

128. Statue of Phil Lynott
at Harry Street, Dublin.
Photo taken by C. Bryan in 2023.

Lynott, the band's de facto leader and composer (or co-composer) of almost all the band's song, would achieve international prominence as the first black Irishman to achieve success in a rock band. Though

Philomena reported experiencing frequent prejudice and abuse in England directed at herself and her son when he was a baby, Lynott reportedly experienced very little direct racism growing up in Ireland. Lynott was inordinately proud of his Irish identity as well as his black heritage, seeing no problem with inhabiting both spaces. In an interview with the *Daily Express* in 1970, he stated that 'to be black and Irish like Guinness is natural…everyone else is a bit weird.' [17] In her article 'The Irish Rover: Phil Lynott and the Search for Identity', Lauren O'Hagan examines Lynott's lyrics to investigate his quest for identity and his "internal conflict between being black, Irish, illegitimate, a rockstar, a Lothario, a son, a father, and a husband, all at the same time."[18]

In an interview with the *Irish Independent* in 2013, the Thin Lizzy guitarist Scott Gorham said "Phil was so proud of being Irish. No matter where he went in the world, if we were talking to a journalist and they got something wrong about Ireland, he'd give the guy a history lesson. It meant a lot to him." Several of Lynott's songs touch on the topic of identity, including 'Halfcaste', the B Side of the group's 1975 single 'Rosalie'.

In 1980, Lynott married Caroline Crowther, the daughter of the British television presenter Leslie Crowther. The pair had two daughters, while Lynott also had a son from his earlier years who was given up for adoption. To the outside world marriage seemed to have tamed down Lynott's partying ways, particularly his drug and alcohol usage. In his last interview with the Irish press, Lynott spoke about his Sunday routine involving taking his daughters to mass and then spending the evenings reacquainting himself with traditional Irish music.

However, in reality his dependency on drugs and alcohol was still significant and by 1984 had led to his marriage falling apart. On Christmas Day 1985, Lynott was discovered by his mother collapsed alone at his home in Kew, West London. He died of pneumonia and heart failure due to septicaemia on 4 January 1986, at the age of 36, and was buried in St Fintan's cemetery in Dublin.

Lynott's legacy as a black Irish rock pioneer has been long-lasting. In 2005, a life-size bronze statue of Lynott was erected in the centre of Dublin (see page 218), and in November 2019, the Central Bank of Ireland issued 3,000 €15 silver commemorative coins as part of the 'Modern Irish Musicians' series, commemorating the 70th anniversary of Lynott's birth.

John Conteh

The son of a West African father and a mother of Irish descent, John Conteh[19] came to fame in the 1970s and 1980s as a boxing champion and celebrity. From 1974 to 1978 he held the World Boxing Council (WBC) light heavyweight title as well as European, British and Commonwealth titles, positioning him as one of Britain's great boxing champions.

Immediately taking to the sport and - after a spell in in his teens at an approved school for breaking into a supermarket with friends - Conteh clocked up an impressive forty-six wins in fifty fights. He went on to win three gold medals at the 1970 Commonwealth Games, as well as the senior Amateur Boxing Association [ABA] championships at middleweight in 1970 and then at light heavyweight in 1971.

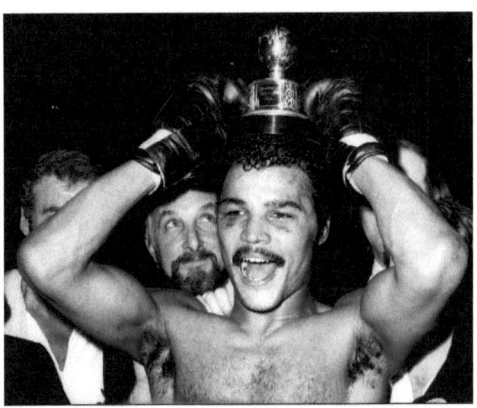

129. John Conteh holds his trophy aloft after becoming the world light heavyweight champion, at Wembley, after beating Jorge Ahumada of Argentina. 10 October 1974. Image @Alamy.

Turning professional at the age of twenty, during the years 1974-1978 Conteh would go on to become the holder of the WBC European, British and Commonwealth titles as well as become the WBC light heavyweight champion.

Outside the ring, Conteh became a well-known celebrity thanks to his good looks and charismatic personality.

As well as appearing on the cover of the Paul McCartney and Wings album *Band on the Run* (1973) (along with Kenny Lynch), he featured in the BBC sports challenge show *Superstars* (winning the 1974 title) and was the subject of *This is Your Life in 1974*,[20] at which his Irish mother made an appearance with him. Conteh also made appearances in a number of films, including *Man at the Top* (1973) and *The Stud* (1978).

130. 'Band on the Run' album was Wings' third and most successful album. Released in 1973, with John Conteh (far right) and Kenny Lynch (second from left). Image @Alamy.

In the late 1970s, Conteh married the model Veronica Smith who he met when she was tasked with looking after him at an exhibition at Earl's Court. The pair would go on to have two children.

131. John Conteh escorting Veronica Smith at the Gala Premiere of the motion picture 'Rollerball', .3 September 1975. Image @Alamy.

Conteh's brilliant boxing career was cut short after a fight in 1980 resulted in a failed brain scan post-match thus causing his boxing licence to be revoked. Unfortunately, the acting and advertising opportunities that lay before him were squandered as Conteh lapsed into an alcoholism that his boxing routine could no longer keep at bay. Regaining sobriety in the early 1990s, Conteh has since been teetotal and in addition to dabbling in acting he is in demand as an after dinner speaker. He was awarded an MBE in 2017 for his services to boxing.

Tara Prem

Born in 1946 to the Indian actor Bakshi Prem and an Irish mother, Tara Prem came to prominence in the 1970s as a young television producer who was instrumental in writing and commissioning British multicultural TV drama.

Educated at the French Lycée in South West London, Prem went on to study drama at the University of Bristol and in Paris before working for a brief spell in the early 1970s as a theatre actor and then in the Indian film industry. However, a stint in Chicago led her to develop an interest in directing and, on her return from America, Prem moved into television, initially working as a trainee script editor for the BBC. Increasingly interested in modern, regional work, in her late twenties Prem moved to Birmingham to work at Pebble Mill Studios alongside David Rose, the head of English Regions Drama, whose role was to enable the regions to supply more programmes to the national television service. In an interview in 2013, with Eleni Liarou, Tara said the following:

> *"So I got up there and, you know, got into the swing of things. And one of the first things I realised, which became really important for me and the whole way things went, was because of my Indian background, is that - I mean, it wasn't as much as it is now - but nevertheless, Birmingham had a huge amount of Indians even in 1974. And you know, you looked out of your window - well, not quite out of your window because Pebble Mill was in a very white area! - but what I mean is, you know, it was there and it was extremely obvious and I said, you know, if we're going to reflect the English regions, the first thing we should do is reflect what's going on in Birmingham and to somehow get this world, into...onto the television."*
>
> *"Because I knew how much it wasn't on the television because of...my father was an actor, my father was an Indian actor. And so ...my father came to England in 1932, he was here before the war. And he'd come to be a doctor and then he'd dropped out and had gone*

into the BBC Indian radio where they all did all…European classics - Shakespeare, Chekhov, Ibsen, Shaw - all in Hindi and Urdu to broadcast it back to India. It was incredible, really." [21]

The first drama in Pebble Mill's newly commissioned series Second Cities First was Prem's *A Touch of Eastern Promise* (1973)[22] which was shot in a predominantly Asian district of Birmingham, emphasising both regionality and the multicultural population of the area. It was the first drama on British television to have an entirely Asian cast, with some of characters speaking with a distinctive Birmingham accent while others spoke Punjabi.

132. A still image: *A Touch of Eastern Promise*.
Courtesy of BBC Archives.

While Prem credited her Indian father for her initial interest in the theatre, in an interview with *The Birmingham Post* in 1975, she notes that it was really her Irish mother who was responsible for guiding her interest in drama and said the following:

"She used to take me to the Old Vic when I was young. It was the time when it was only 1s. 6d. to go up in the gallery, and Richard Burton was taking all the Shakespearean leads." [23]

In 2015, Prem was awarded the Outstanding Contribution to Media Award by the Asian Media Awards for her longstanding work in multicultural programming.

Chris Hughton

Chris Hughton, the son of an Irish mother and a Ghanaian father, was the first black footballer to play for Ireland. In 2019 he said the following to the *Irish Independent* newspaper:

> *"I was the first black player to play for Ireland, which is something I am hugely proud of, even today… It became normal after that for black players to play for Ireland, Paul McGrath came a few years later. There was no black community in Ireland when I played but that's not the case now, Ireland has changed dramatically.*
>
> *I was always conscious that I was a black player, the only one in the team with Ireland and, believe it or not, Tottenham at the time, but I was pleased to see others follow me.*
>
> *I had only been to Ireland twice before I played for the Republic. My mother is from Limerick, but my nan used to come over to us in England every summer. We didn't go to Limerick for our summer holidays the way a lot of the Irish community did.*
>
> *I jumped at the chance to play for Ireland, but also I didn't have this really strong association with the country."* [24]

Born in Forest Gate, London in 1958, Hughton's mother, Christine, was from Ballinacura, Limerick and his father, Willie, was Ghanaian. Along with his sister, Annette, and brother, Henry, who would go to play for Ireland's under-21 team in 1981, Hughton grew up in Upton Park, receiving his education at St Bonaventure's Catholic School and completing an apprenticeship as an engineer before signing with Tottenham Hotspur.

Making his league debut in 1979, one month later Hughton would also don Ireland's green jersey, making his debut for Ireland in a friendly against the USA. Hughton has mentioned that he had only ever been to Ireland twice before he joined the team. His Irish grandmother and aunt come to visit the family in London rather than Hughton and his mother visiting Ireland in the holidays, the way that many Irish families in Britain did. An article on Hughton and his Irish heritage in the Limerick leader in 1988, featured a photo of a six year old Hughton, his mother and siblings visiting relatives in Limerick.

Though Hughton jumped at the chance to play for Ireland, he did not have the strong association with the country, like some of the other British footballers of Irish descent. However, growing up in the East

London of the 1970s, an era when racism was rife, meant that Hughton's identity was not rooted in England either.

133. Extract from 'My Joy at Chris, by Mrs Hughton'.
Limerick Leader, 18 April 1988. Image courtesy of the National Library of Ireland.

In an interview with the *Irish Independent* in 2010, Hughton said:

"I was born in London, therefore I am from England but I have never felt English [...] I don't mean that I'm anti-English, because I am not but as soon as I started working these things out, I saw myself as a sort of United Nations man...." [25]

'*He was Ireland's first black player and now he quietly makes a stand for black managers in Britain who have felt excluded from the closed shop that is the clubbable English management circuit. Hughton won't fit in there easily.*' [26]

As the only black player in the Ireland team, Hughton came up against a range of views on his place there, including those that he describes as 'uncomfortable':

> *"I went through some very uncomfortable situations where you are in company as the only black person there, and things are said, what some would see as banter. For a lot of black people in that environment it would have been very uncomfortable, you do turn a blind eye to some things and get on with it. As you got older and wiser, maybe more confident, you right some of the wrongs and over the years I have had to stand up to people, to tell them I am not 'coloured' but I am black. In those days some would refer to people like me as half-caste, which is an awful term. So, as you get on in life, you stand up and say, 'I am black'."*[27]

At the same time, however, he notes that during his time in Ireland as a black Londoner, he never experienced the level of racist abuse that he received during his career in England during the 1970s and 80s.

> *"It was a difficult time but in all my years playing for Ireland I never experienced what I had in England. From the fans and the people around the team with Ireland I never had a problem. It was a very welcoming place, that dressing-room. Maybe an Irish dressing-room was different as we had a mix anyway, lads born in Ireland with players, like me, who qualified through parentage, different accents, so it was easy to bed in [...] I never remember getting racial prejudice in Ireland.*[28]
>
> *I was brought up in a football environment where we saw a lot of racism – whether it was abuse from other players or huge groups of supporters in away matches. I remember going to stadiums and huge sections of the stand gave you racial abuse. It was never nice but it wasn't a surprise – particularly when I was first at Spurs. I was the only black player in the team followed by Garth Crooks [three years later]. You were used to it if somebody made a racial comment to you on the pitch. I wouldn't say you accepted it, but you had to get on with it."*[29]

Hughton made his professional debut with Tottenham Hotspur at 20, and went on to play for West Ham, and Brentford. He also earned

53 caps representing Ireland and paved the way for other black British and mixed race Irish footballers to play for Ireland. After his retirement, Hughton went into football coaching before becoming a manager making him one of a very small group of black players to become managers. While twenty-five percent of players in English football's four divisions are from a black, Asian and minority ethnic background, over 97% of managers are white. Hughton is a vocal advocate for both addressing the ongoing issue of racism in football, including the lack of diversity at senior management levels of the game.

Chapter 8

Celebrated Personalities

This chapter includes a selection of high profile people of colour across Britain and Ireland in the later part of the 20th Century. They include celebrated writers and campaigners who dared raise their voices, as well as sports stars, actors and others, many of whom struggled in early life and managed, against all odds, to overcome adversity and be the voice and soul of their people and communities. This is by no means an exhaustive list of people, there are countless other great stories, far too many for this publication.

Christine Buckley – Advocate for Survivors of Childhood Abuse
In the *Dictionary of National Biography*, Liz Evers describes Christine Buckley (1946-2014) as a "nurse, midwife and advocate for survivors of childhood abuse in religious and state-supported institutions".

134. Christine Buckley, 20 May 2009.
Release of Report of the Commission
to Inquire into Child Abuse.
Courtesy of the Buckley family
and Charles Collins.

She was "born Christine West on 10 October 1946 at Mile End Hospital, London"[1] in England, and was the daughter of Anna West (née Kershaw) from Longford, and Ariwodo Kalunta, a medical student from Nigeria. Her father was studying at Trinity College Dublin (TCD).[2]

Christine Buckley became prominent in the 1990's as a campaigner for survivors of childhood abuse in Irish childcare institutions, such as orphanages, Industrial and Reformatory Schools. She gave a voice to thousands of people who experienced child abuse, not only to those living in Ireland but also to those living in the United Kingdom and further afield, to where many had fled for safe sanctuary. There were many people of mixed African Irish parentage among the survivors who had been left in these childcare institutions in Ireland and who emigrated to Britain. In writing about Christine Buckley, Patsy McGarry wrote the following in the *Irish Times* in 2014:

> *'Her story is history as driven by one person. She was an original, a pioneer in exposing how badly this State "cherished" many of its children, whatever their age, throughout most of the 20th century, up to 1996 when the last Magdalene laundry closed. If a high point of much of her work was then taoiseach Bertie Ahern's 1999 apology on behalf of the State to all who had been in residential institutions as children, as well as his announcement then of the Commission to Inquire into Child Abuse (Ryan Commission) and the setting up of the Residential Institutions Redress Board, it was not all.'* [3]

Her influence and activism undoubtedly led the way to future investigations such as the Murphy Commission, which investigated clerical sexual abuse in Dublin and Cloyne dioceses, the McAleese committee which investigated the Magdalene laundries, as well as the more recent Commission of Investigation into Mother and Baby Homes set up in 2015.

Her campaign began in earnest when she agreed to participate in a drama-documentary called *Dear Daughter,*[4] produced by Louis Lentin in 1996, which was "the first televised exposure of the horrific abuse of hundreds of children in Ireland's industrial schools."[5] It was broadcast on RTÉ on 22 February 1996. The exposure of the abuse she and others suffered in St. Vincent's Industrial School, run by the Sisters of Mercy, in Goldenbridge, Dublin, was not received well by the establishment, especially the Church. Christine Buckley was a lone voice and was vilified for her actions by so called authoritative figures. The abuses exposed in *Dear Daughter* were subsequently denied on RTE's *Prime Time* programme. Mary Raftery said in an RTE interview in 2010 that:

> *"at the time everything was quite small, it was centred around one institution, the experience of a small number of people. It was basically one person's word against another, was how the public saw it. I knew enough at that stage to know that everything that Christine Buckley had been saying and Bernadette Fahy and all the women in Goldenbridge [was true], not only was it true about Goldenbridge, but it was also true about the other 51 Industrial Schools throughout the length and breadth of the country"* [6]

Following *Dear Daughter*, Mary Raftery had begun to work on another documentary in 1998, called *States of Fear*, to investigate the abuses happening in a wider number of institutions. This documentary was focused on establishing the wider systemic nature of the child abuses across several childcare institutions. By identifying a widespread pattern, she would lend more credibility to the allegations made at that time by Christine Buckley and others. In the 2010 RTE interview Raftery said:

> *"at that time it wasn't an absolute knowledge I had, it was a very well-rounded suspicion and it was very clear that what I had to do was spend a very long time speaking with survivors of Industrial schools, because it was only by doing that, that you could develop, get an incontrovertible picture of what these places were like. It was a question of constructing a series of programmes that wouldn't allow people to go back into denial again. In other words, that the body of evidence would be so overwhelming that it could not be denied anymore. To do that you needed to make a documentary about a system, not about, you know, an individual, you know, one or two or three individual experiences within the system. Though obviously, at the end of the day, it's all about that pain that individuals suffered...As soon as we got into those files we realised actually, the State knew all about this. The State knew that children were starving. The State knew that the children were beaten and the State ignored complaint after complaint even from their own officials."* [7]

Dear Daughter was one of several television documentaries, including Lentin's Stolen Lives (1999) and Mary Rafferty's *States of Fear* (1999) noted above, which raised awareness of the child abuse in religious-run and State-funded institutions, and which lead to the commissioning of the Murphy and Ryan reports, which investigated the sexual abuse scandal in the Catholic archdiocese of Dublin and in Industrial schools, respectively. These documentaries put pressure on the Irish State, which could no longer deny the abuses that had happened and which eventually lead to a full State apology to victims of clerical child abuse by Bertie Ahern, the then Taoiseach (Prime Minister).[8]

Christine Buckley was the daughter of an Irish woman and a Nigerian medical student. "At the age of three weeks old she was given up to be fostered. *Dear Daughter* delves into her traumatic childhood at the orphanage and her persistent determination to find her parents."[9]

Buckley was born in England, after which she was brought to Ireland with her mother. At three weeks old she was placed in the infant hospital run by St. Patrick's Guild, Temple Hill, Blackrock, Co. Dublin and lived there until late 1947. She was placed with a foster family until late 1950, when she was committed by the Children's Court to St Vincent's Industrial School, in Goldenbridge, Dublin, run by the Sisters of Mercy. "Because she was mixed race, it seems that adoption was not considered an option for Buckley, and subsequently no adoption papers were ever signed by her mother."[10] Neither of her parents were informed about the court's decision.

It is worth noting that the *Dictionary of Irish Biography* mentions that when Buckley was doing her general nursing studies in Drogheda, she managed to gain access to her British birth certificate. "In the document Anna West (née Kershaw) was correctly named as her mother, but her father was falsely named as Anna's then-deceased husband William West, at an address in Stepney, London." Some mixed race children found out later in life that the falsification of their birth certificates would make it significantly more difficult to trace their African fathers and establish their true identity.

> *'Her father, however, managed to maintain contact with her during her first two years at Goldenbridge. Paying a donation to the Sisters, he visited her at the orphanage, often accompanied by a woman Buckley had assumed was her mother, but was in fact her father's landlady. Kalunta left Ireland in the 1950s to undertake graduate studies in psychiatry in Newcastle, England, then returned to practice in Nigeria in the 1960s, …'*[11]

Buckley first met her mother in 1985 and she gave permission for her father's name to be released. Buckley was then able to trace her father to Nigeria, where he was a practicing psychiatrist. Dr. Ariwodo Kalunta visited Ireland in 1992, and in November that year, he appeared with his daughter, Christine Buckley, on RTÉ TV's *Late Late Show*. A few days later, they both appeared on the *Gay Byrne Show* on RTÉ Radio One and she spoke about tracing her father and her experiences at Goldenbridge. This was the first time abuses at Goldenbridge had been revealed in public and, as Suzy Byrne said in her book: "that interview would lift the lid on one of Ireland's darkest and most shameful chapters".[12]

135. Christine Buckley with her father, Dr. Ariwodo Kalunta, in November 1992. Image courtesy of the Buckley family.

Later in 1999, Christine Buckley and Carmel McDonnell-Byrne (a fellow survivor), founded the Aislinn Education and Support Centre in Dublin for survivors, which was formally opened by the Minister for Health in early 2000. "The centre provided a safe, judgement-free community environment where abuse survivors could be among people who had similar experiences."

The purpose of the centre was to help survivors to move on with their lives through therapy and education, which helped many gain junior and leaving certificates, further education awards and even admission to universities. This work took up much of Buckley's "time in the latter years, even as she struggled with bouts of cancer" for several decades. In 2009, she was presented with the 'European Volunteer of the Year' award at the European Parliament in Strasbourg. In 2012, she was awarded an honorary doctorate by Trinity College Dublin, her father's alma mater. As McGarry described in his Irish Times article of 29 December 2014, Christine Buckley was truly a "21st century Irish hero".

136. Christine Buckley in 2010 at the Aislinn Centre. Image courtesy of Julien Behal and Alamy.

Christine Buckley remains an inspiration for human rights activists and campaigners in Ireland today.

The Story of M, SuAndi - Poet and Writer
The complexity of mixed race families, as well as their longstanding history, is captured in SuAndi's *The Story of M* (1994), an autobiographical monodrama that pays tribute to her white Liverpudlian-Irish mother who married a Nigerian merchant seaman and raised her children in Manchester during the 1950s and 1960s.

As Deirdre Osborne discusses, *The Story of M*, commissioned in 1994 by the Institute of Contemporary Arts, was born of a time 'when British writers of African descent were beginning to assert their artistic presence in mainstream culture, while maintaining strong grassroots connections.'

The piece, in which SuAndi performs as both daughter and mother, powerfully reflects on both the life and death of SuAndi's white Liverpudlian-Irish mother who had raised mixed race children of

Nigerian descent against the racist backdrop of the 1950s and 1960s, as well as SuAndi's own experiences of growing up in Manchester as the daughter of a white mother and a black father.

The Story of M, in which SuAndi layers her mother's reminiscences with her own, weaves together a history of Britain from the multiracial Liverpool of the 1920s, to the racism of Manchester in the 1950s, as well as life in Britain in the 1990s. In doing so, SuAndi not only highlights the prejudices directed towards mixed race families during the twentieth century, but also shines a spotlight on the norms of daily life for such families that had so long been missing from the 'outsider' accounts typically produced by the media, academia and the arts.

The Story of M[13]

Then there's the media,
desperate for a story,
Headlining,
The Mixed Heritage, confused shows.
They can F***
I know exactly who I am -
I am a Black woman
A mixed race woman.
I am proud to be a Nigerian daughter
whose father loved her.
He loved me so much,
And I am equally proud to be the daughter
of a Liverpool woman of Irish descent.

Racial prejudice was often directed at British soldiers of colour despite their service to Britain. SuAndi's father was a merchant seaman who was captured in the Battle of the Atlantic and he was held as a German prisoner of war.

137. SuAndi's father.
Courtesy of SuAndi.

138. SuAndi, aged 8.
Courtesy of SuAndi.

"The Story of M combines the use of dramatic monologue with the presence of the writer/performer; the character 'M' is Margaret, SuAndi's mother, played by SuAndi, daughter, performer.

This 'heightened form of writing', as Catherine Ugwu describes it, is one that compositionally and aesthetically 'writes' a story that has not been told: a story that 'locates' in the 'space' in between black and white."[14]

A published poet and the freelance Cultural Director of National Black Arts Alliance, in 1999 SuAndi was awarded an OBE for her contribution to the Black Arts Sector. She has also received honorary degrees from Lancaster University and Manchester Metropolitan University for her work in the literature and the arts in general. In recent years, SuAndi has worked to preserve the history of the pre and post-war African community in Manchester, many of whom married white women. The moving memories and histories of these families have been collected into the works Afro Solo UK and Strength of our Mothers.

Outside of *The Story of M*, SuAndi has also described the importance of both her father's Nigerian ancestry and her mother's Irish heritage on shaping her identity and experiences.

Celebrated Personalities

139. SuAndi receiving her honorary degree
From Manchester Metropolitan University, July 2019.
Courtesy of SuAndi.

"My mother was raised by nuns at Knolle Park in Liverpool and I believe she had my brother within the walls of the Magdalena sisters because she used to speak of the laundries. I was raised within the confines of the Catholicism transported from County Wicklow to Liverpool, my mother's place of birth, and married to the missionary zeal of Nigeria [...]. There is nothing clever about my writing and I write for performance, not the page. I come from a family of talkers. From both sides of the globe my family have retold their lives to each other around coal fires in a converted terrace shop with a crooked window installed by whole village of Black men, to whom my father never spoke a word because they were Caribbeans. (another example of the ignorance of those times). I do not attempt to follow any form, it doesn't interest me. I want my work to sound like a conversation - the exchange of secrets, often some that should not really be spoken. My mother's mouth was filled with the over-the-fence chatter of Liverpool, expanding her expressions with an inherited Irish superstitiousness - we never did anything that might tempt fate against us. So we never wrote anything down, preferring to whisper it on." [15]

Joanna Traynor - Writer
As Deirdre Osborne highlights, during the 1990s a body of fiction emerged that portrayed the experiences of those that Valerie Mason-John described as 'trans-raised': i.e. those who grew up in Britain in the 1960s and 70s and who self-identify as black or mixed race, but who were reared by white people either in adoptive or foster care or institutional settings.

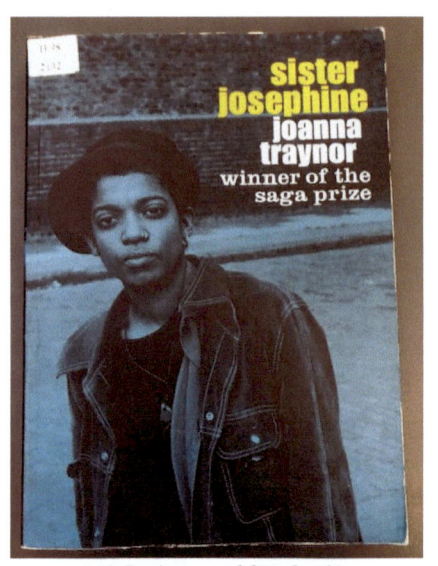

140. Book cover of *Sister Josephine* by Joanna Tryanor. Image courtesy of Bloomsbury Publishing and the British Library Board. Shelfmark: H.98/2132.

Many of these children had mothers of Irish background or descent. Among these was Joanna Traynor who won the Saga Prize in 1997 for her novel *Sister Josephine*, which drew on her harrowing experiences as a mixed race child in foster care. The daughter of a Nigerian father and a mother of Irish descent, Traynor spent the early years of her life in a children's home before being placed with a strict white Catholic family in Liverpool. Years of emotional, physical and sexual abuse were to follow, much of which is reflected in the depiction of her protagonist Josie.[16] In the novel, when Josie finally leaves her foster care to start a nursing course, she receives her birth certificate and realises for the first time that her heritage, which was kept from her all her life, includes an Irish mother. In her book, *Sister Josephine*, she describes receiving her birth certificate for the first time as follows:

> "*The paper was cream-coloured like my O level certificates. It was a certificate of some sort, I could tell. I tried to slide it out of the envelope without creasing the paper. I turned it over. It was my birth certificate.*
> *O'Leary. Mary O'Leary. Name of Father - Blank. Name of Child - Josephine. Occupation of mother - student. The blank bugged me. More than the Mary. I was Josephine O'Leary. And the invisible mother had a name. An Irish name. I went to tell the warden that I was Josephine O'Leary so she could tick me off her list.*" - Extract from *Sister Josephine* [17]

As had long been the case through the twentieth century, and earlier, having a mixed race child often further increased the stigma of illegitimacy, particularly in the Irish community in Britain where birth outside marriage was highly disapproved of. As such, many white women of Irish descent in Britain either gave or were pressured to give their mixed race babies up for adoption. However, these same pressures made people loathe to foster or adopt mixed race children for fear of being exposed to prejudiced attitudes; those who did foster or adopt mixed race children often replicated, consciously or unconsciously, social prejudices towards the children. Consequently, mixed race children placed in care tended to be remain there until adulthood or, if they were taken into a family, experienced difficult upbringings. In an interview in 1998 Traynor said:

> "*I was three and a half when I was taken out of the children's home in Liverpool, and taken to my foster family,*" she says. "*I remember the day I arrived at this place. They stuck me on a chair, and all I remember is people prodding me. I don't think they'd seen a black child before. I had a bright red coat on with big, black buttons. And I wanted them to stop prodding me. It was my first coat and I really liked it. I'd never had one before; probably because I'd never gone anywhere!*" [18]

Bernardine Evaristo - Writer

Lara, Bernardine Evaristo's debut novel published in 1997, draws on Evaristo's own interracial family history over seven generations, including Irish ancestors, to explore life for a mixed race family in the London in the 1960s and 70s.

141. *Lara*, a debut novel by Bernardine Evaristo Published in 2009, featuring a photo of her parents. Reproduced courtesy of Bloodaxe Books.

Semi-autobiographical and written in verse, *Lara* traces the roots of a racially mixed English-Nigerian-Brazilian-Irish family over 150 years, three continents and seven generations. The story follows the journey of the eponymous Lara, the fourth of eight children produced from the marriage of Taiwo, a Nigerian man, and Ellen, a white British mother, as she seeks to understand herself and her heritage beyond the white suburb of Woolwich in the 1960s and 70s.

> "*Lara was very much about excavating my family history; it was about exploring an area of British history that I felt hadn't been covered hardly at all in literature in this country. I wanted to write about a mixed-race African-English marriage in London in the 1950s, which was based on my family history.*"[19]

Yet, as well as Lara's personal journey, Evaristo also explores the lives of generations of people who migrate to other countries in search of a better life and the struggles of acceptance and integration they and their future generations find there, including from the families they marry into.

> *"It is the story of Irish Catholics leaving generations of rural hardship behind and ascending to a rigid middle class in England; of German immigrants escaping poverty and seeking to build a new life in 19th century London; and of proud Yorubas enslaved in Brazil, free in colonial Nigeria and hopeful in post-war London."* [20]

Evaristo's devoutly Catholic mother, Jaqueline, was of English, German and Irish heritage, her own mother coming to England from Birr, Co Offaly, at the end of the 19th century. Evaristo's father, Julius, who had come to Britain in 1949, was of Nigerian and Brazilian heritage. His own Yoruba father was an 'Aguda', an emancipated African 'slave' who returned to Nigeria.

The couple met at a Catholic overseas social club and Evaristo, born in 1959, was the fourth of eight children. Evaristo's Irish grandmother was fiercely opposed to her only daughter's marriage while the rest of her mother's family were so appalled that they 'treated her as if she was dead.

> *"My grandmother could not believe that her only child, into whom she had poured her dreams "like syrup on treacle tart," was going to ruin everything by marrying someone one gene up from an ape: an African. And most importantly, in her curtain-twitching, small-minded, suburban neighbourhood—what on earth would the neighbours think? ...*
>
> *As my grandmother, fictionalised as Peggy, says to my mother (Ellen) in Lara: Do you think I'm going to let you ruin your life by marrying ... a darkie ... a n*****-man? You silly girl! I have sacrificed my whole life for you. How cruel How can you do this to me, your own mother! Peggy gulped a scream down, balled fist to open mouth, a Greek tragic-mask, then fled the room, bawling."* [21]

As Proctor notes, Evaristo's background and diasporic heritage deeply informs her writing, raising important questions around identity, nation and citizenship. 'Her fiction makes clear the fact that it is no longer, and more importantly never was, possible to return to a pure, white, Anglo-Saxon Britain prior to immigration.' *Lara* won the EMMA Best Book Award in 1999. Ten years later, Evaristo would go on to win the Booker Prize for her novel *Girl, Woman, Other* (2019).[22]

Other Irish People of Colour in the Public Eye

Alongside the emerging 'new wave' of mixed race voices in the arts and social sciences, there was increasingly a public recognition that not only could people hold multiple identities at once, such as claiming both Irish and African or Caribbean identities, for example, but that they did not feel their mixed heritages were negative or problematic. Similarly, where experiences had been negative, there was also a growing acknowledgement that these were not the result of some inherent aspect of being 'mixed race' but the result of social attitudes. With Irish citizenship laws stating that no matter where a person is born, anyone whose parent or grandparent is an Irish citizen is entitled to Irish citizenship, football in Ireland under the management of Jack Charlton saw the so-called 'granny rule' open the doors to the recruitment of those from the Irish diaspora to Irish teams. Consequently, the presence of mixed race Irish families in Britain was highlighted in the 1990s by the selection of footballers such as Terry Phelan and Phil Babb to play for Ireland.

Paul McGrath – International Footballer
Paul McGrath, the renowned Irish footballer, was born in Greenford, Middlesex UK in December 1959. His mother, Betty McGrath, was from Dublin in Ireland and his father a Nigerian medical student studying in Dublin.[23]

After a brief relationship, Betty became pregnant and, as frequently happened in Ireland during the twentieth century due to the stigma of having an illegitimate child, she fled to the UK to have her baby. As with the case of Philomena Lynott, Betty McGrath came under immense pressure from the nuns at the Mother and Baby Home in Acton, West London to put her child up for adoption. Despite refusing to sign McGrath away, the Catholic Crusade organisation on St. Anne's Street in Dublin was contacted to arrange fostering. On returning to Dublin, Betty's son was 'yanked' from her grasp by two women from the Catholic Crusade when she arrived on the pier and McGrath was placed in foster care.

142. Paul McGrath, footballer for EIRE & Aston Villa FC
6 June 1994. Image @ Alamy.

After the breakdown of his foster arrangement, McGrath was put into a Smyly Trust Home orphanage, colloquially called 'The Nest', which was run by a Protestant congregation. In 1971 he was sent to another institution called Glen Silva and later to Race Field House in Dublin where he would meet other mixed race children. In his autobiography, McGrath talks of being institutionalised as a child and his later problems in dealing with alcohol addiction.

A talented footballer in junior leagues, McGrath soon attracted the attention of a scout and after a short stint as an apprentice metal worker and security guard in Dublin, in 1981 he became a professional player with St. Patrick's Athletic. Signed by Manchester United in 1982, McGrath returned to the country of his birth, becoming a celebrated footballer in the Premier League, playing for Aston Villa after his departure from Manchester. Married twice, with five children, McGrath retired from professional football in 1998 and returned to Ireland, settling down in Wexford. He is considered one of Ireland's greatest players of all time.

Phil Babb – International Footballer

Babb was born in Lambeth, London, in 1970 and was the son of Guyanese father and an Irish mother. He qualified to play for Ireland at the age of 22 through his mother, who was born in Carlow.

143. Phil Babb, footballer (Front far right) with Paul McGrath (Top second left). 1994 FIFA World Cup USA Group E - Italy v Republic of Ireland - Giants Stadium, New York. Image @ Alamy.

Babb started his football career at Millwall and was transferred to Bradford City in 1990, where he made his entry into the English League. He was described in the Irish Press as a "very versatile player with pace, composure and good passing ability" who was then sold to Coventry City and quickly established himself there as the club's number 1 centre-half and voted player of the year by the Highfield fans in the 1993-94 season. His leadership was recognised by the club who appointed him captain of the team in 1994. He subsequently went on to play for Liverpool, and played in the victorious 1995 Football League Cup Final.

Babb made his first appearance for Ireland as a substitute in their match with Hungary in June 1993 at Lansdowne Road in Dublin.[24] Hungary beat Ireland 4-2, however, as this was a David O' Leary testimonial match, it wasn't regarded as a full international match. The *Irish Press* (20 April 1994) noted that 'for Babb it was anything but a polished introduction as he looked both nervous and over-awed, prompting Jack Charlton to say afterwards that "Phil has a lot to learn about international football."'

He went on the win his first cap against Russia in March the following year "where he handled things quite comfortably". Babb went on to play in defence along with Paul McGrath in the 1-0 win against Italy in the 1994 FIFA World Cup USA at Giants Stadium, New York.

He ended his football career at Sunderland in 2004. Over the course of his football career, he earned 35 caps playing for the Republic of Ireland.

Kanya King – Business Leader in the Music Industry

Growing up in Kilburn, London as one of eight siblings, Kanya King is the youngest daughter of an Irish mother and a Ghanaian father who died when King was 13.

144. Kanya King MOBO Founder and Chief Executive Kanya King promotes the 2009 MOBO Awards at the Clyde Auditorium. Image @ Alamy.

Working as a TV researcher after studying English Literature at Goldsmiths, King realised that there was a gap in mainstream British music awards to acknowledge music originating from black culture.

Putting up her own house as security, King not only funded the awards but persuaded Carlton TV to broadcast the event which she named Music of Black Origin. The 'MOBOs' as the awards would go on to be known, have continued to provide a platform and launch pad for numerous British artists and are recognised as one of the most prestigious global music events. In 1999, King was awarded an MBE for her services to the music industry, and a CBE in the 2018 Birthday Honours List. Interviewed in 2017 Kanya King said of her father:

> *"I didn't realise it at the time but he had a strong African accent, you don't notice as a kid. People would ask what's it like to have one black and one white parent and I'd say 'what's it like not to'?"* [25]

Terry Phelan – International Footballer
Born in 1967, Phelan grew up in Lower Broughton, Salford and would go on to have a successful career playing in the Premier League for Manchester City, Chelsea and Everton.

145. Terry Phelan footballer
for EIRE & Everton FC
20 October 1997. Image @ Alamy.

A rare mixed race face in his white neighbourhood, Phelan faced 'proper abuse' growing up. However, the son of a mother from Tubbercurry, Co. Sligo, Phelan was raised with a fiercely proud Irish identity and had always seen playing for Ireland as his ultimate dream. We have not identified any information about his father.

At the age of 24, he made his Irish debut in a friendly against Hungary and would go on to make 42 appearances playing for Ireland, including at the 1994 FIFA World Cup. From the outset, Phelan had no time for those who questioned his right both to play for Ireland or to see himself as an Irishman. In an interview in 2020 he said:

> *"My mother was Irish, all her family were Irish - it was Irish through and through [...]. There was no talk of being English, that was how I grew up. There was only one place I was ever going to play for and that was Ireland - it was in your blood. My mother was a staunch Irish lady. She was never going to change. I always wanted to put the green jersey on more than anything else. I saw myself as an Irishman [...] I wasn't bothered by what people said, 'Oh you're a plastic this and a plastic that'. That never got talked about at an Irish [team] table. A lot of the players were born in England but that wasn't our fault. I know we used to have hassle from locals in Ireland saying that, 'We should be playing our own players'. I played for the Irish youth team from a young boy at 15-years-of age, so I came right through the ranks; I just didn't land in the first team right away - I had to work hard to get there. I always got overlooked [...] But because my mother went and lived in England for a better life, a better job and she had her children in England - does that make us any different because we don't speak in an Irish accent? That's what annoys me. I've got an Irish passport, I'm Irish through and through but I don't speak with the accent and people have a go at you because of that - they call you a plastic Irishman. I don't agree with that. I'm as Irish as the next person, whether they were born in Dublin, born in Cork, born in Sligo. Why not? Why can't we be?"*[26]

Wilf O'Reilly – Speed Skater

The son of an Irish mother and an American father, Wilf O'Reilly was raised by his mother in Birmingham.[27]

146. Wilf O'Reilly, speed skating champion, Calgary 1988.
Courtesy of BBC Archives.

Taking up figure skating as a boy at his local ice rink, at the age of 13 O'Reilly turned to speed skating. He won two gold medals at the 1988 Calgary Winter Olympics when short track speed skating was held as a demonstration sport, and went on to win the World Championship in the Sydney in 1991. In 1997, O'Reilly was awarded an MBE for his services to sport. He is now coach of the Netherlands short track team. Wilf O'Reilly has spoken about his childhood and career to the BBC in the interview called: *Sochi 2014: Wilf O'Reilly's Sporting Life*.[28]

Racial Mixing, the Irish Ethnic Group and the 2001 Census

With no official category for those who see themselves as 'mixed race Irish', it is difficult to know, now and in the past, the extent of racial mixing involving those of Irish descent. However, data from the 2001 Census gives some idea of the level of racial mixing occurring in Britain that involves those who chose Irish as their ethnic group category.

Celebrated Personalities

147. UK 2001 Census Ethnic categories

In the 2001 census for England and Wales (see the table on page 250) we note that very similar proportions of White Irish men (97.82%) and White Irish women (97.41%) were married to a partner in the White group, primarily White British or White Irish. However, almost twice the proportion of White Irish women (1.00%) were married to an Asian partner than White Irish men (0.48%).

Also, a higher proportion of white Irish women (0.64%) were married to a partner in the black group than white Irish men (0.44%). However, a higher proportion of white Irish men were married to a partner in the Chinese or Any other ethnic groups than white Irish women. Thus, white Irish men and white Irish women were in marital unions with partners from all the detailed ethnic groups but most notably with those in the white group. Marital unions with members of the Asian and black groups were proportionately somewhat higher (especially with respect to the Asian group) amongst White Irish women than White Irish men. The Republic of Ireland was the top non-UK country of birth for foreign born in each census from 1951 until 2001. It fell to fourth position in 2011 (after India, Poland, and Pakistan).

	White Irish men	White Irish women
White British	56.15	57.69
White Irish	38.67	36.92
Other White	3.00	2.80
Any white	**97.82**	**97.41**
White and Black Caribbean	0.12	0.11
White and Black African	0.05	0.06
White and Asian	0.23	0.22
Other Mixed	0.20	0.20
Any Mixed	**0.60**	**0.60**
Indian	0.29	0.53
Pakistani	0.05	0.16
Bangladeshi	0.01	0.03
Other Asian	0.13	0.28
Any Asian	**0.48**	**1.00**
Black Caribbean	0.24	0.37
Black African	0.16	0.21
Other Black	0.04	0.06
Any black	**0.44**	**0.64**
Chinese	0.21	0.12
Any other ethnic group	0.44	0.24
	138,584	145,176

148. White married people by ethnic group. White Irish men and women in marital unions by ethnic group. Numbers of White Irish men (n=138,584) and White Irish women (145,176) in marital unions, by detailed ethnic group, in England and Wales, 2001. Data provided by Dr Peter Aspinall.

The table below shows that the numbers of Irish-born declined in each successive census after 1961.

The size of the born in the Republic of Ireland group in the resident population of England and Wales, 1951-2011	
Census Year	*No.*
1951	492,000
1961	683,000
1971	676,000
1981	580,000
1991	570,000
2001	473,000
2011	407,000

149. UK Census: Irish born and resident in England and Wales.
Information courtesy of Dr Peter Aspinall.

Afterword

~ ◎ ~

In November 2023, while finalising this book, Conrad Koza Bryan was kindly given access to St. Werburgh's Church in Dublin, by staff at Christ Church Cathedral. The church is currently closed due to refurbishment, as it has been neglected for some years and has not been used for religious services for some time. Conrad entered the church with a tour group and was allowed to wander around on his own, the purpose of which was to find and look at the portrait of the African boy, John Mulgrave, and take a high resolution photo of it for this book. Unfortunately, the portrait was not there, perhaps it was stored away somewhere during the refurbishment. However, the tablet about his death was still on the wall to see and he later received another image of the portrait from Stuart Kinsella, Research Advisor at Christ Church Cathedral Dublin, taken some time ago, see below:

150 John Mulgrave, the African Boy.
'neither Bond nor Free'
Image reproduced by permission of the Board of
Christ Church Cathedral.

According to Stuart, the framed picture at St. Werburgh's Church was most likely reproduced from Charles O'Mahony, The Viceroys of Ireland (London, 1912), opp. p. 240, which was based on the original oil painting by Nicholas Joseph Crowley (1813-1857), see page 2. After making more inquiries about the picture's whereabouts and provenance, Conrad was delighted to know that Stuart had been rummaging around archives and that he had finally discovered an oil on canvas portrait, in colour, at the National Gallery of Ireland. This is probably the first time this portrait (see page 2) has been included in a publication, in its full colour, showing John Mulgrave's face. All we need now is to find his original African name. Thanks to Stuart and Christ Church Cathedral, we now know that the framed picture at St. Werburgh's Church was ultimately a reproduction of the oil painting by the Irish artist Nicholas Joseph Crowley (1813-1857).

While standing in St. Werburgh's Church, Conrad felt an eery sense of history and time. John Mulgrave, the 'African Boy', is recorded in the burial register, so he is buried in the church somewhere, but his grave was nowhere to be found. There was a lot of overgrowth outside in the adjoining graveyard. This was a shame and a stark reminder of how easy it is to erase the dead from our history, especially relating to people of colour. The tour guide pointed to a boarded-up door, behind which Lord Edward Fitzgerald was laid to rest in 1798. The door led to a vault underneath the church. There was no access to that either, but hopefully once the refurbishment of the church is completed access to the vault will be allowed. They may even find the grave of 17 year old John Mulgrave when the renovation work gets underway.

The reason St. Werburgh's Church is mentioned here is to highlight the importance of this site in terms of Ireland's place within the British Empire. This is a place that was frequented by Ireland's elite Anglo-Irish ruling class, such as the Lord Lieutenant of Ireland, Earl of Mulgrave (Constantine Henry Phipps) who, like Lord Edward Fitzgerald, took home, to Ireland, African enslaved people. We hope, when fully restored to its former glory, that this church will recognise this connection to people of African descent. Perhaps this book will help to raise awareness of the church's significance and Ireland's relationship with people of colour, who found themselves trapped within the transatlantic slave trade.

Clearly, this book provides only a glimpse into the lives of some Irish people of colour in Britain and Ireland during the three centuries

Afterword

covered by this book. There is so much more research to do. Some of the unresolved questions we have are for example: where did the singer Rachel Baptist and her husband disappear to after their final concerts in Belfast? Where did Pablo the acrobat end his final days? What was life like for John Mulgrave in Dubin living with his 'Godmother', who is noted on the wall tablet in St. Werburgh's Church? Did John Suttoe have a family and where, in Co Louth, is he buried? Who was the real person behind William Love, the 'escaped slave' imposter? Why did Fr. George Paddington, the black Irish priest, leave Ireland to preach in Dominica? Answers to these may never be found, but could possibly inspire some writers to magic up some interesting fictional narratives.

We hope this book will encourage more interest in this fragmented and hidden history and prompt academics and educators to introduce more diverse stories into history textbooks and lessons in our schools and colleges. If there are other similar paintings depicting people of African descent, hidden in the National Gallery of Ireland archives we hope these are one day brought to light. It is also worth noting that 2024 is the last year of the 'International Decade for People of African Descent' adopted by the UN General Assembly in 2013. The theme of this 'Decade' is: recognition, justice and development for people of African descent. One of its key objectives, along with protecting and promoting human rights, is for States to promote greater knowledge and respect for diverse heritage, culture and contribution of people of African descent to the development of societies. This book falls squarely into this category and we hope the Government of Ireland continues to support projects and research such as this, by people of colour, which will enhance our knowledge and understanding of each other as equal human beings.

www.mixedraceirish.ie
https://mixedmuseum.org.uk/amri-exhibition/

Selected Bibliography

Chapter 1: Early Irish History

Bunbury, T. (n.d.) 'Bumper Jack' McClintock (1743-1799), Turtle Bunbury. https://turtlebunbury.com/document/bumper-jack/.

Hart, W. 'Rachael Baptist: The Career of a Black Singer in Ireland and England, 1750–73, *Eighteenth-century Ireland*. Volume 37 (2022).

Hart, W. (2002) Africans in Eighteenth-Century Ireland. Irish Historical Studies.

Jones, P. and Youseph, R. (1994), *The Black Population of Bristol in the Eighteen Century*, Bristol Historical Association.

Laffan, W. and Rooney, B. (2009), *Thomas Roberts 1748-1777. Landscape and Patronage in Eighteenth-century Ireland*, Churchill House Press.

Livesay, D. (2018) *Children of Uncertain Fortune: Mixed Race Jamaicans in Britain and The Atlantic Family, 1733-1833*, University of North Carolina Press.

Mahomet, D. (1997) *The Travels of Dean Mahomet: An Eighteenth-Century Journey through India*. Edited with an introduction and biographical essay by Fisher, M. Berkeley: University of California Press.

Narain, M. (2009) Dean Mahomet's "Travels", Border Crossings, and the Narrative of Alterity. Studies in English Literature, 1500-1900.

Rodgers N. (2000), *Equiano and Anti-Slavery in Eighteenth-Century Belfast*, Belfast Society.

Seymour, J.D. (2013). *Irish Witchcraft and Demonology: A History of Witchcraft in Ireland*. Dublin: Hodges, Figgis & Co. [originally published 1913].

Tillyard, S. (1999) *Aristocrats: Caroline, Emily, Louisa and Sarah Lennox 1740-1832*. London: Vintage.

Chapter 2: Irish Roots

Allen, W.G. (1860). *A Short Personal Narrative*. Dublin: William Curry & Co and J. Robertson.

Cameron, J.S. and Hicks, J. (1996). Frederick Akbar Mahomed and his role in the description of hypertension at Guy's hospital. Kidney International. 49:1488-1506.

Elbert, S. (2002). An Inter-Racial Love Story in Fact and Fiction: William and Mary King Allen's Marriage and Louisa May Alcott's Tale, 'M.L.,' History Workshop Journal, (53): 17-42.

Hanley, R. (2016) 'There to sing the song of Moses': John Jea's Methodism and Working-Class Attitudes to Slavery in Liverpool and Portsmouth, 1807-1817. In Donnington, K., Hanley, R. and Moody, J. (eds.) (2016). *Britain's History and Memory of Transatlantic Slavery: Local Nuances of a 'National Sin'*. Liverpool University Press: Liverpool.

Hodges Russell, G. (ed) (2002) *Black Itinerants of the Gospel: The Narratives of John Jea and George White*. Palgrave Macmillan: New York.

Husainy, A. (n.d). Mahomed's Children, Moving Here: Tracing Your Roots, Archived online at The National Archives.

Jea, J. (c1815) *The Life History and Unparalleled Sufferings of John Jea, the African Preacher, Compiled and Written by Himself*. Portsea: Self Published.

Jones, A. (2003) *Pierre Toussaint: A biography*. New York: Doubleday.

Laffan, W. and Rooney, B. (2009), *Thomas Roberts 1748-1777. Landscape and Patronage in Eighteenth-century Ireland*, Churchill House Press.

Lindfors, B. (2011) *Ira Aldridge: The Early Years*, 1807-1833, Rochester.

Mahomet, D. (1997) The Travels of Dean Mahomet: An Eighteenth-Century Journey through India. Edited with an introduction and biographical essay by Fisher, M. Berkeley: University of California Press.

McLoughlin, N. (2008) 'From our Pastor's Desk', Our Lady of Grace Newsletter, 24 February 2008.

Newman, B. (2018) *A Dark Inheritance: Blood, Race and Sex in Colonial Jamaica*. USA: Yale University Press.

Rodgers, N. (2007) *Ireland, Slavery and Anti-Slavery, 1612-1865*. Palgrave Macmillan: Hampshire and New York.

Tillyard, S. (1998) *Citizen Lord: Edward Fitzgerald, 1763-1798*. London: Vintage.

Toulmin, V. (2018) Black circus performers in Victorian Britain, Early Popular Visual Culture, 16(3): 267-289.

Van Hare, G. (1888) *Fifty years of a showman's life, or, The life and travels of Van Hare*. London: W.H. Allen & Co.

Chapter 3: Racial and Ethnic Diversity in Britain

Ansari, H. (2009) *The Infidel Within: Muslims in Britain since 1800*. London: Hurst & Company.

Blackett, R.J.M. (1980). *William G. Allen: The Forgotten Professor*. Civil War History 26(1): 39-52.

Costello, R. (2001) *Black Liverpool: The Early History of Britain's Oldest Black Community, 1730-1918*. Liverpool: Picton Press.

de Nie, M. *The Eternal Paddy: Irish Identity and the British Press, 1798-1882*. Wisconsin: The University of Wisconsin Press.

Fryer, P. (1984). *Staying Power: The History of Black People in Britain*. London: Pluto Press.

Gerzina, G. (1995) *Black London: Life Before Emancipation*. New Jersey: Rutgers University Press.

Gillis, B.M. (2014). *A Caribbean Coupling Beyond Black and White: The Interracial Marriage of Catherine and Edward Marcus Despard and its Implications for British Views on*

Race, Class, and Gender during the Age of Reform. Master's thesis, Duke University.

Jay, M. (2019) *The Unfortunate Colonel Despard: And the British Revolution that Never Happened*. London: Robinson. First edition 2004.

Linebaugh, P. (2019) *Red Round Globe Hot Burning: A Tale at the Crossroads of Commons and Closure, of Love and Terror, of Race and Class, and of Kate and Ned Despard*. California: University of California Press.

Linebaugh, P. and Rediker, M. (2012). *The Many-Headed Hydra: The Hidden History of the Revolutionary Atlantic*. London: Verso.

Lloyd, A.J. 2007. *Emigration, Immigration and Migration in Nineteenth Century Britain, British Library Newspapers*. Detroit: Gale.

Lorimer, D.A. (1978) *Colour, Class and the Victorians: English attitudes to the Negro in the mid-nineteenth century*. Leicester: Leicester University Press.

Mazimhaka, R. J. (1997) *The Discourse of Difference: The Representation of Black African Characters in English Renaissance Drama*. Unpublished PhD thesis: University of Saskatchewan.

Newman, B. (2018) *A Dark Inheritance: Blood, Race and Sex in Colonial Jamaica*. USA: Yale University Press.

Olusoga, D. (2016). *Black and British: A Forgotten History*. London: Macmillan.

Oman, C. (1922). *The Unfortunate Charles Despard, and other studies*. London: E. Arnold & Co.

Seed, J. (2006). Limehouse Blues: Looking for Chinatown in the London Docks, 1900-1940, History Workshop Journal, 62 (2006): 58-85.

Stephens, H.M. Despard, Edward Marcus, *Dictionary of National Biography*, 1885-1900, Vol. 14.

Trahey, Erin (2018) *Free Women and the Making of Colonial Jamaican Economy and Society, 1760-1834*. PhD thesis, History Department, University of Cambridge.

Wong, M.L. (1989) *Chinese Liverpudlians: A History of the Chinese Community in Liverpool*. Liverpool: Liver Press.

Chapter 4: Early Twentieth Century Migration

Auerbach, S. (2009) *Race, Law, and "The Chinese Puzzle" in Imperial Britain*. New York: Palgrave Macmillan.

Bland, L. (2007) British Eugenics and 'Race Crossing': A Study of an Interwar Investigation, *New Formations*, 60: 66-78.

Caballero, C. and Aspinall, P. (2018) *Mixed Race Britain in the Twentieth Century*. London: Palgrave Macmillan.

Christian, M. (2008) The Fletcher Report 1930: A Historical Case Study of Contested Black Mixed Heritage Britishness. Journal of Historical Sociology 21 (2–3): 213–241.

Costello, R. (2007 and 1997) *Liverpool's Black Pioneers*. Liverpool: Bluecoat Press.

Selected Bibliography

Davis, G. (1991). The Irish in Nineteenth Century Britain. *Saothar*, 16: 130-135.

Jenkinson, J. (1987) *The 1919 Race Riots in Britain: Their Background and Consequences*. Unpublished PhD thesis: University of Edinburgh, p193.]'.

Jenkinson, J. (2009) *1919: Riots, Racism and Resistance in Imperial Britain*. Liverpool: Liverpool University Press.

Kay, J.P. (1832) *The Moral and Physical Condition of the Working Classes of Manchester in 1832*, London: Cass.

Lahiri, S. (2000) *Indians in Britain: Anglo-Indian Encounters, Race and Identity 1880-1930*. London and Portland, Oregon: Frank Cass Publishers.

Menen, A. 'My Grandmother and the Dirty English', *The New Yorker*, 4 July 1953.

Miller, F.J. (2015) *Indian or British? Memoirs of a Rajah's daughter: Pat Cross*, CreateSpace Independent Publishing Platform.

Nasta, S. (2002) *Home Truths: Fictions of the South Asian Diaspora in Britain*. London: Palgrave.

O'Mara, P. (2009) *Liverpool Slummy. Liverpool: The Bluecoat Press*. First published 1933.

Parker, D. (2001). We Paved the Way': Exemplary Spaces and Mixed Race in Britain. In *The Sum of Our Parts. Mixed Heritage Asian-Americans*, eds. T. Williams-Leon and C.L. Nakashima, 185–196. Philadelphia: Temple University Press.

Phillips, M. (n.d.) John Archer (1863-1932), Black Europeans. The British Library. https://www.bl.uk/onlinegallery/features/blackeuro/pdf/archer.pdf.

Qureshi, S. (2011) *Peoples on parade: exhibitions, empire, and anthropology in nineteenth-century Britain*. Chicago and London: Chicago University Press.

Seed, J. (2006). Limehouse Blues: Looking for Chinatown in the London Docks, 1900–40. History Workshop Journal 62: 58–85.

Shepherd, B. (1986) Showbiz imperialism: the Case of Peter Lobengula. Mackenzie, J.M. (ed.) (1986) *Imperialism and Popular Culture*. Manchester and New York: Manchester University Press.

Swift, R. (ed.) (2002). *Irish Migrants in Britain 1815-1914 A Documentary History*. Cork, Ireland: Cork University Press.

Taylor, M. (2020) *Sport on the Home Front: Wartime Britain at Play, 1939-1945*. Oxon and New York: Routledge.

Teo, H. (2004) Romancing the Raj: Interracial Relations in Anglo-Indian Romance Novels. History of Intellectual Culture, 4(1):1-18.

Wong, M.L (1989) Chinese Liverpudlians. Liverpool: Liver Press.

Chapter 5: Racial Mixing During and Post - WW2

Bland, L. (2019). *Britain's 'Brown Babies': The stories of children born to black GIs and white women in the Second World War*. Manchester: Manchester University Press.

Bourne, S. (2010) Mother Country: Britain's Black Community on the Home Front

1939-45, London: The History Press.

Bourne, S. (2012) *The Motherland Calls: Britain's Black Servicemen and Women 1939-45*, London: The History Press.

Bourne, S. (2015) Leading Aircraftwoman in the WAAF and one of the first black women to join the British Armed Forces, The Independent, 6 April 2015.

Broad, I. (2016) Marcus Bailey, African Stories in Hull & East Yorkshire, [dated viewed: 27.06.2020].

Caballero, C. And Aspinall, P. (2018) *Mixed Race Britain in the Twentieth Century*, London: Palgrave Macmillan.

Dewjee, A. (2016) Lilian Bader, African Stories in Hull & East Yorkshire, [date viewed: 13.05.2020].

Iroko Theatre Company (2013) *Homage to Canning Town African Ancestors*. Available at http://www.irokotheatre.org.uk/projects/6.pdf [viewed 13.05.2020].

McDonald, A. 'Architects 'are not a luxury'', The Irish Times, 13 February 2014.

Nevins, P. (2019) *'Fudge': The Downs and Ups of a Biracial, Half-Irish British War Baby*. USA: Pauline Nevins.

Padfield, D. (ed) (1999) *Hidden Lives: Stories from the East End by the people of 42 Balaam Street*. London: Eastside Community Heritage.

Rob, A. (2015) Black History Month Firsts: Lilian Bader, Black History 365, [date viewed: 13.05.2020].

Sherwood, M. (1994) *Pastor Daniels Ekarte and the African Churches Mission Liverpool 1932-1964*. London: The Savannah Press.

Smith, G.A. (1987) *When Jim Crow Met John Bull: Black American Soldiers in World War II*. London: I.B. Tauris & Co.

Webster, W. (2018) *Mixing It: Diversity in World War Two Britain*. Oxford: Oxford University Press.

Wong, M.L. (1989). *Chinese Liverpudlians: A History of the Chinese Community in Liverpool*. Birkenhead: Liver Press.

Chapter 6: Racial Mixing in the Era of Mass Migration

Bauer, E. (2010) *The Creolisation of London Kinship: Mixed African-Caribbean and White British Extended Families, 1950-2003*. Amsterdam University Press.

Caballero, C. and Aspinall, P. (2018) *Mixed Race Britain in the Twentieth Century*. London: Palgrave Macmillan.

Jenkinson, J. (2012) 'All in the same uniform?' The participation of black colonial residents in the British armed forces in the First World War. *Journal of Imperial and Commonwealth History*. 40(2):207-230.

Lynott, P. and Hayden, J. (2011) My Boy: The Full Story of Philip Lynott & The Family He Never Knew. Dublin: Hot Press Books.

McGrath, P. (2010) *Back from the Brink: The Autobiography*. London: Arrow Books.

'My Irish Heritage by Kit de Waal', writing.ie, 3 April 2017.

'My Secret Life: Craig Charles, 47, DJ and actor', *The Independent*, 30 June 2012.

Nwanokwu, G.M. (2016) *Black Shamrocks: Accommodation Available - No Blacks, No Dogs, No Irish.*

Chapter 7: Racism and Daily Life

Belcham, J. (2014) *Before the Windrush: Race Relations in 20th Century Liverpool.* Liverpool: University of Liverpool.

Bourne, J. (2007) The Beatification of Enoch Powell, *Institute of Race Relations*, available at http://www.irr.org.uk/news/the-beatification-of-enoch-powell/ [viewed 17 May 2020].

Caballero, C. and Aspinall, P. (2018) *Mixed Race Britain in the Twentieth Century.* London: Palgrave.

Davis, F. (2002) *Who is Black? One Nation's Definition.* Pennsylvania: Pennsylvania State University Press.

Fanning, D. 'Hughton's steady presence restores order on Tyneside', *Independent.ie*, 18 April 2010. Available at https://www.independent.ie/sport/soccer/hughtons-steady-presence-restores-order-on-tyneside-26650753.html [viewed on 03/10/2023].

Fiddy, D. (2018) How lost British TV sci-fi Thwum was rediscovered. BFI. Available at https://www.bfi.org.uk/news-opinion/news-bfi/features/thwum-pete-postlethwaite-sci-fi [viewed 03.09.2023].

Fitzmaurice, A. 'I'm proud to be Ireland's first black player' - Chris Hughton, 40 years since his debut in green, *Independent.ie*, 29 October 2019. Available at https://www.independent.ie/sport/soccer/im-proud-to-be-irelands-first-black-player-chris-hughton-40-years-since-his-debut-in-green-38639891.html [viewed 03.10.2023].

Jaafar, A. 'Curry and Chips' (1969). *BFI Screenonline, available at http://www.screenonline.org.uk/tv/id/535237/index.html [viewed on 03/10/2023].*

John Conteh, *Big Red Book.* Available at https://www.bigredbook.info/john_conteh.html [viewed 03.10.2023].

Liarou, E. (2013) Tara Prem: Pioneer of Multicultural TV Drama. Women's Film and Television History Network UK/Ireland. Available at https://womensfilmandtelevisionhistory.wordpress.com/2013/11/30/tara-prem-pioneer-of-british-multicultural-tv-drama/ [viewed 03.10.2023].

Lynott, P. and Hayden, J. (2011) *My Boy: The Full Story of Philip Lynott & The Family He Never Knew.* Dublin: Hot Press Books.

McNeil, D. (2010) *Sex and Race in the Black Atlantic: Mulatto Devils and Multiracial Messiahs.* New York: Routledge.

McRae, D. 'Chris Hughton ploughing a lonely furrow for black managers', *The Irish Times*, 28 April 2017. Available at https://www.irishtimes.com/sport/soccer/english-soccer/chris-hughton-ploughing-a-lonely-furrow-for-black-managers-1.3065170 [viewed on 03/10/2023].

McRae, D. 'Chris Hughton: 'I have a thirst for knowledge. I won't always be a manager'', *The Guardian*, 28 April 2017. Available at https://www.theguardian.com/football/2017/apr/28/chris-hughton-brighton-thirst-knowledge-manager [viewed on 03/10/2023].

Moody, J. (2014) *The Memory of Slavery in Liverpool in Public Discourse from the Nineteenth Century to the Present Day*. Unpublished PhD thesis, University of York.

My review of "Across the Water Irish Women's Lives in Britain" (1988) Mary Lennon Marie McAdam Joanne O'Brien, *Lipstick Socialist*, 4 December 2018, available at https://lipsticksocialist.wordpress.com/2018/12/04/my-review-of-across-the-water-irish-womens-lives-in-britain-1988-mary-lennon-marie-mcadam-joanne-obrien/.

O'Toole, F. 'From the archives: Don't believe a word – The life and death of Phil Lynott', *The Irish Times*, 2 January 2016. https://www.irishtimes.com/culture/music/from-the-archives-don-t-believe-a-word-the-life-and-death-of-phil-lynott-1.2482658 [viewed 03.10.2023].

Olusoga, D (2016) *Black and British: A Forgotten History*. London: Macmillan.

Power, Ed. 'Life After Lizzy', *Irish Independent*. 7 December 2013. See https://www.independent.ie/entertainment/music/life-after-lizzy-29817116.html [viewed 3.09.2023].

Roberts, M. (2017) Where are they now? John Conteh. *Playing Pasts*. Available at https://www.playingpasts.co.uk/where-are-they-now/where-are-they-now-john-conteh/ [viewed 03.10.2023].

Rossum, D. (1997) "A Vision of Black Englishness": Black Intellectuals in London, 1910–1940. *Stanford Electronic Humanities Review* 5 (2).

Walter, B. (2013) Transnational networks across generations: childhood visits to Ireland by the second generation in England. In M. Gilmartin and A White (eds) (2013) *Migrations: Ireland in a global world*, Manchester: Manchester University Press: 17-35.

Zanon, P. (2019) John Conteh - Brilliantly British. *British Vintage Boxing*. Available at https://www.britishvintageboxing.com/post/john-conteh-brilliantly-british [viewed 03.10.2023].

Zanon, P. (2019b) Royal Seal: The Career of John Conteh, *Hannibal Boxing Media*. Available at https://hannibalboxing.com/royal-seal-the-career-of-john-conteh/ [viewed 03.10.2023].

Chapter 8: Celebrated Personalities

Aston, E. (2003) *Feminist views on the English stage: Women playwrights, 1990-2000.* Cambridge: Cambridge University Press.

Bernardine Evaristo, British Council. See: https://literature.britishcouncil.org/writer/bernardine-evaristo.

Bernardine Evaristo, *Lara*, Bloodaxe Books. See: https://www.bloodaxebooks.com/ecs/product/lara-927.

Brenkley, S. 'O'Reilly seeks break in the cloud: Stephen Brenkley meets the Olympian whose ideal survives a terrible ordeal', *The Independent*, 6 February 1994.

Browne, PJ (2020) 'After 17 Years Travelling The World, Terry Phelan Wants To Repay Ireland', *Balls.ie. See:* https://www.balls.ie/football/terry-phelan-india-irish-indentity-413421 [viewed10.06.2020].

Evaristo, B. 'My Father's House: Bernardine Evaristo tours her childhood home', Five Dials. See: https://fivedials.com/reportage/my-fathers-house-bernardine-evaristo/.

Evaristo, Bernardine (1959-) encyclopedia.com. See: https://www.encyclopedia.com/arts/educational-magazines/evaristo-bernardine-1959 .

'Ex-con shoots for the straight and narrow thanks to former Blues star Terry Phelan', *Manchester Evening News*, 11 June 2014.

McGrath, P. (2010) *Back From the Brink: The Autobiography*. London: Arrow Books.

Osborne, D. (2013) 'Being alone together' (Pinney 2006): the ego-histoire of indigenous Black British Writers' Adoption Aesthetics, Conference Paper, Summer Series: Deirdre Osborne, UNSW. JRMC Research Blog. Available at http://jmrcresearch.blogspot.com/2013/03/seminar-series.html [accessed 18.06.2020].

Osborne, D. (2017) 'Mothertext: Restoring the Mixed Matrilineal Routes to Heritage', *The Story of M*. London: Oberon Books.

Pizzichini, L. 'Suicide attempts, drug abuse, sexual assault. Author Joanna Traynor's life has been a series of triumphs over adversity', *The Independent*, 30 August 1998.

SuAndi OBE, Moving Manchester Writers Gallery, University of Lancaster. Available at https://www.lancaster.ac.uk/fass/projects/writersgallery/content/SuAndi.htm [date accessed 08.06.2020].

References

Foreward

[1] See article by Schaffer and Nassar (April 2018), 'The white essential subject: race, ethnicity, and the Irish in post-war Britain'.

Preface

[1] AMRI is The Association of Mixed Race Irish.

Chapter 1: Early Irish History

[1] Seymour, J.D. (2013). *Irish Witchcraft and Demonology: A History of Witchcraft in Ireland.* Dublin: Hodges, Figgis & Co. [originally published 1913], see: http://www.gutenberg.org/files/43651/43651-h/43651-h.htm [viewed 24/10/2023].

[2] Hart, W. (2002) Africans in Eighteenth-Century Ireland. Irish Historical Studies, 33(129), pp. 19-32.

[3] Ibid.

[4] Casey, Martin, 'PHIPPS, Constantine Henry, Visct. Normanby (1797-1863), of 19 Grosvenor Street, Mdx', in *The History of Parliament: the House of Commons 1820-1832*, ed. D.R. Fisher, 2009, Cambridge University Press. Available at https://www.historyofparliamentonline.org/volume/1820-1832/member/phipps-constantine-1797-1863 [viewed 30/10/2023].

[5] See https://en.wikipedia.org/wiki/Constantine_Phipps,_1st_Baron_Mulgrave [viewed 30/10/2023].

[6] Wright, G. N. (1825) *An Historical Guide to the City of Dublin*, London: Printed for Baldwin, Cradock, and Joy. Available online at https://web.archive.org/web/20071031094153/http://www.chaptersofdublin.com/books/Wright/wright10.htm [viewed 30/10/2023].

[7] Rodgers N. (2000), *Equiano and Anti-Slavery in Eighteenth-Century Belfast*, Belfast Society.

[8] McEvansoneya P. 'The black figure in Angelica Kauffman's earl of Ely family group portrait'. Published in *18th-19th Century Social Perspectives, 18th–19th - Century History, Features*, Issue 2(March/April 2012), Vol. 20. See: https://www.historyireland.com/the-black-figure-in-angelica-kauffmans-earl-of-ely-family-group-portrait/ [viewed 25/09/2023].

[9] Ibid.

[10] Laffan, W. and Rooney, B. (2009), *Thomas Roberts 1748-1777. Landscape and Patronage in Eighteenth-century Ireland*, Churchill House Press*, p. 164.*

[11] Hogan, L. (2019) An Irish Slave in Antigua. Medium. See:

265

https://medium.com/@Limerick1914/an-irish-slave-in-antigua-7acfb106a8e9 [viewed 04.10.2023].

[12] Hart, W. 'Rachael Baptist: The Career of a Black Singer in Ireland and England, 1750–73, *Eighteenth-century Ireland*. Volume 37 (2022); pp. 151-163.

[13] Ibid, p. 153.

[14] Ibid.

[15] Livesay, D. (2010) Children of Uncertain Fortune: Mixed Race Migration from the West Indies to Britain, 1750-1820. Unpublished PhD thesis: University of Michigan, pp. 92 – 110.

[16] O'Keefe, J (1826). *'Recollections of the life of John O'Keefe'*. London: Henry Colburn, p. 66.

[17] Ibid.

[18] Ibid p. 68.

[19] Black, Annette, 'Death in the Music Room', Dublin Bridges, 10 July 2014. Available at http://www.bridgesofdublin.ie/stories/death-in-the-music-room [viewed 15/10/2014].

[20] Gerrad, Francis (1898) *Picturesque Dublin Old and New*, London: Hutchinson & Co, p. 361.

[21] Hart. W. 'Baptist (Crow), Rachael', Dictionary of Irish Biography, October 2009. See https://www.dib.ie/biography/baptist-crow-rachael-a2219 [viewed 20/10/2023].

[22] Rigg, Danny 'Mysterious Irish singer who performed in gardens where Adelphi now stands', *Liverpool Echo*, 10 October 2021. Available at https://www.liverpoolecho.co.uk/news/liverpool-news/mysterious-irish-singer-who-performed-21811553 [viewed 15/10/2023].

[23] Costello, Ray (2001) *Black Liverpool - The Early History of Britain's Oldest Black Community 1730-1918*, Liverpool: Picton Press, p. 22.

[24] England Marriages, 1538–1973, database, FamilySearch. See Rachel Baptist in entry for Thomas Ellis, 1758 at https://www.familysearch.org/ark:/61903/1:1:NLWT-KXJ [viewed 17/10/2023].

[25] England, Cheshire Bonds and Allegations, Cheshire Records Office, Chester; FHL microfilm 1,538,304. Available at https://www.familysearch.org/ark:/61903/1:1:FBJ7-96X [viewed 19/10/2023].

[26] Sir William Barker, 3rd Bt. The Peerage, A genealogical survey of the peerage of Britain as well as the royal families of Europe. Available at https://www.thepeerage.com/p13216.htm#i132151 [viewed 20/10/2023].

[27] Paul, GM Main, 'The Story of the Hotwell at Bristol', *The West of England Medical Journal*, Vol 117 No. 4 Article 2. 15 October 2018. Available at http://www.bristolmedchi.co.uk/content/upload/1/wemj-vol117-no-4/2the-story-of-the-hotwells-medium-res.pdf [viewed 17/10/2023].

[28] Hart, W. (n 12), p. 155.

[29] *Public Advertiser*, 7 September 1767.

[30] 'London Stage Event: 07 September 1767 at Haymarket Theatre.' London Stage Database. https://londonstagedatabase.uoregon.edu/event.php?id=33780, [viewed 21/10/2023]. See also: *The London Stage 1660-1800: A calendar Of Plays, Entertainments & Afterpieces, Together With Casts, Box-Receipts And Contemporary*

Comment, Compiled From the Play Bills, Newspapers And Theatrical Diaries Of The Period, Part 4: 1747-1776, ed. By G. W. Stone Jr., 3 vols (Carbondale: Southern Illinois University Press, 1962), II, p. 1264.

[31] Bunbury, T. (n.d.) 'Bumper Jack' McClintock (1743-1799), Turtle Bunbury, see https://turtlebunbury.com/document/bumper-jack/.

[32] *The Dublin Evening Post*, 23 April 1785. Also see Bunbury, T. (n 31).

[33] McClintock, Henry (transcribed by P. O'Neill 2021). *Journal of Henry McClintock*, The County Louth Archaeological and Historical Society.

[34] Ibid p. 147.

[35] Ibid p. 149.

[36] 'Harvest Home at Drumcar, County of Louth', *Saunders Newsletter*, 11 October 1814.

[37] 'Surrender of the French. Official Accounts' *Chester Chronical*, 14 September 1798.

[38] 'Ireland', *The Gloucester Journal*, 9 July 1798.

[39] Clare Bi-Election hustings details available at: https://www.clarelibrary.ie/eolas/coclare/history/clare_election_1828.htm.

[40] 'Elections', Supplement to the *Limerick Evening Post and Clare Sentinel*, 1 July 1828.

[41] Letters, *Freemans Journal* 12 August 1783.

[42] Postscript, *Freemans Journal*, 19 August 1783.

[43] Forbes J. (1868), *Memoirs of the Earls of Granard*, London, p. 197.

[44] Livesay, D. (2010) *Children of Uncertain Fortune: Mixed Race Migration from the West Indies to Britain, 1750-1820*. Unpublished PhD thesis: University of Michigan.

[45] Livesay, D. (2018) *Children of Uncertain Fortune: Mixed Race Jamaicans in Britain and The Atlantic Family, 1733-1833*, University of North Carolina Press, p. 399.

[46] Calnan baptisms on 28 June 1796, 'Jamaica, Church of England Parish Register Transcripts, 1664-1880', FamilySearch available at https://www.familysearch.org/ark:/61903/1:1:VHD6-3QS [viewed 21/10/2023].

[47] With thanks to Daniel Livesay for this information.

[48] Sabina Eleanor Tierney. Legacies of Slave Ownership, UCL. https://www.ucl.ac.uk/lbs/person/view/13594 [viewed 04.10.2023].

[49] Cherry, B. (2013) 'Mapping slave ownership on to London and its districts: the Portman estate as a case study. London Topographic Society Newsletter (77): 5-7. https://londontopsoc.org/wp-content/uploads/2018/07/Newsletter-No-77-November-2013_20pp.pdf [viewed 04.10.2023].

[50] Tillyard, S. (1999) *Aristocrats: Caroline, Emily, Louisa and Sarah Lennox 1740-1832*. London: Vintage.

[51] Mahomet, D. (1997) *The Travels of Dean Mahomet: An Eighteenth-Century Journey through India*. Edited with an introduction and biographical essay by Fisher, M. Berkeley: University of California Press.

[52] Narain, M. (2009) Dean Mahomet's "Travels", Border Crossings, and the Narrative of Alterity. Studies in English Literature, 1500-1900.49(3): 693-716.

[53] Ibrahim, V. (2010) 'Seeing a vision in a pool of ink': The Mir' of India in Ireland. History Ireland. 3:18. www.historyireland.com/18th-19th-century-history/integration-seeing-a-vision-in-a-pool-of-ink-the-mir-of-india-in-ireland/ [viewed 04/10/2023].

[54] See 'The Royal Scots, The Late 18th Century' at: https://www.nam.ac.uk/explore/royal-scots [viewed 04/10/2023].

[55] George Montagu Dunk, 2nd Earl of Halifax (1716-1771), Known as 'The Father of the Colonies', see https://www.npg.org.uk/collections/search/personextended?linkid=mp01974&tab=biography [viewed 26/09/2023].

[56] Jones, P. and Youseph, R. (1994), *The Black Population of Bristol in the Eighteen Century*, Bristol Historical Association, p. 22. Available at: https://www.bristol.ac.uk/Depts/History/bristolrecordsociety/publications/bha084.pdf [viewed 27/09/2023].

[57] Ibid, p. 14.

[58] *Belfast Newsletter*, 10 October 1766.

[59] See Waddell Cunningham in *Centre for the Study of the Legacies of British Slavery* database at https://www.ucl.ac.uk/lbs/person/view/2146645349 [viewed 27/09/2023].

[60] See Thomas Greg in in *Centre for the Study of the Legacies of British Slavery* database at https://www.ucl.ac.uk/lbs/person/view/2146662339 [viewed 28/09/2023].

[61] Converted to today's prices at: https://www.officialdata.org/uk/inflation/1835?amount=2830 [viewed 27/09/2023].

[62] See 'Dominica 319 ([Hillsborough])', *Centre for the Study of the Legacies of British Slavery* at https://www.ucl.ac.uk/lbs/claim/view/10275 .

[63] See: Woods, C. J. 'Cunningham, Waddle', *Dictionary of Irish Biography*, at https://www.dib.ie/biography/cunningham-waddell-a2312 .

[64] Converted to today's prices at: https://www.officialdata.org/uk/inflation/1797?amount=17000 [accessed 27/09/2023].

[65] Jones, P. and Youseph, R. (n 56) p. 22.

[66] *Somerset v Stewart* (1772) 98 ER 499, (Court of King's Bench).

[67] Ibid p. 510.

[68] Ibid p. 499–500.

[69] 'Lynch Law in Cork', *Irish Examiner*, 28 August 1848, p. 2.

Chapter 2: Irish Roots

[1] Hanley, R. (2016) "There to sing the song of Moses': John Jea's Methodism and Working-Class Attitudes to Slavery in Liverpool and Portsmouth, 1807-1817'. In Donnington, K., Hanley, R. and Moody, J. (eds.) (2016). Britain's History and Memory of Transatlantic Slavery: Local Nuances of a 'National Sin'. Liverpool University Press: Liverpool, p. 39-59.

[2] Jea, J. (c1815) The Life History and Unparalled Sufferings of John Jea, the African Preacher, Compiled and Written by Himself. Portsea: Self Published.

[3] Rodgers, N. (2007) Ireland, Slavery and Anti-Slavery, 1612-1865. Palgrave Macmillan: Hampshire and New York.

[4] Newman, B. (2018) A Dark Inheritance: Blood, Race and Sex in Colonial Jamaica. USA: Yale University Press.

[5] Hodges Russell, G. (ed) (2002) Black Itinerants of the Gospel: The Narratives of John Jea and George White. Palgrave Macmillan: New York.

References

[6] *Cheltenham Chronicle and Gloucestershire Advertiser*, 6 November 1817.

[7] Tillyard, Stella (1998) Citizen Lord: Edward Fitzgerald, 1763-1798. London: Vintage.

[8] Bunbury, T. (n.d.) 'Bumper Jack' McClintock (1743-1799), Turtle Bunbury. https://turtlebunbury.com/document/bumper-jack/ [viewed 04.10.2023].

[9] Donal (2013) Tony Small: The escaped slave who lived in Leinster House. Come Here to Me! https://comeheretome.com/2013/01/29/tony-small-the-escaped-slave-who-lived-in-leinster-house/ [viewed 04.10.2023].

[10] Allen, William, G. 1860. A Short Personal Narrative. Dublin: William Curry & Co and J. Robertson.

[11] Elbert, S. (2002). An Inter-Racial Love Story in Fact and Fiction: William and Mary King Allen's Marriage and Louisa May Alcott's Tale, 'M.L.,' History Workshop Journal, (53): 17-42.

[12] Lot 39, The Property of a Gentleman: Thomas Roberts 1748-1778, 'Gerald Fitzgerald's Negro Servant Holding Bold Sir William in a Landscape, A Poodle Beside'. See: www.sothebys.com/en/auctions/ecatalogue/2005/important-british-pictures-paintings-drawings-watercolours-and-portrait-miniatures-l05123/lot.39.html [viewed 4/10/2023].

[13] Mason, I.L. (1996). A World Dictionary of Livestock Breeds, Types and Varieties. Fourth Edition. C.A.B International. p. 273. See also: https://breeds.okstate.edu/horses/barb-horses.html.

[14] Laffan W. & Rooney B. (2009), *Thomas Roberts 1748-1777. Landscape and Patronage in Eighteenth-century Ireland*, Churchill House Press, p. 161.

[15] Ibid.

[16] McKenna, L. (2020). 'Every man is exactly what he makes himself', History Ireland, available at https://www.historyireland.com/every-man-is-exactly-what-he-makes-himself/ [viewed 10/12/2023].

[17] Mahomet, D. (1997) The Travels of Dean Mahomet: An Eighteenth-Century Journey through India. Edited with an introduction and biographical essay by Fisher, M. Berkeley: University of California Press.

[18] See http://news.bbc.co.uk/1/hi/england/london/4290124.stm [viewed 17/11/2023].

[19] Cameron Stewart, J. and Hicks, J. (1996). Frederick Akbar Mahomed and his role in the description of hypertension at Guy's hospital. Kidney International.49:1488-1506.

[20] See Desmond, R. (1994). Dictionary of British & Irish Botanists and Horticulturalists Including Plant Collectors, Flower Painters and Garden Designers. Taylor and Francis and the Natural History Museum: London.

[21] 'Cooke's Olympic Circus' advertisement with Carlo Pablo Paddington as the 'Flying Indian', *The Manchester Mercury*, 5 April 1825.

[22] 'A Pair of Imposters', *Nottingham Journal*, 3 February 1827.

[23] *Belfast Commercial Chronicle*, 20 January 1927.

[24] Toulmin, V. (2018) Black circus performers in Victorian Britain, Early Popular Visual Culture, 16(3): 267-289.

[25] Van Hare, G. (1888). *Fifty years of a showman's life, or, The life and travels of Van Hare*. London W.H. Allen & Co.

References

[26] See Heidelberg University, James W.C. Pennington Award at https://www.hca.uni-heidelberg.de/forschung/pennington_en.html [viewed 21/12/23].

[27] Jones, A. (2003) *Pierre Toussaint : A Biography*. New York: Doubleday.

[28] Identified by Conrad Bryan in Cork Church Records.

[29] Ireland Valuation Office Books, St Peter's Parish, Cork, Ireland held at the National Library of Ireland.

[30] *Bristol Mercury*, 8 July 1854.

[31] *The Era*, 18 May 1856.

[32] 'A Negro Adventurer' *The Londonderry Standard*, 3 September 1857.

[33] 'A Negro Adventurer', *Newry Telegraph*, 8 September 1857.

[34] Celeste-Marie Bernier, Hannah-Rose Murray(eds) (to be published in March 2024) *Nineteenth-Century African American Speeches in Britain and Ireland*, Edinburgh University Press. Available at https://edinburghuniversitypress.com/book-nineteenth-century-african-american-speeches-in-britain-and-ireland-hb.html [viewed 16/10/2013].

[35] *Stonehaven Journal*, 19 February 1857. Jacksons first speech was reported in the *Dunfries and Galloway Standard* on 3 December 1856, six weeks after he arrived.

[36] *Alloa Advertiser*,18 April 1857.

[37] *Paisely Herlad and Renfrewshire Advertiser*, 13 June 1857.

[38] *Adrossan and Salts Herald*, 12 September 1857.

[39] 'Potter Hill Chapel', *Sheffield and Rotherham Independent*, 7 February 1857.

[40] 'Caution. – Real Fugitive Slave! – Darlington', *The Morpeth Herald*, 7 February 1857.

[41] 'Negro Imposter', *Montrose Arbroath and Brechan Review*, 6 February 1857.

[42] Ibid.

[43] 'A Negro Imposter Lecturing on Slavery', *The Kings County Chronicle*, 26 November 1856.

[44] Doyle, M. "Those the Empire Washed Ashore: uncovering Ireland's multiracial past" in *Ireland in an Imperial World: Citizenship, Opportunism, and Subversion*, ed. Michael de Nie, Timothy McMahon, and Paul Townend. London: Palgrave, 2017.

[45] Hart, W. 'Black Joe the Life of a Black Man in Nineteenth-Century Belfast', *ResearchGate*, April 2022. Available at https://www.researchgate.net/publication/359938849_Black_Joe_the_Life_of_a_Black_Man_in_Nineteenth-Century_Belfast [viewed 21/10/2023].

[46] *Belfast News-Letter* 24 March 1879.

[47] *Belfast Telegraph* 24 March 1879.

[48] This piece was kindly provided by Dr. Maurice J Casey who curated the exhibition *Revolutionary Routes: Ireland and the Black Atlantic*, at EPIC, The Irish Emigration Museum, in 2022.

[49] Lynnette G. Geary, 'Jules Bledsoe: The Original "Ol' Man River", The Black Perspective in Music, 17:1&2 (1989), p. 43.

[50] '"Up Abyssinia" Cry at Traitor' Irish Workers' Voice, 4 April 1936.

[51] Ibid.

[52] Geary, 'Jules Bledsloe', p. 43.

[53] William Hart's superb exploration of Africans in eighteenth-century Ireland is a model worth replicating for other centuries in modern Irish history, see: Hart, W. 'Africans in Eighteenth-Century Ireland', 33:129 (May, 2002), pp. 19-32.

[54] Several theatres titled Theatre Royal were built on the same site over the century, see: 'The Theatre Royal Years', RTE Archives, https://www.rte.ie/archives/category/arts-and-culture/2021/0614/1228025-the-story-of-the-theatre-royal/ (viewed 04/10/2023).
[55] Aldridge's early life is detailed in Bernth Lindfors, Ira Aldridge: The Early Years, 1807-1833 (Rochester, 2011).
[56] Hebert Marshall and Mildred Stock, Ira Aldridge: The Negro Tragedian (London, 1958), p. 98.
[57] Nini Rodgers, Ireland, Slavery and Anti-Slavery: 1612-1865 (Basingstoke, 2008), p. 278.
[58] Marshall and Stock, Aldridge, p. 156.
[59] Hazel Waters, 'Ira Aldridge's Fight for Equality', in Bernth Lindfors (ed.), Ira Aldridge: The African Roscius (Rochester, 2007), p. 110.
[60] Elaine Sisson, "Irish Black Bottom Blues": Race, Modernity and the City' in Darragh Gannon and Fearghal McGarry (eds.), *Ireland 1922: Independence, Partition, Civil War* (Dublin, 2022), pp. 51-52.
[61] Stuart Redden, 'Bombs and boxers on this week in Civil War-era Dublin', available at //www.thejournal.ie/battling-siki-mike-mctigue-1923-dublin-1369744-Mar2014/ [viewed 04/10/2023].
[62] Campbell, Ministry of Industry and Commerce to the Secretary, Ministry of Home Affairs, 8 September 1923, National Archives of Ireland, Department of Justice, JUS 2019/90/183.
[63] 'Paul Robeson Tells of Soviet Progress', Irish Workers' Voice, 23 February 1935.

Chapter 3: Racial and Ethnic Diversity in Britain

[1] Mayhew, Henry (1851) *London Labour and the London Poor,* vol. 3. Available at: https://dl.tufts.edu/teiviewer/parent/5x21ts300/chapter/c18s11 (accessed 13/11/2023).
[2] Further reading. McGrady, R. Joseph Emidy: An African in Cornwall. The Musical Times, 27(1726): 619-621 and 623.
[3] See: https://www.bbc.co.uk/news/uk-england-cornwall-33211440 [viewed on 06/10/2023].
[4] "Diaspora: The Irish in Britain". Encyclopaedia of Irish History and Culture. https://www.encyclopedia.com/international/encyclopedias-almanacs-transcripts-and-maps/diaspora-irish-britain [viewed 06.10.2023].
[5] Crymble, A. Cultural Diversity in London, 1821. The Migration Museum. https://www.migrationmuseum.org/cultural-diversity-in-london-1821/ [viewed 06/10/2023].
[6] Newman, B. (2018) *A Dark Inheritance: Blood, Race and Sex in Colonial Jamaica*. USA: Yale University Press.
[7] J. Ewing Ritchie, (1857) *The Night Side of London*, London: W. Tweedle, quoted in John Seed, "Limehouse Blues: Looking for Chinatown in the London Docks, 1900-1940," History Workshop Journal 62 (2006): 58-85.
[8] Pierce Egan's *Life in London* series (published in 1821 in a single collection).
[9] Ibid, p. 286.

[10] Costello, R. (2001) *Black Liverpool: The Early History of Britain's Oldest Black Community, 1730-1918*. Liverpool: Picton Press.
[11] Lloyd, A.J. (2007). Emigration, Immigration and Migration in Nineteenth Century Britain, British Library Newspapers. Detroit: Gale.
[12] Gibbs, J. M (2008) *Performing the Temple of Liberty: Slavery, Theatre, and Popular Culture in London and Philadelphia, 1760-1850*. Baltimore: John Hopkins University Press. Frazier, T. (2019) The Invention of Mungo: Race and Representation in the Eighteenth Century Atlantic World. International Journal of Arts and Humanities, 5(2): 17-27.
[13] Silliman, B. (1820) A journal of travels in England, Holland, and Scotland, and of two passages over the Atlantic, in the years 1805 and 1806. New Haven: S. Converse.
[14] Caballero and Aspinall (2018) Mixed Race Britain in the Twentieth Century. London: Palgrave Macmillan, p 2.
[15] Fryer, P. (1984). *Staying Power: The History of Black People in Britain*. London: Pluto Press.
[16] Lorimer, D.A. (1978) *Colour, Class and the Victorians: English attitudes to the Negro in the mid-nineteenth century*. Leicester: Leicester University Press.
[17] Mazimhaka Rwanyonga, J. (1997) *The Discourse of Difference: The Representation of Black African Characters in English Renaissance Drama*. Unpublished PhD thesis: University of Saskatchewan,
[18] Olusoga, D. (2016) *Black and British: A Forgotten History*. London: Macmillan.
[19] Blackett, R.J.M. (1980). William G. Allen: The Forgotten Professor. Civil War History 26(1): 39-52.
[20] Ibid. Letter from William G. Allen to Miss Edwards, 21 April 1869.
[21] Ibid. In a letter from William G. Allen to William Lloyd Garrison, 20 June 1853.
[22] Catherine Gordon, baptismal record dated 15 February 1758, at St Catherine's parish church, 'Jamaica, Church of England Parish Register Transcripts, 1664-1880', database with images, See FamilySearch at https://www.familysearch.org/ark:/61903/1:1:VHDB-2NY [viewed 21/10/2023].
[23] Trahey, Erin (2018) *Free Women and the Making of Colonial Jamaican Economy and Society, 1760-1834*. PhD thesis, History Department, University of Cambridge. Will of Sarah Gordon, 19 May 1799, LOS 66, fol. 6, Registrar General, Twickenham Park, Jamaica.

Chapter 4: Early Twentieth Century Migration

[1] Beauchamp Forde Gordon Caulfield-Stoker files, ref. no. WO 339/24054, National Archives, Kew, London.
[2] *Western Mail*, 20 April 1920.
[3] Higgins, M.D. (2012) John McAuliffe: President Higgins on Manchester's Irish Connection, The Manchester Review, May 2013. Available at https://www.themanchesterreview.co.uk/?p=2976 [viewed 21/10/2023].
[4] Kay, J.P. (1832) The Moral and Physical Condition of the Working Classes of Manchester in 1832, London: Cass.

References

5. Thompson, P. (1970) 'Family Life and Work Experience Before 1918'. Interviews. Available at http://cadensa.bl.uk/uhtbin/cgisirsi/x/0/0/5?searchdata1=CKEY1307197&library=ALL [accessed 21/10/2023].
6. Barnett, Marcus, 'In the Red Corner', *Jacobin*, 24 July 2017, available at https://jacobin.com/2017/07/len-johnson-boxer-color-line-segregation-sports-communist-party-internationalism [viewed 17/11/2023].
7. Phillips, M. (n.d.) John Archer (1863-1932), Black Europeans. https://www.bl.uk/onlinegallery/features/blackeuro/archermayoral.html [viewed 21/10/2023].
8. Costello, R. (2007) *Liverpool's Black Pioneers*. Liverpool: Bluecoat Press.
9. Costello, R. (1997) *Liverpool Black Pioneers*. Liverpool: The Bluecoat Press.
10. Rand, Lisa 'Black History Month 2020: The Liverpool lifeguard who has a street named after him', Liverpool Echo, 26 October 2020. Available at https://www.liverpoolecho.co.uk/news/liverpool-news/black-history-month-2020-liverpool-19148597 [viewed 23/10/2023].
11. Ibid.
12. Nugent, Father (2001), 'A Hundred Years of Works of Catholic Charity in Liverpool', *The Nugent Care Society*. Available at https://wearenugent.org/app/uploads/2017/10/NC-History.pdf [viewed 23/10/2023].
13. Bowcott, Owen, 'Brown apologises for Britain's 'shameful' child migrant policy', *The Guardian*. 24 February 2010. Available at https://www.theguardian.com/society/2010/feb/24/british-children-sent-overseas-policy [viewed 23/10/2023].
14. 'Gala at Runcorn Baths', *Runcorn Guardian*, 17 June 1910.
15. Caballero, C. and Aspinall, P. (2018) *Mixed Race Britain in the Twentieth Century*. London: Palgrave Macmillan, 60-63.
16. Jenkinson, J. (2009) *1919: Riots, Racism and Resistance in Imperial Britain*. Liverpool: Liverpool University Press.
17. Jenkinson, J. (1987) *The 1919 Race Riots in Britain: Their Background and Consequences*. Unpublished PhD thesis: University of Edinburgh, p193.
18. *The Yorkshire Evening Post*, 13 June 1919.
19. O'Mara, P. (2009) *Liverpool Slummy*. Liverpool: The Bluecoat Press. First published 1933.
20. Caballero, C. and Aspinall, P. (2018) *Mixed Race Britain in the Twentieth Century*. London: Palgrave Macmillan, pp 97, 103-105.
21. History of Chinatown in Liverpool, see: https://www.liverpoolecho.co.uk/news/nostalgia/liverpools-original-chinatown-move-22641559 [viewed 06/10/2023].
22. Wong, M.L (1989) *Chinese Liverpudlians: Liverpool*. Liver Press.
23. Auerbach, S. (2009) Race, Law, and "The Chinese Puzzle" in Imperial Britain. New York: Palgrave Macmillan.
24. Seed, J. (2006). Limehouse Blues: Looking for Chinatown in the London Docks, 1900–40. History Workshop Journal 62: 58–85.
25. Bland, L. (2007) British Eugenics and 'Race Crossing': A Study of an Interwar

Investigation, 60: pp66-78.

[26] Christian, M. (2008) The Fletcher Report 1930: A Historical Case Study of Contested Black Mixed Heritage Britishness. Journal of Historical Sociology 21 (2–3): 213–241.

[27] *The Western Daily Mail,* 9 July 1935.

[28] The Original Chinatowners. Available at www.bbc.co.uk/videonation/articles/1/london_theoriginal.shtml [viewed 06.10.2023].

[29] Leslie Hoe, cited in Parker, D. (2001), 'We Paved the Way': Exemplary Spaces and Mixed Race in Britain, in Williams-Leon, Teresa, (2001) *The Sum of Our Parts. Mixed Heritage Asian-Americans,* ed. p191.

[30] Lahiri, S. (2000) *Indians in Britain: Anglo-Indian Encounters, Race and Identity 1880-1930.* London and Portland, Oregon: Frank Cass Publishers.

[31] 'Aubrey Menen', Making Britain: Discover how South Asians shaped the nation, 1870-1950. The Open University. http://www.open.ac.uk/researchprojects/makingbritain/content/aubrey-menen [viewed 06/10/2023].

[32] Nasta, S. (2002) *Home Truths: Fictions of the South Asian Diaspora in Britain.* London: Palgrave.

[33] Menen, A. 'My Grandmother and the Dirty English', The New Yorker, 4 July 1953.

Chapter 5: Racial Mixing During and Post-WW2

[1] Caballero, C. and Aspinall, P. (2018) *Mixed Race Britain in the Twentieth Century.* London: Palgrave Macmillan pp 307-308.

[2] Oakley, M. (2014) Second World War Bombing Raid South Hallsville School, East London History. https://www.eastlondonhistory.co.uk/second-world-war-bombing-raid-south-hallsville-school/ [viewed 06/10/2023].

[3] 'Homage to Canning Town African Ancestors', Iroko Theatre Company, 2013. http://www.irokotheatre.org.uk/projects/6.pdf [viewed 06.10.2023].

[4] Maps of London. http://www.maps-of-london.com/ [date accessed 06.10.2023].

[5] Padfield, D. (ed) (1999) Hidden Lives: Stories from the East End by the people of 42 Balaam Street. London: Eastside Community Heritage.

[6] Smith, G.A. (1987) When Jim Crow Met John Bull: Black American Soldiers in World War II. London: I.B. Tauris & Co.

[7] Caballero, C. And Aspinall, P. (2018) *Mixed Race Britain in the Twentieth Century,* Palgrave Macmillan: London.

[8] Bland, L. (2019*). Britain's 'Brown Babies': The stories of children born to black GIs and white women in the Second World War. Manchester:* Manchester University Press.

[9] Nevins, P. *(2019) 'Fudge': The Downs and Ups of a Biracial, Half-Irish British War Baby'.* USA: Pauline Nevins.

[10] McDonald, F. Architects 'are not a luxury', The Irish Times, 13 February 2014.

[11] Bourne, S. (2010) Mother Country: Britain's Black Community on the Home Front 1939-45, London: The History Press. Bourne, S. (2012) The Motherland Calls: Britain's Black Servicemen and Women 1939-45, London: The History

References

Press.
[12] Broad, I. (2016) Marcus Bailey. African Stories in Hull & East Yorkshire, https://www.africansinyorkshireproject.com/lilian-bader.html [viewed 06/10/2023].
[13] Rob, A. (2015) Black History Month Firsts: Lilian Bader, Black History 365, https://www.blackhistorymonth.org.uk/article/section/bhm-heroes/black-history-month-firsts-lilian-bader/ [viewed 06/10/2023].
[14] Dewjee, A. (2016) Lilian Bader, African Stories in Hull & East Yorkshire, https://www.africansinyorkshireproject.com/lilian-bader.html [viewed 06/10/2023].
[15] Wong, M.L. 1989. *Chinese Liverpudlians: A History of the Chinese Community in Liverpool.* Birkenhead: Liver Press.
[16] Caballero, C. And Aspinall, P. (2018) *Mixed Race Britain in the Twentieth Century*, Palgrave Macmillan: London, pp 241-244.

Chapter 6: Racial Mixing in the Era of Mass Migration

[1] Lynott, P. and Hayden, J. (2011) My Boy: The Full Story of Philip Lynott & The Family He Never Knew. Dublin: Hot Press Books.
[2] Williams, H. 'My Secret Life: Craig Charles, 47, DJ and actor', The Independent, 30 June 2012.
[3] Jenkinson, J. (2012) 'All in the same uniform?' The participation of black colonial residents in the British armed forces in the First World War. Journal of Imperial and Commonwealth History. 40(2):207-230.
[4] See the National Archives copy of letter from the Office of the Superintending Aliens Office, 11 June 1919 at https://www.nationalarchives.gov.uk/education/resources/1919-race-riots/1919-race-riots-source-4/# .
[5] Nwanokwu, G.M. (2016) Black Shamrocks: Accommodation Available - No Blacks, No Dogs, No Irish, CreateSpace Independent Publishing Platform.
[6] 'My Irish Heritage by Kit de Waal', writing.ie, 3 April 2017. See: https://www.writing.ie/interviews/my-irish-heritage-by-kit-de-waal/ [viewed 06/10/2023].
[7] See https://youtu.be/VBihdZys2qk [viewed 07/10/2023].
[8] 'Reluctant to adopt babies', Irish Independent, 28 September 1970.
[9] Longmate N. 'The little Boy from Two Worlds', *Daily Mirror*, 30 January 1957.
[10] McGrath, P. (2006). *Back from the Brink* (2006). Arrow Books, London, p 3.
[11] Small, J. W. The Crisis in Adoption. International Journal of Social Psychiatry, 1984;30(1-2):129-142.

Chapter 7: Racism and Daily Life

1. Paul, K. (1996). A Case of Mistaken Identity: The Irish in Postwar Britain. *International Labor and Working-Class History*, doi:10.1017/S0147547900001733, 49:116-142.
2. Powell, E. 'Rivers of Blood Speech, 20 April 1968. See https://anth1001.files.wordpress.com/2014/04/enoch-powell_speech.pdf [viewed 07/10/2023]. Shrimsley, A. 'Enoch: Stop this flow of Coloured Immigrants, Sunday Mirrow, 21 April 1968.
3. Olusoga, D (2016) *Black and British: A Forgotten History*. London: Macmillan.
4. Williams, H. 'My Secret Life: Craig Charles, 47, DJ and actor', The Independent, 30 June 2012. Available at https://www.independent.co.uk/news/people/profiles/my-secret-life-craig-charles-47-dj-and-actor-7893368.html [viewed 07/10/2023].
5. Frost, D., and Phillips. (2011). *Remembering the Riots: Liverpool 1981* Liverpool: Liverpool University, 32. See also Moody, J. (2014) *The Memory of Slavery in Liverpool in Public Discourse from the Nineteenth Century to the Present Day*, Unpublished Phd thesis, University of York, 81-82.
6. 'Curry and Chips', Nostalgia Central, available at https://nostalgiacentral.com/television/tv-by-decade/tv-shows-1960s/curry-chips/ [viewed 06/10/2023].
7. Ibid, note that O'Grady's entrance in the first episode of this series and this conversation can be viewed from 03.50 on you tube at: https://www.youtube.com/watch?v=d2vaDFHtD2s [viewed 24/10/2023].
8. See the O'Grady's scene with Alf Garnett and his family on Youtube video from 19:50 available at: https://youtu.be/nsQQn9outRg [viewed 07/10/23].
9. 'It's not black and white', *The Guardian*, 22 October 2001. Available at https://www.theguardian.com/media/2001/oct/22/tvandradio.television1 [viewed 25/11/2023].
10. Gbadamosi, G. (2013) *VAUXHALL*, Telegram Books.
11. Ginsborg, 'Vauxhall - Gabrielle Gbadamosi', video interview, 5 April 2013. Available at https://vimeo.com/63403887 and https://mixedmuseum.org.uk/amri-exhibition/experiences-of-mixed-race-irish-families-in-the-1970s-and-1980s/ [viewed 24/10/2023].
12. Lennon, Mary, McAdam, Marie, O'Brien, Joanne, (1988), *Across The Water: Irish Women's Lives in Britain*, Little, Brown. M. 'My review of "Across the Water Irish Women's Lives in Britain" (1988) Mary Lennon Marie McAdam Joanne O'Brien', Lipstick Socialist, 4 December 2018, available at https://lipsticksocialist.wordpress.com/2018/12/04/my-review-of-across-the-water-irish-womens-lives-in-britain-1988-mary-lennon-marie-mcadam-joanne-obrien/ [viewed on 08/10/2023].
13. Walter, Bronwen (2001). The second-generation Irish: a hidden population in multi-ethnic Britain. Anglia Ruskin University. Report. https://hdl.handle.net/10779/aru.23783430.v1 [viewed 08/10/2023].
14. Walter, B. (2013) Transnational networks across generations: childhood visits to Ireland by the second generation in England. In M. Gilmartin and A White (eds)

(2013) Migrations: Ireland in a global world, Manchester: Manchester University Press: 17-35.

[15] O'Toole, 'From the archives: Don't believe a word – The life and death of Phil Lynott', Irish Times, 2 January 2016. Available at https://www.irishtimes.com/culture/music/from-the-archives-don-t-believe-a-word-the-life-and-death-of-phil-lynott-1.2482658 [viewed 08/10/2023].

[16] Lynott, P. and Hayden, J. (2011) *My Boy: The Full Story of Philip Lynott & The Family He Never Knew*. Dublin: Hot Press Books.

[17] 'The Black Rose with Shamrock Roots', Daily Express, 17 April 1979.

[18] O'Hagan, L. (2021) The Irish Rover: Phil Lynott and the Search for Identity, Popular Music and Society, 44:1, 26-48, DOI: 10.1080/20567790.2019.1653623.

[19] Roberts, M. (2017) Where are they now? John Conteh. Playing Pasts. Available at https://www.playingpasts.co.uk/where-are-they-now/where-are-they-now-john-conteh/ [viewed 03.10.2023].

[20] John Conteh, Big Red Book. Available at https://www.bigredbook.info/john_conteh.html [viewed 03.10.2023].

[21] Liarou, E. (2013) Tara Prem: Pioneer of Multicultural TV Drama. Women's Film and Television History Network UK/Ireland. Available at https://womensfilmandtelevisionhistory.wordpress.com/2013/11/30/tara-prem-pioneer-of-british-multicultural-tv-drama/ [viewed 03.10.2023].

[22] Fiddy, D. (2018) How lost British TV sci-fi Thwum was rediscovered. BFI. Available at https://www.bfi.org.uk/news-opinion/news-bfi/features/thwum-pete-postlethwaite-sci-fi [viewed 03.09.2023].

[23] Metcalf, Teresa, 'Taking the stage at Pebble Mill', *Birmingham Post*, 30 September 1975.

[24] Fitzmaurice, A. 'Chris Hughton Proud to be First Black Player for Ireland', *Irish Independent*, 29/10/2019. Available at https://www.independent.ie/regionals/herald/hughton-proud-to-be-first-black-player-for-ireland/38640133.html [viewed 09/10/2023].

[25] Fanning, D. 'Hughton's steady presence restores order on Tyneside', *Irish Independent*, 18 April 2010. Available at https://www.independent.ie/sport/soccer/hughtons-steady-presence-restores-order-on-tyneside/26650753.html [viewed 09/10/2023].

[26] Ibid.

[27] Fitzmaurice, A (n 24).

[28] Ibid.

[29] McRae, Donald, 'Chris Hughton: 'I have a thirst for knowledge. I won't always be a manager'', *The Guardian*, 28 April 2017.

Chapter 8: Celebrated Personalities

[1] Evers, Liz, 'Dictionary of Irish Biography: Buckley, Christine', Royal Irish Academy, 14 March 2021. Available at https://www.dib.ie/biography/buckley-christine-a10166 [viewed 22/10/2023].

[2] Ibid.

References

[3] McGarry, Patsy, 'Christine Buckley helped shift cultural axis on child abuse', *The Irish Times*, 12 March 2014.

[4] Lentin, Louis (1996) *Dear Daughter*, TV Documentary. Available at https://ifiarchiveplayer.ie/dear-daughter/ [viewed 13/10/2023].

[5] Ibid.

[6] Raftery, Mary, RTE Interview with Michael Murphy, 'The Big Story Mary Raftery', 16 April 2010. Available at https://www.rte.ie/archives/2019/0424/1045440-mary-raftery-states-of-fear/ [viewed 13/10/2023].

[7] Ibid.

[8] Lentin, Louis (n 4).

[9] Ibid.

[10] Evers, Liz (n 1).

[11] Ibid.

[12] Byrne, S. (30 November 2023) *Dear Gay: Letters to The Gay Byrne Show – a handwritten history of Ireland*, Gill Books, p. 139.

[13] Osborne, D. (2017) 'Mothertext: Restoring the Mixed Matrilineal Routes to Heritage', The Story of M. London: Oberon Books.

[14] Aston, E. (2003) *Feminist views on the English stage: Women playwrights, 1990-2000*. Cambridge: Cambridge University Press.

[15] SuAndi OBE, Moving Manchester Writers Gallery, University of Lancaster. Available at https://www.lancaster.ac.uk/fass/projects/writersgallery/content/SuAndi.html [viewed 09/10/2023], and personal correspondence.

[16] Battersby, Eileen, 'Unpublished debut novel wins prize', *Irish Times*, 22 October 1996. Available at https://www.irishtimes.com/culture/unpublished-debut-novel-wins-prize-1.98224 [viewed 30/10/2023].

[17] Traynor, Joanna (1997), *Sister Josephine*, London: Bloomsbury Publishing.

[18] Pizzichini, L. 'Suicide attempts, drug abuse, sexual assault. Author Joanna Traynor's life has been a series of triumphs over adversity', *The Independent*, 30 August 1998. Available at https://www.independent.co.uk/life-style/a-life-less-ordinary-but-no-sympathy-thanks-interview-joanna-traynor-1174978.html [viewed 10/10/2023].

[19] Hooper, K. 'On the Road: Bernardine Evaristo interviewed by Karen Hooper', The Journal of Commonwealth Literature, March 2009, available at https://doi.org/10.1177/0021989406060628 [viewed 30/10/2023].

[20] Evaristo, B. 'My Father's House: Bernardine Evaristo tours her childhood home', *Five Dials*. See: https://fivedials.com/reportage/my-fathers-house-bernardine-evaristo/.

[21] Bernadine Evaristo, *encyclopedia.com*, available at https://www.encyclopedia.com/arts/educational-magazines/evaristo-bernardine-1959 [viewed 30/10/2023].

[22] Bernadine Evaristo, British Council.org, available at https://literature.britishcouncil.org/writer/bernardine-evaristo [viewed 30/10/2023].

[23] McGrath, P. (2010) *Back From the Brink: The Autobiography*. London: Arrow Books.

[24] Phil Babb, Irish Press, 20 April 1994.

References

[25] 'Kanya King ... Single mum at 16, now the power broker for urban music riding the rise of grime', Evening Standard, 13 October 2017. Available at https://www.standard.co.uk/business/kanya-king-single-mum-at-16-now-power-broker-for-urban-music-riding-the-rise-of-grime-a3658081.html [viewed 30/10/2023].

[26] Browne, PJ (2020) 'After 17 Years Travelling The World, Terry Phelan Wants To Repay Ireland', Balls.ie. Available at https://www.balls.ie/football/terry-phelan-india-irish-indentity-413421 [viewed 30/10/2023].

[27] Brenkley, S. 'O'Reilly seeks break in the cloud: Stephen Brenkley meets the Olympian whose ideal survives a terrible ordeal', *The Independent*, 6 February 1994. Available at https://www.independent.co.uk/sport/o-reilly-seeks-break-in-the-cloud-stephen-brenkley-meets-the-olympian-whose-ideal-survives-a-terrible-ordeal-1392441.html [viewed 30/10/2023].

[28] See BBC interview 'Sochi 2014: Wilf O'Reilly's Sporting Life' here https://www.bbc.co.uk/sport/av/get-inspired/25939632 [viewed 30/10/2023].

Index

Abolition Act of 1833, 27
Abyssinia, 95
Achi,
   Canton Kitty, 164, 166
   Mr., 164, 166
Across the Water, a book about
   Irish immigration, 215
Adoption, 156, 193, 204, 206, 219, 232, 238, 239
African, 69, 100, 118, 142, 166, 196, 206, 234, 242
African American, 189
African Churches Mission, 190
African diaspora,
   Dublin Theatre Stage, 95
   Irish Communist Party, 95
   La Scala Theatre, 96
   Southern Syncopated
      Orchestra, 96
   the *Black Doctor*, 96
   The Capitol theatre in
      Dublin, 97
   The Irish Workers' Voice, 95
   Theatre Royal in Dublin, 96, 97
   West Africans, 96
Afro Solo UK bySuAndi, 150
Agecroft cemetary, 147
Aldridge, Ira, 95, 96
Ali,
   Arthur, 30
   Mir Aulad, 30
   Rebecca, 30
Allen,
   Mary, 98
   William G., 48, 98, 118, 119
Amateur Boxing Association, 220
American War of
   Independence, 121, 126
AMRI, xxv
AMRI exhibition, v
AMRI Exhibition, xxiv
Anglo-Indians, 183
Anglo-Saxon, 168, 242
Angus, John, 36
Anionwu,
   Dame Professor Elizabeth
      Nneka, v, xxii, 192
   Lawrence, 193
Anti-Slavery Society, 48
Arab, 159, 196
Archbishop of Canterbury, 149
Archer,
   Bertha, 151, 152
   John R., 150, 152, 153, 155, 211
   Richard, 150
Arne, Thomas, 6
Asian, 108, 177, 207, 223, 249
Aspinall, Peter, v, 209
Association of Black Social
   Workers and Allied
   Professionals, 206
Aston Villa football club, 243
Atlantic Slave Trade, 38

Index

Atteridge, Captain, 39
Babb, Phil, 242, 244
Baden-Powell, Lord, 149
Bader (neé Bailey), Lillian, 194, 195
Bader, Ramsay, 195
Baker, Godfrey Evans, 29, 51
Baker, William Massey, 29
Baptist, Rachel, 6, 7, 10, 11, 13, 28
Barbadian, 150, 203, 211
Barker, Sir William, 3rd Bt., 9
Barnardos, 190
Battersby, Sarah, 161
Bauer, Eaine, 201
Bay of Honduras, 128
Belgium, 183
Belize, 127, 128
Belle,
    Dido Elizabeth, 24
    Maria, 24
Black Brown and Fair, an etching, 104
Black community, 142, 153
Black culture, 246
Black Doctor, a play, 96
Black GIs, 189, 191, 196, 197
Black Irish priest, 69, 149
Black Mayor of Battersea, 153
Black people, 33, 113, 114, 115, 142, 150, 159, 162, 163, 175, 199, 207, 208
Black Power Movement, 211
Black, Emma Louisa, 57
Blake, Mary, 26
Bledsoe, Jules, 95
Bloomsbury Group, 181
Bombay, 181
Boyce, William, 6

Brady Mary, 142
Brazilian, 69, 240
Brennan, Annie, 142
Brentford football club, 226
Brice, Fanny, 26
Brien, Margaret, 16, 18, 19, 98
Britain, 15, 39, 149, 197, 207, 213, 215, 230, 239, 248
British, 199, 212, 223
British Boxing Board of Control (BBBC), 149
British Music, 246
British South Africa Company, 145
Broken Blossoms (1919), silent film by D.W. Griffiths, 168
Brown, Geoff, 150
Bryan, Conrad, v, xxi, 48, 71
Buckley, Christine, 229, 230, 234
Burdett, Sir Francis, 129
Burk, Patrick, 35
Burke, Dick, 68
Burke, Thomas, 168
Burns, Mary Theresa, 150
Caballero, Chamion, v, xxi, xxiv
Cairns, Magistrate J.A.R., 168
Calabar, 41
Calnan,
    Eugene, 25
    John, 25
    William, 25
Cameron and Hicks report, 58
Camm, Thomas, 89
Canning, Constable Samuel, 89
Canning, George, MP, 129
Caribbean, 24, 34, 100, 203, 237, 242

Index

Casey, Maurice, v
Catholic, 70, 77, 81, 88, 104, 142, 149, 150, 151, 181, 183, 184, 194, 201, 205, 206, 217, 224, 237, 238, 241
Catholic Children's Protection Society, 206
Catholic Church, 184
Catholic Crusade, 243
Catholic Girls Home, 195
Catholic orphanage, 156
Catterick Camp, 195
Caulfield-Stoker, Captain Beauchamp, 136, 137, 139
Census categories, 248
Cetwayo, the Zulu king, 92
Charles, Craig, 200, 209
Charlton, Jack, 242
Chelsea footbal club, 246
Children of WW2 – the 'brown babies', 189, 191, 196, 197, 202, 204, 207
Chinese, 100, 105, 108, 113, 117, 136, 142, 160, 163, 164, 165, 167, 169, 196, 197, 200
Chingie, short story by Dorata Flatau, 170
Chinkeke! Orchestra, 201
Christian, Mark, 176
Church of England, 57, 183, 194
Church of Ireland, 30
Churchill, Winston, 149
Circus,
    Astley's Amphitheatre, in London, 66
    Astley's in England, 61
    Batty's in Cork, 60, 71
    Batty's in Ireland, 60
    Royal Amphitheatre Fishamble Street Dublin, 72
    Ryan's in Cheltenham, 59
Clarke, James, 156
Cochrane, Sir Basil, 53
Cold Bath Fields Prison, 129
Colenso, Bishop, 147
Coleridge-Taylor, Samuel, 211
Colour bar, 149
Compulsory repartiation, 196
Conteh, John, 220, 222
Cooke, 'Mr Cooke, 62
Coromanti tribe, 35
Costello, Ray, 156
Cottingham, Captain, 21
Coventry City Football Club, 244
Cowper, Mr., 61
Crooks, Garth, 226
Cross (née Rikh),Pat, 180, 183, 186
Crosswell, Detective Joshua, 77
Crowley (artist), Nicholas Joseph, 2, 253, 254
Crowther,
    Caroline, 219
    Leslie, 219
Crozier, Thomas, 89
Cruickshank,
    George, 105, 108
    Robert, 105
Cudjo, the State Trumpeter, 34
Cunningham, Waddle, 37
Curragh Military College, Kildare, 98
Curry and Chips (1969) sitcom, 211

Index

Daly, Jane, 51
Davenport Army Service Corps, 137
Davis, Linda, 197
de Waal, Kit, 201
Deane, Frederick, 58
Dear Daughter, 1996 drama documentary, 230
Dearden, Basil, 203
Despard,
   Catherine, 120, 121, 123, 125, 127, 130, 131, 132
   Col. Edward Marcus, 119, 120, 121, 123, 126, 128, 130, 139
   James, 123, 128, 131, 132
   Jane, 120
   William, 120
Dewjee, Audrey, 47
Diamond, Joe 'Black', 163
Dickens, Charles, 42, 108
Doherty, Constable Andrew, 77
Dominica, 37
Doré, the artist, 103
Douglas, Frederick, 73
Doyle, Mark, v, 76, 82
Drury, Sir William, 1
Duke of Leinster, 46
Duke of Portland, 129
Dunlop, Robert, 84, 92, 94
Duquey, Mr., 23
Durney, John, 26
East India Company, 29, 51, 177
Egan, Enya, v
Egan, Pierce, 105
Ekarte, Pastor G Daniel, 190
Ellen Lowther, 61

Ellis, Thomas, 8
Ely family, 4, 102
Emidy, Joseph, 102
Employment and Occupations,
   Acrobats, xxii, 6, 59, 69, 71, 72
   Actors, 96, 200, 215, 222
   Boxers, 96, 143, 148, 149, 220, 221
   Business owners, 11, 47, 55, 56
   Circus entertainers, 6, 72
   Craftsmen, 101
   Doctors, 70, 92, 93, 141, 151, 154, 180, 222
   Drummers, 34, 99
   Equestrian, 59, 63
   Factory workers, 169, 194, 202
   Footballer, 224
   Footballers, 205, 227, 242, 243
   Labourers, 101
   Law, 179
   Mayors, 150
   Medicine, 30, 58, 98, 179, 182
   Merchant seamen, 194, 234
   Ministers, 101
   Musicians, 101
   Performers, 101
   Poets, 150, 214, 234
   Priests, xxi, 52, 66, 69, 72, 156, 184, 204
   Prostitutes, 44, 107
   Sailors, 36, 101, 107, 109, 163, 164, 192, 196, 197, 203
   Seamstresses, 101, 202

Servants, 1, 16, 29, 32, 35, 44, 46, 100, 108, 111, 113, 114
Singers, 6, 7, 8, 9, 12, 14, 28, 45, 97, 199, 203
Soldiers, 101, 125, 174, 178, 189, 192
Songwriters, 203, 217
Students, 108, 179
Trumpeter, 34
Writers, 215, 234, 236, 238
Enslavement, 1, 35, 41, 44, 99, 100, 102, 108, 113, 127
Equiano Olaudah, 4
Equitable Life Assurance Society of New York, 84
Ethiopia, 95
Eugenics, 187
Evaristo,
   Bernardine, 240, 241
   Jaqueline, 241
   Julius, 241
Everton football club, 246
Everts, Liz, 229
Fall, Louis 'Battling Siki', 96
Fanque, Pablo, 63
First World War, 135, 194
Fisher, Michael, 29, 51
Fitzgerald,
   Anna-Maria, 28
   Charles, 1st Baron Lecale, 28
   Emily 1st Duchess of Leinster, 28, 50
   Gerald, 50
   Lady Emily Lennox, 46
   Lord Edward, 46, 49, 129
   Pamela, 46
   the Hon. Henry,, 28
Flatau, Dorota, 170

Fleming, Rachel, 174
Fletcher Report (1930), 176, 210
Fletcher, Muriel, 174, 210
Fleure, Herbert, 174
Foley, Yvonne, 197
Foote, Samuel, 11
Forbes, George – 6th Earl of Granard, 20, 21, 23, 34
Ford, Sir Richard, 129, 130
Forshaw, Annie, 150
Foster care, 238, 239, 243
Fourth Dragoon Guards, 32
French Revolution, 126
Fury, a drummer major, 21
Garnett, Alf, 213
Garrick, David, 111
Gbadamosi, Gabriel, 214
Geary, Lynette, 95
Ghana, 35
Ghanaian, 202, 224, 245
Gibbs, Joseph, 9
Gold Coast, 35
Gordon,
   Catherine, 128
   Sarah, 127, 128
Gore, Henry, 23
Gorham, Scott, 219
Goudy, Rev., 73
Grant, Mary Ellen, 163
Great Exhibition in 1851, 143
Great Famine, 103, 115
Greg,
   John, 37
   Samuel, 37
   Thomas, 37
Gregs and Cunningham, Messrs, 36, 37

Grenville (Lord), William Wyndham, 1st Baron Grenville, 123
Griffiths, D. W., 168
Grotius, 38
Growler, an American brig, 39
Guyanese, 156, 199, 217, 244
Guy's Hospital, 56
Habib, Imtiaz, 112
Haiti, 70
Haiti Revolution, 126
Hamilton, Lady Emma, 131
Handel, G. F., 6
Hargrave, Mr., 38
Harman, Mr., 23
Hart, William, v, 1, 6, 11, 84
Hastley, Constable Gilbert, 77
Havana, 34
Hertford Estate, Dominica, 37
Hillsborough Sugar Plantation, Dominca, 37
Hindostanee Coffee House, 53
Hindus, 179
Hirsch, Dr Shirin, 150
Hoe,
    Connie, 177
    Leslie, 177
Holden, John, 88
Holnicote House, 189
Hughes, Geoffrey, 212
Hughton,
    Annette, 224
    Chris, 224, 227
    Christine, 224
    Henry, 224
    Willie, 224
Hurst,
    Edward, 73
    Mrs., 74

Hylands, Bridgett, 163
Illegitimacy, 204, 205, 218, 239
India, 179, 209, 249
Indian, 69, 100, 142, 177, 180, 182, 185, 192, 196, 222
Indian restaurants, 56
Indonesian, 136
Industrial and Reformatory Schools - Ireland, 230
Institutionalisation, 238
International exhibitions, 143
Ireland, v, 15, 16, 39, 47, 140, 185, 201, 216, 224, 242
Ireland football team, 247
Irish, 108, 142, 163, 167, 180, 185, 190, 192, 199, 200, 202, 205, 207, 210, 214, 217, 224, 238, 239, 240, 242, 248, 249
Irish community, 201
Irish diaspora, 215, 242
Irish mothers, 190, 191, 192, 214, 215, 217, 224, 230, 234, 238, 244, 247, 248
Irish Parliament, 38
Irish presence in Britian, 103
Irish Rebellion, 126
Irish Women, 113
Irish,
    Second generation, 216
Irish-Indian, 180
Jackson, John, A. – lecturer on slavery, 73
Jamaica, 3, 24, 121, 127, 128
Jamaican, 201
James, Norton, 161
Jay, Mike, 121, 127
Jea,
    Charity, 42
    Elizabeth, 42

Index

family, 114
   Hephzabah, 45
   Jemima, 45
   John, 41, 45
   Mary, 42, 45
Jenkinson, Jacqueline, 160, 200
Jerrold, Blanchard, 103
Jewel, Florence 'Kitty', 145
John Chinaman, 167
John Polson, 121
Johnson,
   Len, 143, 148, 150
   Margaret, 150
   William 'Billy', 148, 149
Johnson, Galley, 163
Johnson, Jack, 149
Johnson, Joseph, 100
Johnston, David, 93
Johnstone, Clarence, 95
Jones, Arthur, 70
Jones, Domillie, 197
Jones, Joshua, 122
Jordan, James, 39
Joseph, Tam, v
Kalunta, Ariwodo, 230
Kane, Darby, 36
Kauffman, Angelica, 4, 102
Kaufmann, Miranda, 112
Kay, James Philip, 141
Kennedy, John, v
Kerri McLean, 128
Kevin O'Grady, 211
Khan, Mirza Abu Talib, 52
King George III, 125
King George IV, 56
King William IV, 56
King, 'Miss King', 61
King, Kanya, 245
King, Mary, 48

Kingsley, Charles, 115, 116
Kingsley, Fanny, 116
Kingston, Jamiaca, 127
Kinsella, Stuart, v, 253
Knowles, Captain, 38
Koo,
   Dr. Wellington, 137
   Madame Wellington, 137
La Scala Rhythm Kings, 96
Labourers, 121, 142, 158
Lady Anne Coventry, 102
Laffan, William, v, 5, 50
Lascars, 100, 105, 108, 164, 177
Lauwyck, Bernard, 70
Lawless, Valentine, Lord Cloncurry, 131
Lawson, Margaret, 85, 92
Lawson, Mr Justice, 83
Ledger, William, 36
Lee, Richard, 14
Leeds, 148
Leeds Irish Centre, v
Legacies of British Slavery Database, 37
Lennon, Mary, 215
Lentin, Louis, 230
Liarou, Eleni, 222
Limehouse Nights by Thomas Burke, 168
Lindsay, Sir John, 24
Liverpool Association for the Welfare of Half-Caste Children, 174
Liverpool Slummy by Pat O'Mara, 163
Livesay, Daniel, v
Livesay, Dr Daniel, 24
Lloyd, Mr., 65

Lobengula,
   King on Matebeleland, 145
   Lily (née Magowan), 147
   Prince Peter, 143, 146
Lock, 38
Longford Militia, 24
Louisburg, 34
Love, William, 73, 74, 75, 98
Lowther, Ellen, 63
Lynch,
   Gladys, 204
   Kenny, 203, 212, 220
   Oscar, 203
Lynott,
   Phil, 199, 201, 205, 217, 219
   Philomena, 199, 200, 201, 205, 217, 219
Magdalene laundries, 230
Magowan, Lily, 145, 147
Maharajah of Cooch Behar's sisters,
   Princess Pretiva, 136
   Princess Sudhira, 136
Maher,
   Margaret, 148
   William, 148
Mahomed,
   Amelia, 53
   Arthur, 56, 58
   Dean Jnr, 52
   Eleanor, 29
   family, 114
   Frederick, 56, 58
   Frederick Henry Horatio Akbar (grandson), 56
   Henry Edwin, 53
   Horatio, 56
   James, 58
   James Dean Keriman, 56
   Jane, 53, 56, 58
   Janet, 58
   Rev. James, 58
   Rosanna, 56
   Sake Dean, 29, 51, 52, 58
   William, 29, 52, 53
Mahomed's Baths, 54
Mammoth Screen, v
Manchester City footbal club, 246
Manchester United, 243
Mandal, Robin, 192
Mander,
   Alan, 136
   family, 136, 155
   Lionel Henry, 136
   Samuel, 136
   Sir Charles, 136
Mansfield, William Murray, 1st Earl of, 25, 38, 100
Mantez, Dolores, 202
Martiniaz, 160
Mary Ann ship, 16
Mary Ann, the Sloop, 36
Mary Seacole Statue Appeal, 194
Maryland, 70
Mason-John, Valerie, 238
Maynard Keynes, John, 181
Mayor of Battersea, 150
Mazimhaka, Jolly Rwanyonga, 115
McAdam, Marie, 215
McAleese committee, 230
McCarthy, Michael, 70, 71
McCartney, Paul, 220
McClintock,
   Henry, 19
   John, 19

McCoy, Maggie, 163
McEvansoneya, Phillip, 5
McGrath,
   Betty, 242
   Paul, 205, 242, 245
McGuire, Mollie, 163
McLean, Kerry, v
McLoughlin, Father Nicholas, 70
Menen,
   Aubrey, 180, 181
   Natayana, 180
Migration, 139, 141, 143, 148, 151, 164, 194, 199, 207, 215, 230, 238
Miller, Fenella J., 186
Milligan, Spike, 211, 212, 213
Milligan, Tommy, 149
Minns, Allen Glaser, 151
Miscegenation, 145
Mixed marriages, 19, 30, 58, 115, 117, 118, 119, 124, 128, 131, 135, 137, 139, 142, 143, 145, 150, 166, 179, 184, 189, 202
Mixed Museum, v, xxiv, xxv
Mixed race children, 24, 171, 193, 197, 199, 202, 204, 205, 210, 218, 238, 239, 243
Mixed race families, 234, 240
Mixed race people, 24, 26, 27, 28, 29, 30, 32, 48, 113, 114, 122, 134, 139, 143, 155, 163, 170, 172, 182, 190, 194, 199, 201, 208, 214, 215, 227, 235
Mohamedans, 179
Montagu Dunk, George 2nd Earl of Hallifax, 34
Moody, Harold, 211

Mosquito Shore, 121
Mother and Baby Institutions, 193, 230, 242
Mr Ma and Son, 1929 novel by Lao She, 170
Mulatto, 26, 173
Mulatto Jack, 5, 24
Mulgrave, John, 2, 253
Multiracial Britain, 99, 108
Mungo, 19, 23, 38
Murphy Commission, 230
Murphy, Elizabeth, 157
Murphy, Paddy, 32
Music of Black Origin, 246
Musicians, 102
Muslim, 217
Mussen, William, 89
Mustee, 25, 26
Narain, M., 30
National Front, 208
National Gallery of Ireland, 2, 4, 254, 255
Navy Army and Air Force Institutes (NAAFI), 195
Negro boarding house, 163
Nelson, Admiral Horatio, 121, 125, 130, 131
Neville, Sylas, 13
Nevins, Pauline, v, 190
New York, 31, 32, 41, 48, 96
Newbolt, Dr. and magistrate, 43
Newman, Brooke, 44, 104
Nigeria, 193, 230
Nigerian, 193, 200, 214, 234, 238, 240, 242
North America, 34
Nova Scotia, 197

Index

Nubia, Onyeka, writes as 'Onyka', 112
Nwanoku, Chi-chi, 201
Nwanokwu, Gus, 200
O'Brien, Joanne, 215
O'Coigley, Father James, 124
O'Connell, Daniel, 22
O'Donnell, Mr., 82
O'Grady, Kevin, 211, 212
O'Keefe, John, 7
O'Leary David, 245
O'Mara, Pat, 163
O'Reilly, Wilf, 248
Olusoga, David, 118, 208
Orange Order, 79
Orr, James Speers, 92, 94
Osborne, Deirdre, 234, 238
Our Lady & St Nicholas Church, Liverpool, 8
Oxford, Chief Constable Kenneth, 210
Paddington,
   Father George John, 69, 70, 71
   Father. George John, 149
   Joseph, 'Pablo', 59, 61, 63, 66, 71, 72
   Mary Anne, 70
   the Celebrated Corkonian, 60
Padmore, George, 211
Paine, Thomas, 123
Pakistan, 209, 212, 249
Palma, Bernardo, 6
Pan-Africanism, 150, 151, 211
Paris, 222
Parris, Cecil, 199, 200, 217
Party Processions Acts, 76
Paul, Kathleen, 207

Pebble Mill Studios, 222
Pennington, James W.C., 70
Percy, Algernon, 1st Earl of Beverly, Lord Lovaine, 28
Percy, the Hon. Algernon, 28
Phelan, Terry, 242, 246
Phipps,
   Constantine 1st Baron of Mulgrave, 3
   Constantine Henry Lord Mulgrave, 3
Pitt, William, Prime Minister, 123, 124
Places in Britain,
   Bath, 11
   Birmingham, 199, 201, 217, 222, 223, 248
   Birmingham,
      New Theatre, Kings Street, 11
      Sawyer's Room in the Square, 11
   Bocking Hall, 9
   Bristol, 9, 13, 35, 37, 66, 72, 108, 134, 197, 222
   Bristol,
      Hot Wells, 9
      Widows and Ophans Fund, 72
      Zoological Gardens, 72
   Cambridge, 192
   Cardiff, 108, 159, 161, 163, 168, 169, 174, 176
   Darlington, 74
   Dedham, 9
   Dublin, 205
   Essex, 9
   Glasgow, 73, 108, 169

Liverpool, 8, 14, 89, 108, 139, 140, 151, 153, 156, 160, 163, 164, 168, 169, 174, 176, 194, 196, 200, 202, 209, 238
Liverpool,
  Cleveland Square, 164
  Frederick Street, 164
  Knolle Park, 237
  Merseyside, 210
  Ormskirk District, 200
  Pennywell, 164
  Pitt Street, 164
  Toxteth, 194, 209
London, 11, 52, 101, 103, 104, 107, 112, 114, 118, 119, 120, 123, 125, 126, 128, 129, 131, 132, 138, 139, 140, 141, 144, 150, 160, 161, 168, 170, 174, 180, 184, 192, 199, 200, 203, 214, 215, 217, 222, 224, 240, 241
London,
  Acton, 242
  Agate Street, 187
  Battersea, 151, 211
  Battersea Labour Party, 155
  Canning Town, 172, 187, 188, 204
  Corresponding Society, 123
  Drury Lane, 117
  Forest Gate, 224
  Graylands Augustus Road, 137
  Kew, 219
  Kilburn, 245
  Lambeth, 214, 244
  Limehouse, 164, 167, 168, 169, 170, 177
  Marylebone, 47
  Mile End, 229
  Oakley Arms, 125
  Pennyfields, 170
  Piccadilly, 47
  Portman Square, 53
  Saffron Hill, 117
  Seven Dials, 103
  Shadwell, 164
  Somers Town, 132
  St Giles, 104, 106
  Stepney, 204, 232
  Union Street, 132
Manchester, 139, 140, 142, 150, 199, 217, 234
Manchester,
  'Little Ireland', 140
  Clayton, 148
  Greengate Dixie, 142
Middlesborough, 195
Newcastle, 108
Newport, 160
Portsmouth, 42, 44
Salford, 142, 147
Stafford, 193
Swansea, 135
Thetford, Norfolk, 151
Wellingborough, 190
York, 195
Places in Ireland,
  Adare, 9
  Ballinamuck, battle of, 21, 24
  Ballinasloe, 75
  Bandon, 14
  Belfast, 4, 14, 35, 85, 86, 94, 95

Belfast,
  1872 riots, 76
  Camptown Races, 80
  Conservative Party, 88
  Crimea Street, 78
  Falls Road, 77
  Liberal Party, 87
  Poor Law Union, 89
  Shankill Road, 77, 80
Carlow, 244
Castle Forbes, 20
Castlebar, 21, 24, 191
Cavan, 31
Clare, 22
Clintontown in Louth, 18
Clonmel, 14
Connaught, 163
Cork, 4, 14, 29, 30, 32, 35, 39, 51, 60, 65, 66, 68, 69, 71, 149, 183, 216
Cork,
  Castle White Gardens, 66
  Cremorne Gardens, 66
  Millard Street, 70
  Western Road, 66
Derry, 73, 75
Donagheady, 73
Donagheay, 73
Donegal, 73
Down, 161
Drogheda, 18, 232
Drumcar, 16, 17, 20
Dublin, 4, 6, 7, 8, 11, 13, 14, 16, 33, 36, 46, 48, 68, 73, 75, 80, 87, 95, 96, 97, 98, 137, 199, 201, 218, 230, 232, 242, 245, 247
Dublin,
  Ashton's Key, 36

Bethseda Chapel, 137
Dublin Castle Viceregal Apartments, 3
Fishamble Street, 72
Marlborough Green, 7
Music Hall in Crow Street, 6
Parnell Square, 137
Pembroke Road, 30
Pemroke Road, 31
St Fintan's Cemetery, 219
Temple Hill Hospital, 232
The Royal Amphitheatre, 72
Dunany, 16, 17
Dundalk, 19
Dunneanny, 17
Durrow, 14
Galway, 75
Granard, 21
Holywood, 87
Kilcooley Abbey, 9
Kilkenny, 9, 14, 15
Killarney, 183
Kilrush, 22
Limerick, 9, 14, 26, 215, 224
Longford, 20, 21, 24, 38
Moville, 73, 94
Newry, 36
Newtownforbes, 20
Offaly, 241
Ramelton, 73
Strabane, 73
Stranorlar, 73
Tipperary, Roscrea, 148
Wexford, 3, 244
Wicklow, 237
Planters, 24, 26, 29, 46, 121, 178

Index

Polly Peacham, a character in *Beggar's Opera*, 13
Polygamy, 179
Porter, Mr., 73
Powell, Enoch, 207, 209
Prem, Bakshi, 222
Prem, Tara, 222, 223
Prince of Wales, 144
Protestant, 51, 77, 243
Provisional IRA, 210
Prufendorf, 38
Quadroon, 26
Queenstown Regatta, 66
Quill, Thomas, 17
Quin, Valentine, 9
Qureshi, Sadiah, 143
Race Relations Bill - UK, 207
Race Relations Board, 213
Race riots, 159, 160, 168, 194
Racial mixing, 159, 161, 163, 167, 168, 170, 174, 177, 179, 187, 189, 197, 199, 204, 207, 208, 248
Racism, xxii, 82, 95, 96, 115, 116, 118, 135, 141, 150, 151, 153, 191, 195, 203, 208, 211, 213, 226, 235, 239
Raftery, Mary, 231
Ranelagh Gardens, Liverppol, 8
Rees, Reverend, 147
Reid, Maria, 150
Repatriation scheme, 161
Richardson, Captain, 176, 210
Rivers of Blood speech by Enoch Powell, 207
Robers, Thomas (1748-1777) - artist, 50
Robeson,
　Eslanda, 95, 97
　Paul, 95, 96
Rodgers, Nini, 43
Rohmer, Sax, 168
Romeo and Juliette, 13
Rooney, Brendan, v, 5, 50
Roper, Moses, 73
Rose, David, 222
Rossington, Norman, 212
Rowlandson, Thomas, 44, 104, 105
Royal Academy show, 108
Royal Irish Constabulary, 89
Royal Navy, 44
Royal Scotch Guards, 33
Saint Kitts, 201
Saint Lucian, 161
Salter, Joseph, 166
San Juan expedition, 121
Sapphire (1959), a film by Basil Dearden, 202
Scotland, 73
Scott, Sir John, 129
Second World War, 196, 197
Seven Years War, 34
Shadow Squad, TV series, 203
Shampooing Surgeon, 56
Sidthorpe, Stephen, 17
Sie-Jalloh, Jenneba, 215
Sierra Leone, 148, 215
Singh, Victor Duleep, 102
Sinophobia, 170
Sister Josephine, novel by Joanna Traynor, 238
Slave Trade Act, 37
Slaves, 24, 27, 41, 121
Sligo, 247
Small,
　Edward, 48

Harriet Pamela, 47
Julie, 46, 129
Moirico, 46, 48
Tony, 46, 47, 48, 129
Small, Julia, 98
Small, Tony, 98
Smith, John Thomas, 100
Smith, Veronica, 221
Smyly Trust Orphanages, 205, 243
Smyth, Chestnutte, 92, 94
Smyth, Dr. James, 93, 94
Sneinton, 113
Society of Artists, 48
Somerset Case, 38
Somerset, James, 38
South Carolina, 46
South Hallsville School, 187
Southampton, 144
Spearing, Mr., a magistrate, 39
Speight, Johnny, 211, 213
Spring,
 James, 203
 Robert, 203
SS Rowan, 96
St. Lucia, 161
St. Patrick's Guild, 232
St. Patrick's Orphan Asylum, 64
St. Patrick's Athletic, 243
St. Vincents Industrial School, Goldenbridge, 230
St. Werburgh's Church, 1, 4, 253, 254
States of Fear, TV documentary, 231
Steele, Mr, 22
Stewart, Charles, 38
Stewart, Robert, 92

Stoker,
 Countess Oei Hui-lan 'Hoey', 136
 family, 155
 Lionel, 139
Strength of our Mothers by SuAndi, 150
SuAndi, v, 150, 234
Suttoe, John, 16, 17, 20, 98
Sydney, Thomas Townshend, 1st Viscount Sydney, 122
Sykes, Eric, 212
Tariq, 217
Teirney, Samuel, 85, 87, 92
The Avengers, TV series, 203
The *Beggar's Opera*, 13
The Busy Body, a play, 12
The Mayor of Garratt, a play, 12
The Mystery of Fu Manchu by Sax Rohmer, 168
The Story of M (1994) by SuAndi, 234
Theatre Royal, Haymarket, London, 12
Thin Lizzy, 205, 217
Thompson, George Henry, 76, 79, 81, 82, 98
Thompson, Paul, 142
Threat to white British men's Jobs, 200
Thro' the Wood laddie, a Scottish air, 13
Tierney,
 Ebeneezer, 27
 Eleanor Frances, 26
 family, 103
 George MP, 26, 124
 James, 26, 124
 Sabina Eleanor, 26

Index

Til Death Us Do Part (1974) sitcom, 211
Tillyard, Stella, 28, 46
Tippen, James, 71
Tobias, Andrew, 31, 32
Tottenham Hotspur football club, 224, 226
Toulmin, Vanessa, 63
Toussaint, Pierre, 70
Toxteth Riots, 210
Trans-raised, 238
Traynor, Joanna, 238
Trinity College, 30, 97
Trinity College Dublin (TCD), 230
Truro Philharmonic Orchestra, 102
Tucker, Henry Anthony, 47
Tudor, xxv, 103, 113
Tussaud, Madame, 126
UFO, 1970 sci-fi drama series, 203
United Irishmen, 123
University College, Aberystwyth, 174
University of Heidlberg, 70
University of Liverpool, 175
Van Hare, George, 65, 66
Vauxhall (2013), novel by Gabriel Gbadamosi, 214
Victorian, 173, 183, 203
Villet, Alice, 180
Virginia, 38
Wade, George, 167
Walsh, Jane, 120
Walter, Bronwen, 216
Wapping bathhouse, 104
Waters, Bronwen, 113
Waters, Hazel, 96
Wells, Bombardier Billy, 149
West (née Kershaw), Anna, 230, 232
West African, 163, 220
West Ham football club, 226
West Indian, 29, 178, 196, 197, 203
West Indies, 24, 35, 70, 119, 128
Wheatstone, Francis, 22
White women, 163, 170, 175, 176, 196
White, Captain, 39
Wickham, William, 129
Williams, Charlie, 209
Williams, Sir Ralph, 160
Wilson, George, 85
Wilson, Joseph, 84, 85, 86, 87, 90, 91, 94
Wilson, Kathleen, 30
Witchard, Anne, 170
Women's Auxiliary Air Force (WAAF), 195
Woods, Billy, 157
Woolf, Virginia, 181
Working class, 100, 103, 111, 113, 114, 118, 134, 135, 145, 170, 191, 200
Wyatt,
  Captain Felix, 57
  James, 58
Yemeni, 142